KT-388-435

GLASGOW UNIVERSITY
LAW LIBRARY

*Into Europe*

*The Structure and Development*
*of the Common Market*

*Also by*
*A. E. Walsh & John Paxton*

Trade in the Common Market Countries

Trade and Industrial Resources of the
Common Market and EFTA Countries

# INTO EUROPE

*The Structure and Development
of the Common Market*

A. E. Walsh
John Paxton

HUTCHINSON OF LONDON

HUTCHINSON CO (PUBLISHERS) LTD
*3 Fitzroy Square, London W1*

London Melbourne Sydney Auckland
Wellington Johannesburg Cape Town
and agencies throughout the world

*First published 1968*
*Second edition July 1972*

GH1416/1

WITHDRAWN FROM
GLASGOW
LIBRARY

© First edition A. E Walsh and John Paxton 1968
This edition A. E. Walsh and John Paxton 1972

*This book has been set in Times Roman,*
*printed in Great Britain on antique wove paper*
*by The Camelot Press Ltd, London and Southampton,*
*and bound by Wm. Brendon & Son Ltd, of Tiptree, Essex*
ISBN 0 09 112570 7   (cased)
     0 09 112571 5   (paper)

Initials: D3155/5

CANCELLED
LIBRARY

TO LILIAN & JOAN

# Contents

# Acknowledgements

Over many years we have received help from officials of the Commission of the European Communities in Brussels and also from the Press and Information Office in London.

We should also like to thank Dr. Walter Rosenberger of Keesing's Contemporary Archives and officials of the National Farmers' Union.

Again our gratitude goes to our indexer, Mrs. Fetherstonhaugh.

# *Preface*

The Treaty of Rome is one of the most remarkable documents in the social and economic history of the western world. It is explicit in providing for complete economic union so that goods, people and capital will be able to pass over the national boundaries of the member countries as freely as they can move inside any one country today. On the horizon lies political union.

No past attempt at federation, whether successful or not, can be compared with the magnitude of the task formally begun in 1957. Six countries with separate traditions and institutions developed over a thousand years pledged themselves, for all time, to a programme of progressive unity.

It is impossible to foresee the extent to which Britain's economy and industries will be changed by joining the Six, but above the economic detail will lie the central purposes of the Treaty of Rome.

Our aim in presenting this new edition of our book is to show how far these purposes have been achieved at the time of Britain's accession. From our description of the way joint-thinking and policy making has developed, we hope the reader may feel more confidence in understanding the *nature* of the Common Market and to some extent in his prediction of its impact on his future.

A. E. WALSH
JOHN PAXTON

# CHAPTER 1

## Post-War Europe

If history demands a date for the most important event in the movement which led to the creation of the European Economic Community that date might well be Tuesday, 9 May 1950. It was on that day, at four o'clock in the afternoon, that the French Minister of Foreign Affairs, M. Robert Schuman, announced at a press conference that his Government had decided to place the entire complex of coal and steel production in France and Germany under a common High Authority in an organisation which would also be open to participation by other West European countries.

If history demands names with which to associate the process of crystallising out the solution containing all the ingredients of a new order in Europe, these names are certainly Jean Monnet and Robert Schuman. Monnet was an administrator. Administrators need politicians to put forward their ideas. Throughout the entire period of the chain of events from which the European Economic Community evolved, it is the partnership between Monnet, the administrator, and Robert Schuman, the politician, to which must be attributed the responsibility for the preparation of the plan and for its launching.

Throughout the long period of the instability of successive governments in France from 1945 onwards and their short and tempestuous lives, the name Schuman persists, once as Premier for a short time, but for almost all the time as Foreign Minister. Even the Bidault Government, which was in office at the time of the announcement of the Schuman Plan, only lasted until 24 June 1950; but Schuman still remained Foreign Minister in the subsequent governments.

Although he was neither by temperament nor by political education a believer in economic determinism, it was Schuman, above all his contemporaries, who demonstrated that while economic motives had for generations supplied the reason and the temptation to resort to war to settle national aspirations economic motives and resources could equally be orientated towards making war impossible.

The war left behind in its aftermath many Europeans with faith that they had a part to play in making a further war between France and Germany 'not merely unthinkable but materially impossible' and that, if a start could be made by the pooling of coal and steel production in the area in which nature had laid the resources but in which political conflict had divided them there might be created in Europe a new order in which motives and the resources for war would no longer exist.

Of these Europeans, it was Robert Schuman who recognised that he had the talent, and, as Foreign Minister of France, the power to change the face of Europe. Fortune was perhaps kind to him in the response which his ideas evoked from other European statesmen and in the chords which his bold and imaginative plan struck in the minds of men at the particular time and in the particular conditions which were rife in Europe. This is how history is often made.

Jean Monnet by contrast was an administrator. He was neither a member of the French Government nor of the French National Assembly. He was Director-General of the French Reconstruction Plan and as such he had, since the Liberation, achieved an almost unique international reputation and influence, despite the fact that his primary concern was with the French economy.

To Monnet must be credited the working out of the Schuman Plan. Of Monnet, Schuman declared that he played a predominant role from the very beginning in the conception of the plan and in elaborating the text of the treaty under which the European Coal and Steel Community was formed.

The Schuman Plan has something at once banal and romantic in the manner of its unfolding. Once completed, the problem was to get it adopted. M. Bidault, the Prime Minister, had as late as April 1950 made some suggestions for another scheme for co-ordinating economic and defence action between the United States and their allies. This idea had found no response in the United States but it made it difficult for Bidault to follow it up with ideas for a totally different plan.

Monnet had, however, a powerful ally in Robert Schuman, the Foreign Minister. Both sought the same solution to Europe's difficulties. Both saw that political unity must be sought as the result of economic unity and that the formation of a Franco-German Coal and Steel pool was the first stage towards greater achievements in the future.

Events moved quickly in the last stages in the preparation and presentation of the Plan.

On the fateful days which preceded M. Schuman's announcement of the plan to set up the European Coal and Steel Community, it fell to Monnet to bring the project to its definitive stage and to set in motion the machinery which he had so skilfully devised.

On 4 May 1950 he called the men who had been collaborating with him in its preparation to a meeting in the rue Martignac in Paris— M. Clappier, permanent head of M. Schuman's Ministry, M. Jacques Gascuel, M. Hirsch and M. Uri. The 'conspirators' agreed upon their respective roles for the drafting and presentation of the announcement of the project. On 8 May all the drafts which had been used in its preparation were destroyed. On the morning of 9 May the text of the announcement was finally completed and it was left to M. Clappier to take it personally to M. Schuman to expound at a Cabinet meeting which was being held that day at the Elysée Palace. Would M. Schuman be able to persuade his ministerial colleagues to listen to what he had to say? M. Monnet and his team waited impatiently by their telephones. No news came. M. Monnet telephoned the Elysée; he thought that the Cabinet might have broken up before reaching M. Schuman's exposition.

The minutes of Cabinet meetings remain secret and one can only surmise the course of the discussions. Only a few ministers besides the Prime Minister, M. Bidault, and M. Schuman himself, had any prior knowledge of the subject. For the others it must have been a complete surprise.

As they listened to M. Schuman, few of them can have grasped the full significance of what he was saying. Few can have realised that afternoon that they were listening to a project which would have a profound effect upon the history of Europe and affect the destinies of millions of people. This was not just another occasion for a routine exchange of ideas to be conducted through conventional diplomatic channels, but a solemn declaration to which France would be irrevocably committed. Probably no one who did not take part in the deliberations of that meeting will ever know all the facts.

Suffice it to say that M. Schuman secured the Cabinet's agreement to the form and text of the announcement which he submitted, and went straight to a press conference which, such was his confidence of his success, he had called in advance, and made his announcement.

His declaration had the effect which he had sought in France and abroad. The surprise element had been complete. The psychological impact was immeasurable. Certainly M. Schuman had secured the support of Germany for the German Chancellor had on 8 May referred to the project as 'magnanimous' and on 13 May he described it as an act of historical significance. It seems doubtful, however, that Adenauer was told precisely of the form and text of Schuman's announcement before the morning of 9 May. The British Government did not know what was coming, nor, indeed, did the U.S. Secretary of State, Mr. Dean Acheson, who was in Paris on 8 May. In one master stroke, Robert Schuman had enabled France to gain the initiative in European affairs and a new era in Europe had begun.

The march of events after M. Schuman's announcement on 9 May 1950 was swift. On 20 June 1950 delegates from the Governments of France, Germany, Belgium, Luxembourg, the Netherlands and Italy met in Paris. They started work at once on drafting a treaty and 10 months later, on 18 April 1951 the draft treaty establishing the European Coal and Steel Community was signed and ready for ratification. It was put to the vote in the Parliaments of the six countries and ratified. Britain had been invited to take part in the discussions but declined. The Prime Minister, Mr. Attlee, told the House of Commons that Britain could not agree to the fundamental conditions that she should commit herself in advance to be bound by the future decisions of a higher coal and steel authority.

The European Coal and Steel Community was formed without Britain. The treaty came into force on 25 July 1952 and the High Authority, which had been installed in Luxembourg, assumed its duties.

\*         \*         \*

The history of the coal and steel industries in France and Germany forms a significant part of the history of the two countries themselves and in particular of those areas on their joint frontier which had been for so long in dispute—the Saar Basin with its coal mines and Lorraine with its resources of iron ore.

In modern times no one European country has had within its own borders a balanced supply of iron ore and coking coal. Even the return of Lorraine to France in 1919, although it altered the pattern of Germany's coal-ore balance, did not have the effect which was expected, because Germany had for years been organising her industry, as had other steel producing countries including Britain, on the basis of rich imported ores from other countries.

Indeed, the interdependence of the European countries on one another for both coal and iron ore had brought about all kinds of international integration in the industry. This integration was particularly evident between France and Germany between the wars when industrial collaboration was the only way of maintaining coal and steel equilibrium in the face of all the political upheavals of the period.

For obvious reasons, this process of integration became one of enforced collaboration during the Second World War. It is not surprising therefore that when all the turmoil of the immediate post-war years had passed, there existed, at all levels in France and Germany, a framework of personal relationships upon which collaboration directed to peaceful industrial purposes could be constructed. Though the factories had been destroyed, the men who had run and directed them in peace and in war remained.

It is impossible to say exactly who first had the idea of a Franco-German Iron and Steel Pool. According to Bernard Lavergne it came originally from Hugo Stinnes, the coal and steel magnate of the Ruhr, in 1931. Paul Wergner in his biography of Konrad Adenauer says that as far back as 1923 at the time of the French occupation of the Ruhr, Adenauer, then Mayor of Cologne, had believed in the unification of the heavy industries of France and Germany.

The concept of the European Coal and Steel Community—and, as we shall show later, the European Economic Community (the Common Market)—is a political one. The Schuman Plan on which it was based was approved by the French Cabinet 'as a first step in the federation of Europe'.

When the war in Western Europe ended in 1945, victors and vanquished alike were in a state of utter political and economic exhaustion. Physically, Britain had suffered grievously, but not in the same way as the Continental countries. She was operating under a system of stringent controls and regulations imposed to mobilise her resources for total war. The unwinding of these controls was a tedious and frustrating process which necessitated prolonging almost all the restrictions to the reopening of external trade that the war had made necessary.

In Europe conditions were infinitely worse. Physical damage had paralysed roads and railway transport and most of the large factories. From 1940 to 1944 Germany had made herself into the axis upon which the entire production of the countries of Western Europe turned. Everything short of the necessities of life itself (and often even these) which these countries produced flowed into Germany to meet her demands for food and war materials.

The defeat and collapse of Germany brought in their train nothing less than the complete collapse of the framework of economic links which Germany had built up during the war and there was nothing left to take its place. It is estimated that in 1945, pig iron production in the countries that now form the Common Market, was less than one-third the level of 1939 and coal production even less.

Such chaos demanded palliative measures. The first of such measures to relieve the desperate economic situation in the worst-hit countries was provided by UNRRA, the United Nations Relief and Rehabilitation Administration, which, by its charter, was designed primarily to help the peoples in countries which had opposed the German axis nations before and during the war.

The first positive step to revive international industrial economic relationships was the Anglo-American loan agreement of 1946 by which Britain received a net sum (after provisions for the repayment of outstanding lend-lease claims) of £1,300m. from the United States. One of the conditions of this loan was a return to convertibility of currency. In her attempt to carry out this condition Britain vitiated the purpose of the loan and dissipated much of the loan itself.

The period between the summer of 1946, when the bulk of American assistance to Europe virtually came to a standstill and the winter of 1947, when Britain brought matters to a head by informing the United States that she could no longer maintain her share of the combined military and economic aid to support the Greek Government against Communism, was a period of great confusion in Europe. Communism was rapidly gaining ground. The consolidation of the Communist domination in Eastern Europe was having its effect on the Communist parties in Western Europe. The Communist Party had become the strongest party in France and Italy was expected to move in the same direction.

America reacted quickly to a situation which had been brought about by the failure of the West to assess the magnitude of the task of rehabilitating Europe. On 12 March 1947 President Truman announced the Truman Doctrine which warned the Soviet Union against further political pressure in South East Europe. In June 1947 General George C. Marshall, newly appointed Secretary of State, announced his plan, which was later approved by Congress, for large scale economic help to the European countries to finance the purchase abroad of the machinery and equipment which they needed but which they lacked the dollar resources to pay for.

The Marshall Plan was described at the time as the blood trans-fusion which sustained the weakening European economies and gave them strength to work their own recovery.

To administer the aid given under the Marshall Plan the Organisa-tion for European Economic Co-operation was set up by the signing of the Convention for European Economic Co-operation on 16 April 1948. Under this Convention the member governments pledged themselves 'to combine their economic strength, to join together to make the fullest collective use of their individual capacities and poten-tialities, to increase their production, develop and modernise their industrial and agricultural equipment, reduce progressively barriers to trade amongst themselves, promote full employment and restore or maintain the stability of their economies and general confidence in their national currencies'.

O.E.E.C. comprised the following countries: Austria, Belgium, Denmark, France, Germany, Greece, Iceland, Ireland, Italy, Luxem-bourg, the Netherlands, Norway, Portugal, Sweden, Trieste, Turkey and the United Kingdom.

Even with such massive external assistance, which by June 1950 had amounted to some £3,300m. the efforts to restore economic health in Western Europe were subjected to strain and pressures. Inflation, rising prices and devaluation were discounting much of the value of the external aid.

Nevertheless by the end of 1949 European currencies were suffi-ciently aligned to allow a start to be made on dismantling the com-plicated structure of bilateral trade and payments and to return to a system of multilateral clearing of payments.

Between 1948, when it began, and 1956 O.E.E.C. had achieved most of its major objectives. In addition to the arrangements through the European Payments Union for multilateral clearing it had suc-ceeded in getting some 90 per cent of European trade freed from quota restrictions. The countries with moderate import tariffs con-sidered, however, that they could not proceed with the elimination of their remaining quotas until a start had been made on the reduction of tariff disparities.

In 1948, shortly after the signing of the Convention setting up the O.E.E.C. the first moves designed to achieve political federation in Europe became apparent. At The Hague Congress in May 1948 leading Europeans, Bidault, Blum, Churchill, de Gasperi, Monnet, Spaak, van Zeeland and others called for measures which could lead to the political and economic integration of Western Europe. As a result in 1949 the Council of Europe was inaugurated in Strasbourg.

The Council of Europe has two political chambers, a Committee of Ministers, usually the Foreign Ministers of the member States, and a consultative assembly of Representatives, made up of members of the Parliaments of the member States.

The Council of Europe never assumed or was given any legislative authority. Within its corridors of power, there have been consultation and pressure, proposal and counter-proposal, but none of these met the aims of the European federalists.

Political debate was no substitute for action. Even during the first year of the existence of the Council of Europe, the real movement towards European integration began to emerge.

If political unity could not be achieved as a primary aim in Europe there were statesmen who felt that, if a basis for economic integration would be found, political unity would follow.

Prominent amongst them was M. Spaak, the Foreign Minister of Belgium. In the autumn of 1955 a Committee was appointed under the chairmanship of M. Spaak to consider a plan for a Common Market. At the deliberations of this committee a United Kingdom delegate attended as observer.

Between 1952 and 1957 the door to Britain's close participation in the moves towards European integration was wide open. This is the period of lost opportunity. A Free Trade Area would have been possible then but for Britain's reluctance to help O.E.E.C. to move towards tariff reductions. By the time the Spaak Committee had prepared its plan for the Common Market opinion was hardening. Britain faced with the choice of coming in or staying out made her disastrous decision to remain aloof.

For all practical purposes the decision to form the European Economic Community was taken at the Messina Conference held in June 1955 and attended by Ministers from France, W. Germany, Italy, the Netherlands, Belgium and Luxembourg. The Treaty itself was signed in Rome on 25 March 1957.

Between these two dates, there was considerable activity on the part of the other member countries of O.E.E.C., led by Britain, to avoid being left out of the new economic order in Europe. Negotiations were opened in March 1957, to form a Free Trade Area made up of the six members of the Common Market and of seven European countries, Britain, Norway, Sweden, Denmark, Switzerland, Austria and Portugal.

In the light of all subsequent developments it seems strange that it was the Customs Union aspect of the European Economic Community that dominated the scene of these negotiations. The Free Trade Area was to be an association of six countries who observed all the disciplines of the Treaty of Rome and seven others who maintained a large measure of independence including freedom for their own external trade policies. Tariffs on goods passing from one Free Trade Area country to another were to be abolished progressively. The Common Market common external tariff against all other countries not members of the Free Trade Area was to go ahead as laid down in the Treaty.

Such advantages as for instance, duty free imports of food, raw materials and manufactured goods from the Commonwealth as were enjoyed by Britain were to remain. It was said of Britain at the time that she was seeking the best of both worlds. 'With its different institutional structures, inspired by a different purpose yet performing some of the same tasks, the Free Trade Area would have been likely to exert a weakening influence on the Common Market' (*The Economist*, 25 April 1959).

The plan for a Free Trade Area of the Six and the Seven non-member countries was worked out in London during 1956 and a decision to open discussion was taken in 1957. In October 1957, O.E.E.C., including France, approved the principle of a Free Trade Area. On 17 October 1957 the Council of O.E.E.C. passed a resolution in which it declared its determination to secure the establishment of a European Free Trade Area which, taking into consideration the objectives of the European Economic Community, would take effect parallel with the Treaty of Rome. To this resolution France subscribed.

West Germany wanted a Free Trade Area. So did the Netherlands and, to a lesser extent, Belgium. The German Foreign Ministry had certain reservations because it did not want to upset its new relationships with France. Italy was somewhere half way between the two. France paid lip service to the O.E.E.C. Plan but, because her trade policy was protectionist and because she was beginning to see the prospects of putting a curb on West Germany through her dominant position in the European Economic Community she showed signs in January 1958 of her intention to sabotage the Free Trade Area idea. One of France's Junior Ministers, M. Maurice Faure, was strongly pro-Free Trade Area. Opposed to him was the head of the Economic side of the French Foreign Ministry M. Wormser who, throughout the whole period of discussions relating to Britain's place in Europe, was a most formidable adversary.

The French pinned their faith on the problem of 'Origin' as the most plausible grounds in which to oppose a Free Trade Area, on the pretext that the privileges enjoyed within the Commonwealth would distort conditions of competition for the Common Market and make it difficult to prevent many Commonwealth products which enjoy duty free entry into Britain from getting into Europe by the back door. For over a year the French delegation raised one technical objection after another to the system which was emerging from the negotiations and which is now successfully used in Efta.

Challenged on this, the Community produced the Ockrent Report which, while reaffirming that the Community was determined to arrive at an agreement for a Free Trade Area associated with the Community on a multilateral basis, nevertheless reiterated many of the supposed difficulties. France then fell back upon her second line of defence by raising every conceivable obstruction on the step-by-step examination of the difficulties as they emerged.

Looking back on these negotiations for a Free Trade Area, it must be admitted that Britain's position was weak and her approach naïve especially in view of the relative isolation of France at that time. It is not surprising that Britain was suspected of wanting to set up an organisation which at best was regarded as defensive and which at worst could seriously undermine the purpose of the European Economic Community and its disciplines.

At the end of 1958, the political game came into full play and M. Soustelle speaking for the French Government at a Press Conference abruptly denounced the whole plan and the negotiations were immediately broken off.

THE EUROPEAN FREE TRADE ASSOCIATION

In May 1959 Sweden took the first steps towards forming a Free Trade Area of the seven European countries which had attempted to set up a Free Trade Area with the European Economic Community. Sweden invited Austria, Denmark, Norway, Portugal, Switzerland and the United Kingdom to discussions in Stockholm for this purpose.

On 20 November 1959, these seven countries agreed the Stockholm Convention setting up the European Free Trade Association (Efta) to come into effect on 1 July 1960.

The main purpose of the Convention was to stimulate trade between the member countries by giving 'Area tariff treatment' to industrial goods traded from one member country to another. For this purpose, the protective tariffs for elimination were all customs duties which had not been declared as revenue duties. Agricultural products were excluded from the Efta Convention.

The essential difference, in terms of its existence as a Customs Union, between the Common Market and Efta was that while the Treaty of Rome lays down a common external tariff to be levied on all goods coming from non-member countries, the members of Efta maintained their own existing levels of tariffs towards goods coming from the rest of the world.

By a series of tariff reductions between 1960 and 1966, Efta became a completely free trade area for trade between its members on 1 January 1967 with the exception of special provisions for delayed tariff reductions by Portugal.

One of the many obstacles which were raised by France in the 1958 negotiations for a Free Trade Area in Europe concerned the question of origin. How would it be possible so to define the origin of goods as to ensure that the elimination of tariffs within the area did not open a back door for goods from outside the area to get through the tariff wall?

This difficulty was met in the Efta Convention by the simple expedient of specifying origin criteria. Goods entitled to free entry could conform to one of three conditions. They qualified (1) by having been produced wholly within the Area of Efta; (2) by having been produced within the area by a qualifying process specified in the Process List; (3) or, in place of (2) by containing not more than 50 per cent by value of non-Area materials, except for textiles which were excluded from the percentage criterion.

Very few of the disciplines of the European Economic Community were written into the Efta Convention. Indeed, apart from the elimination of customs duties between the member states of Efta there was no provision for integrating them economically in the way in which the Treaty of Rome integrated its six members. Nor had the Efta countries any aims of political union. The Secretariat of Efta consists of an organisation with offices in Geneva.

Finland became an associated member of Efta in 1961 and Iceland a member in 1970.

Britain's partners in Efta have taken advantage of the abolition of tariffs by increasing their trade with one another to a much greater degree than has Britain in her trade with the rest of Efta.

With the accession of four members to the European Economic Community, Efta will cease to exist as an effective trading group but the Community and the Efta Governments have expressed the wish that the free trade already established between them will be maintained and that all should co-operate in avoiding the re-erection of tariff barriers between the Efta countries who are joining the Common Market and those who are not.

These non-candidate countries are Austria, Iceland, Portugal, Sweden, Switzerland and Finland.

In the summer of 1961, the British Government decided upon two steps towards overcoming the difficulties with which the economy has been beset since the end of the second world war. The first step was the programme of the Chancellor of the Exchequer, Mr. Selwyn Lloyd, to improve the balance of payments situation which was experiencing one of the crises which have been phenomena of the post-war period. The second was the announcement by the Prime Minister, Mr. Harold Macmillan, that an attempt was to be made to negotiate Britain's entry into the Common Market.

This decision called for consultation with the Commonwealth countries and three Cabinet Ministers were nominated to visit all the Commonwealth countries to smooth the path of the Government in preparation for its discussions with the Six.

On the whole, the reaction of the Commonwealth countries was lukewarm. Most feared the effects of the common agricultural policy of the Common Market on their exports of foodstuffs and of the loss of Commonwealth preference for much of their other exports to Britain.

In the event, on 10 August 1961 Britain, joined by Denmark, requested negotiations aimed at membership of the European Economic Community and on 8 November 1961 negotiations started in Brussels.

The talks were long, difficult and often acrimonious. Britain made every concession that she deemed possible in the light of her obligations to the Commonwealth and to dependent territories. The story is told of a journalist who at one point asked a French delegate how the negotiations were going. The Frenchman replied 'Terrible. Things couldn't be worse. The English are agreeing to everything.'

By the end of 1962, agreement had, in fact, been reached on all but a hard core of problems. It was agreed that the enlarged Community would help the temperate Commonwealth countries (Australia, New Zealand and Canada) in a broadly based move towards world-wide agreements to include price and production policies, minimum and maximum quantities to enter international trade and special safeguards for developing countries. The main subjects left for agreement concerned processed foodstuffs (canned and dried fruits), safeguards for New Zealand's exports of dairy produce, and Britain's request for zero tariffs on certain important raw materials, notably aluminium, zinc, lead, wood pulp and newsprint.

At this point in the discussion, on 14 January 1963, President de Gaulle made one of his customary 'ex cathedra' announcements and said that Britain was not ready for membership of the European Economic Community and on 29 January 1963 on the initiative of the French the Brussels negotiations were abruptly broken off, in much the same manner as the Free Trade Area negotiations had been broken off in Paris four years earlier.

It was not until 2 July 1967, some two and a half years after its election, that the Labour Government applied again for Britain's membership of the European Economic Community and 11 July 1967 lodged a formal application. On 19 December 1967 President de Gaulle once again decided the issue and vetoed all Community discussions on the applications from Britain and those from Norway, Denmark and the Republic of Ireland. De Gaulle resigned as President of France on 25 April 1969. He was succeeded on 16 June 1969 by M. Georges Pompidou. The door to Britain's membership remained closed but not bolted and barred.

The European Economic Community Summit Conference at The Hague on 2 December 1969 changed the course of events when the Community formally agreed to reopen negotiations with Britain, Norway, Denmark and the Republic of Ireland. At this meeting, M. Jean Rey, President of the Commission, said that even if negotiations began straight away the time needed for negotiation and ratification would mean that it would not be until the end of 1972, at the earliest, that the enlargement of the Community could be fully accomplished.

At a press conference after the final Summit Meeting M. Pompidou said, 'Preparatory talks for the admission of Britain and the three other countries can now open in a positive spirit.'

On 18 June 1970 the General Election in Britain resulted in a Conservative majority and Mr. Edward Heath succeeded Mr. Harold Wilson as Prime Minister.

On 29 June 1970, talks began in Luxembourg between the Six and Britain, Norway, Denmark and Ireland on their applications for membership of the European Economic Community. After nearly twelve months of intensive negotiations, a break-through came in the small hours of 13 May 1971.

At the 11–13 May Ministerial-level negotiating session agreement was reached on two of the most difficult issues: Britain's transitional arrangements for aligning its farm prices with those of the Community and a framework for calculating Britain's contribution to the Community's system of direct income. Several vital issues remained unsolved. The first and possibly the most sensitive one concerned the future of New Zealand's dairy exports to Britain. Others were the role of sterling in the enlarged Community. For a favourable issue on these outstanding items it was essential that France should establish once and for all that she accepted Britain's readiness to participate in the fullest sense of the word in European economic and monetary union and that Britain should abandon her suspicion that France was prepared to use any pretext to impose a new veto to the entry of Britain to the Community.

The way was cleared at the meeting in Paris between Mr. Heath and President Pompidou on 20–21 May 1971.

After that meeting events moved swiftly. Final agreement, apart from a few minor points, came in Luxembourg at 4.30 a.m. on 23 June. Although it had become clear at the previous Session on 7–8 June that France and Britain had reached a large measure of understanding on the main issues, France had been holding back her final assent for the unanimity required for the admission of new members to the Community.

The following is a short chronology of the principal events connected with the European Communities:

1946 19 September Winston Churchill, in Zurich, urges Franco-German reconciliation within 'a kind of United States of Europe'.

1947 5 June        General Marshall proposes American aid to stimulate recovery in Europe.

| | |
|---|---|
| 29 October | Creation of Benelux—economic union of Belgium, Luxembourg and the Netherlands. |
| 1948 16 April | Convention for European Economic Co-operation signed—the birth of O.E.E.C. |
| 1949 5 May | Statute of the Council of Europe signed. |
| 1950 9 May | Robert Schuman makes his historic proposal to place French and German coal and steel under a common Authority. |
| 1951 18 April | The Treaty setting up the European Coal and Steel Community (E.C.S.C.) is signed in Paris. |
| 1952 10 August | E.C.S.C. High Authority starts work in Luxembourg under its first president, Jean Monnet. |
| 10 September | E.C.S.C. Common Assembly holds its first session in Strasbourg, and elects Paul-Henri Spaak as its first president. |
| 1953 10 February | E.C.S.C. common market for coal, iron ore, and scrap is opened. |
| 1 May | E.C.S.C. common market for steel is opened. |
| 1954 21 December | An association agreement between United Kingdom and E.C.S.C. is signed. |
| 1955 1–3 June | Messina Conference: the Foreign Ministers of the Community's member states propose further steps towards full integration in Europe. |
| 1957 25 March | Signature of the Rome Treaties setting up the Common Market and Euratom. |
| 1958 1 January | The Rome Treaties come into force: the Common Market and Euratom are set up. |
| 9 February | E.C.S.C. transition period ends—full operation of common market for coal and steel. |
| 19–21 March | First session of the European Parliament—Robert Schuman elected president. |
| 1959 1 January | First tariff reductions and quota enlargements in the Common Market. Establishment of common market for nuclear materials. |
| 20 November | European Free Trade Association convention signed between Austria, Denmark, Norway, Portugal, Sweden, Switzerland and the United Kingdom. |
| 1960 10–12 May | Community decides to speed up its timetable for implementing the Common Market. |

1961  9 July       Greece signs association agreement with E.E.C. (entry into force 1 November 1962).

     18 July       The six Community countries issue Bonn Declaration aiming at political union.

     1 August      The Republic of Ireland applies for membership of the Common Market.

     10 August     Britain and Denmark request negotiations aiming at membership of the Common Market.

     8 November Negotiations with Britain open in Brussels.

     15 December The three neutrals, Austria, Sweden and Switzerland, apply for association with the Common Market.

1962 14 January    Community fixes basic features of common agricultural policy, and regulations for grains, pigmeat, eggs and poultry, fruit and vegetables, and wine.

     9 February   Spain applies for association with the Common Market.

     2, 5 March   Britain applies for membership of the E.C.S.C. and Euratom.

     30 April      Norway requests negotiations for membership of the Common Market.

     15 May       Community decides on second speeding-up of Common Market timetable.

     16 July       Conclusion of 1960–62 negotiations for worldwide tariff cuts in G.A.T.T. Community substantially reduces common external tariff.

     30 July       First regulations implementing the common agricultural policy comes into effect.

1963 14 January    President de Gaulle declares that Britain is not ready for Community membership.

     22 January   Franco-German Treaty of Co-operation signed in Paris.

     29 January   British negotiations with Six broken off.

     1 July        Signature of Yaoundé Convention, associating 18 independent states in Africa and Madagascar with the Community for five years from 1 June 1964.

     12 September Turkey signs association agreement with Community (entry into force 1 December 1964).

| | |
|---|---|
| 23 December | Common farm-policy regulations for rice, beef and dairy products agreed. |
| 1964 14 April | Council of Ministers accepts Commission's proposals for fighting inflationary trends in Community. |
| 4 May | Kennedy Round negotiations open in Geneva. |
| 23 September | Common Market Commission bans Grundig-Consten exclusive-sales agreement as contravening monopoly rules. |
| 1 November | Common policy regulations for beef, dairy products and rice come into effect. |
| 9 December | First meeting of the Parliamentary Conference of members of European Parliament and parliamentarians from Yaoundé associated states. |
| 15 December | Council adopts the Mansholt Plan for common prices for grains. |
| 1965 31 March | Common Market Commission proposes that, as from 1 July 1967, all Community countries' import duties and levies be paid into Community budget and that powers of European Parliament be increased. |
| 8 April | Six sign treaty merging the Community Executives. |
| 31 May | Common Market Commission publishes first memorandum proposing lines of Community policy for regional development. |
| 1 July | Council fails to reach agreement by agreed deadline on financing common farm policy; French boycott of Community Institutions begins seven-month-long crisis. |
| 26 July | Council meets and conducts business without French representative present. |
| 1966 17 January | Six foreign ministers meet in Luxembourg without Commission present and agree to resume full Community activity. |
| 3 May | Common Market Commission publishes memorandum on legal means of forming 'Community law' companies. |
| 7 May | Medium-term Economic Policy Committee |

|            | publishes first five-year outline programme, which is adopted by Council on 8 February 1967. |
|------------|-----------------------------------------------------|
| 11 May     | Council agrees that on 1 July 1968, all tariffs on trade between the member states shall be removed and that the common external tariff should come into effect, thus completing the Community's customs union. It agrees also on the completion of the common farm policy by the same date. |
| 13 July    | European Court of Justice upholds principle of Commission's ban on Grundig-Consten agreement. |
| 16 July    | Nigeria signs an association agreement with the Community. |
| 24 July    | Common prices for beef, milk, sugar, rice, oilseeds and olive oil agreed by Council, enabling free trade in agricultural products by 1 July 1968. |
| 10 November | British Prime Minister Harold Wilson announces plans for 'a high-level approach' to the Six with intention of entering E.E.C. |
| 1967 January–March | Mr. Wilson and Foreign Minister George Brown visit Rome, Paris, Brussels, Bonn, The Hague and Luxembourg and discuss the possibility of British membership. |
| 2 May      | Mr. Wilson announces in the House of Commons that Britain is preparing a formal application for membership of the E.E.C. |
| 11 May     | Britain lodges formal application for membership of the European Economic Community. |
| 1968       | Britain's application for membership of the European Economic Community remains on the table with the Community. |
| 1969 25 April | General de Gaulle resigns as President of France. |
| 16 June    | M. Georges Pompidou elected President. |
| 2 December | At a Summit Conference at The Hague the Community formally agree to open membership negotiations with Britain, Norway, Denmark and the Republic of Ireland on their applications of 1967. |
| 1970 18 June | Conservatives win a majority at the General |

|            |                                                                       |
|------------|-----------------------------------------------------------------------|
|            | Election; Mr. Edward Heath succeeds Mr. Harold Wilson as Prime Minister. |
| 29 June    | Talks begin in Luxembourg between the Six and Britain, Norway, Denmark and the Republic of Ireland. |
| 1971 20–21 May | Meetings in Paris between Mr. Edward Heath and M. Georges Pompidou. |
| 23 June    | The Council of Ministers of the Community announces that agreement has been reached with the United Kingdom for the basis of the accession of the United Kingdom to the Communities. |
| 11–13 July | At a Ministerial-level negotiating session, agreement is reached on major outstanding issues: the transitional period for the U.K., Commonwealth Sugar, Capital Movements and the common commercial policy. |
| 28 October | Vote in the House of Commons on the motion 'That this House approves her Majesty's Government's decision of principle to join the European Communities on the basis of the arrangements which have been negotiated.' The voting figures in the House of Commons were 356 For, 244 Against, majority of 112; and in the House of Lords 451 For, 58 Against, majority of 393. |
| 1972 22 January | Treaty of Accession was signed in Brussels between the European Communities (France, Belgium, Germany, Italy, Luxembourg and the Netherlands) on the one side and the four new member States (United Kingdom, Denmark, Norway and the Republic of Ireland) on the other side. |

The U.K. Government issued its famous White Paper in July 1971, *The United Kingdom and the European Communities*. After debates in the House of Commons lasting from 21 to 28 October 1971 and ending with a Government majority of 112, the way was now clear for the Treaty of Accession and for the mass of legislation that will be required to be embodied in a Bill to make the legislative changes which will enable the United Kingdom to comply with the obligations of membership of the Communities and to exercise her rights of membership. The Treaty of Accession was signed in Brussels on 22 January 1972 and *the European Communities Bill*, summarised in Chapter 3, was published on 25 January 1972.

Germany ratified the Treaty on 5 July 1957 by an overwhelming majority in the Bundestag. The French National Assembly voted 341 to 235 for the Common Market Treaty on 9 July 1957. The Belgian Chamber of Deputies voted 174 to 4 in favour of ratification and the Senate 134 to 2. The Italian Chamber of Deputies and later the Senate ratified by a large majority with only the Communists voting against. Luxembourg's single Chamber Parliament voted 46 to 3. In the Netherlands, the last country to ratify, the Lower House approved the Treaty by 112 to 12 on 5 October 1957 with 24 abstentions and the Upper House completed the process in December 1957.

Unlike Britain, each of the other three Efta countries who have signed the Treaty of Accession (Norway, Denmark and the Republic of Ireland) will be holding a referendum. The Norwegian referendum will only be consultative, the vote in Parliament being decisive. In Denmark the result of the referendum alone will decide the issue. In Ireland the votes in the referendum and in Parliament will be complementary: a positive vote in both being needed before Ireland can ratify.

The crucial point in all the parliamentary processes leading to the ratification of the Treaty of Accession is that Britain and the other new member-states accept in advance, as part of their own law, past and future Community decisions. Any British statute that conflicts with her obligations to the Community goes by the board because national law is subordinated to Community law in every field covered by the Treaty of Rome and its Regulations. Past dictates of the Community are adopted, except where provision has been made otherwise in the Treaty of Accession. From the date of their membership the new member-states will, however, have a share in the making of future dictates.

# CHAPTER 2

## The Terms of Britain's Entry into the European Economic Community

The following sets out, in outline, the main points of agreement for Britain's entry into the Community.

(1) *Transitional Period.* Five years from 1 January 1973.

(2) *Industrial Tariffs.* The removal of tariffs on goods traded amongst the Ten will be made in five stages each of 20 per cent, the first on 1 April 1973 and the last on 1 July 1977.

The Common External Tariff will be adopted in four stages, the first being an alignment of 40 per cent of the differences on 1 January 1974 followed by three further moves each of 20 per cent on 1 January 1975, 1 January 1976 and 1 July 1977 respectively. For thirteen products (twelve industrial raw materials and tea) Britain will continue to import more than 90 per cent of her requirements duty-free. (The Common External Tariff will apply, with certain exceptions, to Britain's imports of Commonwealth manufactures.)

(3) *Agriculture.* Britain will adopt the Community system of support, but not Community prices, in the first year of membership. Thereafter Britain will increase her threshold and intervention prices to full Community levels by six stages over the five year transitional period. Tariffs on Horticulture will be dismantled in five equal stages of 20 per cent at the end of December 1973 and ending in 1977.

(4) *Community Finance.* Britain accepts the Community 'own resources' system of finance. From its inception until 1970, the Community's expenditure was financed by a combination of the proceeds from levies on agricultural imports which were made over to the Community and financial contributions from the member-states.

On 21 April 1970, the Council of Ministers adopted a new system designed to make the Community self-financing and to bring its expenditure into one central budget. Between 1971 and 1977, the Community is phasing in the provision of its funds by payment from member countries of 90 per cent of the import levies they collect on imported farm produce and of the import duties on all other goods and the proceeds of up to a one per cent value added tax.

B

It was necessary to find a method to enable Britain gradually to adopt to the Community system over a period of years without placing an undue burden on her economy.

A percentage or *key* has been set, broadly corresponding to Britain's share of the total gross national product (GNP) in the ten countries of the enlarged Community. This represents the proportion of the budget which Britain would nominally be expected to pay in the first year of membership. This key will then increase marginally in each of the four subsequent years under similar arrangements to those agreed by the Six for themselves.

However, Britain will pay only a proportion of her nominal contribution for the first five years. The proportion will increase in annual stages.

The effect of these arrangements is shown in the following table. Column 2 sets out the nominal key.

3 shows the proportion which Britain will, in practice, be required to pay.

4 gives Britain's resulting share of the Community budget in each year.

| (1) Year | (2) U.K. Percentage of Community Budget | (3) Percentage of key to be paid | (4) U.K. contribution as percentage of Community Budget |
|---|---|---|---|
| 1973 | 19·19 | 45·0 | 8·64 |
| 1974 | 19·38 | 56·0 | 10·85 |
| 1975 | 19·77 | 67·5 | 13·34 |
| 1976 | 20·16 | 79·5 | 16·03 |
| 1977 | 20·56 | 92·0 | 18·92 |

After the first five years, there will be a further period of two years, during which the size of Britain's contribution will be limited by reference to the previous year's contribution.

In 1980 and subsequent years, Britain will be required to pay 90 per cent of her agricultural levy and customs duties and such value added tax (VAT) (not exceeding the yield of a 1 per cent VAT) as is necessary to close any gap between Community expenditure and Community revenue.

This gap cannot be estimated, but it is important to note that in common with other members Britain is entitled to receive payments from the Community budget as well as to make contributions to it.

If Community expenditure moves away from agricultural subsidies and assistance towards industrial and regional activities as seems likely in the course of time, Britain could expect to enjoy larger receipts from the Community budget for her needs under a wider regional policy.

(5) *Institutions.* Britain will have the same representation and voting weight in the enlarged Community as the other three large countries, Germany, France and Italy. Most decisions of the Council of Ministers are taken on the basis of a proposal by the Commission. For certain Council decisions, unanimity is required. In cases where qualified voting with weighting of votes is provided in the Treaty, the members of the Council have the following weightings:

Germany 10, Italy 10, France 10, U.K. 10, Belgium 5, Netherlands 5, Denmark 3, Norway 3, Ireland 3, Luxembourg 2. Total 61.

In these cases, where the Council decision follows a proposal by the Commission, the decisions of the Council are to be effective only if at least forty-three votes are cast in favour out of sixty-one.

Where the decision is one on which the Commission has not made a proposal, it is approved only if forty-three votes are cast in favour by at least six members. In cases in which a simple majority is required, a majority will, of course, be six out of the ten States.

(6) *Sugar.* The U.K. Governments contractual obligations to buy agreed quantities of sugar under the Commonwealth Sugar Agreement will be fulfilled until 1974 and domestic beet sugar production continues to be limited until then.

Thereafter, it has been agreed that the arrangements for sugar imports from developing Commonwealth sugar producers should be made within the framework of an association or trading agreement with the enlarged Community.

(7) *New Zealand.* The quantities of New Zealand butter and cheese on which import levies will not be payable will be run down to a figure of 80 per cent of New Zealand's current butter exports to Britain and 20 per cent of her cheese exports by the end of five years. The butter situation will be reviewed in the third year of Britain's membership and the enlarged Council of Ministers will decide on measures for assuring the exceptional treatment granted to New Zealand to be continued after 1977.

(8) *Sterling.* Britain has agreed to an orderly and gradual rundown of sterling balances after joining the Community and in the meantime they will be stabilised. No time-table has been set for the dismantling of sterling's reserve role.

(9) *Coal and Steel.* Britain needs no transitional period for applying

the rules of the European Coal and Steel Community, but the alignment of tariffs on steel products will be made at the same rate as the alignment of tariffs on industrial goods generally.

(10) *Fiscal Harmonisation.* Britain will adopt the various measures of fiscal harmonisation. Her use of Value Added Tax will be in advance of membership of the Community and she will also adopt other harmonisation measures according to her terms of membership. She will convert customs duties at present levied on hydrocarbon oils, beer, spirits and tobacco into internal taxes similar to VAT to allow free movement of these commodities in accordance with the Treaty.

(11) *Channel Islands and Isle of Man.* There will be free trade in agricultural and industrial goods between the islands and the members of the Community, but the islands will be exempt from other Community rules and regulations, including the Value-Added Tax, free movement of labour, freedom of establishment and competition policy.

(12) *Export Credits.* Britain's present system of export credits operated by the Export Credits Guarantee Department requires adjustment to comply with the Community's rules and will be changed during a two-year transitional period.

(13) *Independent Commonwealth Countries* in Africa, the Caribbean, the Indian Ocean and the Pacific will be able to choose between (a) association under a renewed Yaoundé Convention (see page 206); (b) some other form of association exemplified by the Arusha Convention (see page 210) or (c) a commercial agreement.

(14) *All British dependent territories*, except Gibraltar and Hong Kong, will be offered association under part IV of the Treaty of Rome.

(15) *Gibraltar.* The Treaty provisions will apply to Gibraltar as a European Territory for whose external relations a member state is responsible. Gibraltar will not, however, be included in the customs area of the enlarged Community as she is not part of U.K. customs territory.

(16) *Hong Kong* is included in the Community scheme of generalised preferences.

(17) *India, Pakistan, Ceylon, Malaysia and Singapore* are also included in the generalised system of tariff preferences. After enlargement, the Community will examine trade problems, including Indian exports of sugar and textiles. The Community tariff on tea, as stated elsewhere, has also been suspended.

(18) *Malta and Cyprus.* Association agreements for preferential trading arrangements.

(19) *Fisheries.* Notwithstanding the policy of the Community to limit restrictions on fishing to within six miles of the coast of member-states, the limit will be extended to twelve miles for certain coastal waters of Denmark, France, Ireland, Norway and the United Kingdom for a period of five years after accession. At the end of five years, the Council, acting on a proposal from the Commission, will determine conditions for fishing to ensure protection of fishing grounds and the conservation of resources.

# CHAPTER 3

## *Treaties of Rome and Brussels*

### THE TREATY OF ROME

European history is, as every schoolboy knows to his cost, littered with Treaties. Some have altered the political and economic face of Europe. Most have been signed following a period of war and the aim has been that the vanquished should not regain its former power.

In our lifetime another Treaty has been signed and mention of it has already entered the history books. This Treaty has as its aim the raising of living standards for European peoples.

On 1 January 1958 the Treaty of Rome establishing the European Economic Community came officially into force.

This chapter deals with the principal provisions of the Treaty setting up the European Economic Community or Common Market. Subsequent chapters deal in greater detail with developments and interpretation of the Treaty from 1 January 1958.

The final drafts of the Treaty had been completed by the inter-governmental committee in Brussels on 9 March 1957, and the Treaty was signed in Rome by Belgium, France, West Germany, Italy, Luxembourg, and the Netherlands on 25 March 1957. The signing ceremony took place at the Palazzo dei Conservatori on the Capitoline Hill. The signatories being Signor Segni (then Italian Prime Minister); Dr. Adenauer (then Federal German Chancellor); the Foreign Ministers of Belgium (then M. Spaak); France (then M. Pincau); Italy (then Dr. Martino); Luxembourg (then M. Bech); and the Netherlands (Mr. Luns); The West German State Secretary for Foreign Affairs (Professor Hallstein, representing the then Foreign Minister, Dr. von Brentano, who was on a visit to Australia).

Between July and December 1957 the Treaty was ratified by the Parliaments of all the six member-countries.

The Treaty, which was concluded for an unlimited period, consists of 248 Articles, 15 Annexes, 4 declarations of intention, and 3 protocols.

In the preamble to the Treaty, the six signatory countries declared their intention of establishing 'the foundations of an enduring and closer union between European peoples' by gradually removing the economic effect of their political frontiers. It was agreed that a common market and a common external tariff (Customs union) would be established for all goods; common policies would be devised for agriculture, transport, labour mobility, and important sectors of the economy; common institutions would be set up for economic development; and the overseas territories and possessions of member-States would be associated with the new Community. All these measures had one 'essential aim'—the steady improvement in the conditions of life and work of the peoples of the member-countries.

The tasks of the Community were defined in Article 1 of the Treaty as 'the achievement of a harmonious development of the economy within the whole Community, a continuous and balanced economic expansion, increased economic stability, a more rapid improvement in living-standards, and closer relations between the member-countries'.

INSTITUTIONS

A system of institutions is laid down in the Treaty, and they consist of:

    (a)   The Assembly
    (b)   The Council of Ministers
    (c)   The Commission
    (d)   The Court of Justice

and, acting in a consultative capacity

    (e)   The Economic and Social Committee.

The power of decision is entrusted, in the main, to the Council of Ministers with the Assembly exercising political power over the other institutions of the Community. As the economic and political character of the E.E.C. develops the Assembly should obtain greater power and delegates chosen from the Parliaments of the member-states make up the Assembly. These institutions are discussed in greater detail in Chapter 3.

One of the principal characteristics of the process of creating a Common Market is its irrevocable character. This constitutes an important safeguard for the smaller member-countries in as much as their sacrifices in adjusting themselves to the new conditions do not involve the risk of a complete standstill and a subsequent return to the previous status after a period of time.

The Common Market was planned to be established in three stages within a transitional period of 12 years which could be extended to 15 years.

Within the basic 12-year period there were to be three stages, each lasting, in principle, four years. However at the end of the first four years if the Council of Ministers and the Commission had not unanimously agreed that the objectives of that stage had been essentially accomplished, the stage would automatically have been extended for one year. At the end of the fifth year there could be another one-year extension on the same condition, whilst at the end of the sixth year a further extension could be granted only if a request by a member-state for such an extension was recognised as justified by an ad hoc arbitration tribunal of three members appointed by the Council of Ministers. In deciding whether the objectives of the respective stages had been essentially accomplished, and the obligations under the Treaty carried out, no member-country could prevent a unanimous decision by basing its protest on non-compliance with its own obligations.

The second and third stages could have been either prolonged or shortened by unanimous decision of the Council of Ministers, subject to the maximum limit of 15 years for the whole transitional period.

The member-countries co-ordinate their economic policy to the extent required for achieving the aims of the Treaty. The institutions of the Community ensure that the internal and external financial stability of the member-countries was not endangered. Any discrimination against nationals or companies of other member-countries is prohibited, except in the special cases expressly laid down in the Treaty.

THE BASIS OF THE ECONOMIC COMMUNITY

The European Economic Community is based on a Customs Union covering the whole trade of member-countries and entailing (a) a prohibition on imposing import or export duties or similar levies between member-countries; (b) the introduction of a common tariff on imports from non-Community countries; (c) the abolition of all quantitative import and export restrictions and other similar measures between member-countries. The free exchange of goods within the Community applies not only to goods produced in the member-countries but also to those which have been imported by a member-country from outside the Community, and on which Customs duties have been paid on entry.

*Internal Tariffs* Agreement was reached that tariff restrictions on trade between member-countries would be abolished entirely by the end of the transitional period at the latest. In fact the reductions took place much quicker than initially envisaged.

*External Tariffs* A common tariff on imports from the non-Community countries were established in full not later than the end of the transitional period. As a general rule, the final tariff for each product will be the arithmetical average of the corresponding national tariffs in force on 1 January 1957. National tariffs which vary initially by no more than 15 per cent from the average tariff will be replaced by the latter within four years; in other cases the gap will be reduced by 30 per cent after four years, by 60 per cent after eight years, and will be eliminated entirely by the end of the transitional period. Certain exceptions to these general provisions were permitted and are explained in greater detail in the chapter dealing with tariffs.

*Quantitative Restrictions* It was planned that all quantitative restrictions on trade within the Community would be progressively eliminated by a series of quota increases. (This procedure differed from the one applied by the O.E.E.C., which provided for the immediate complete removal of import quotas in respect of a growing range of individual products.)

Thus, one year after the coming into force of the Treaty, 1 January 1959, the member-states converted all their existing bilateral import quotas into global quotas in favour of all other member-countries, without any discrimination between them. All these global import quotas would be increased annually by at least 20 per cent as regards their overall value, and by at least 10 per cent as regards each individual product; bigger increases were made in the case of quotas amounting initially to less than 3 per cent of the domestic output of a given product. While Governments had a certain amount of discretion as to the incidence and timing of quota increases, they were nevertheless required to work towards the ultimate objective, viz. that by the end of the tenth year each individual quote should be equivalent to at least 20 per cent of the national production of the article concerned.

Special provisions regulated the position of those member-countries that had already introduced high global import quotas on the coming into force of the Treaty, or had gone beyond the obligations assumed within the then O.E.E.C. as regards the liberalisation of imports. If the Commission found that the imports of a certain commodity into a member-country during two successive years had been below the respective import quota, the quota was abolished altogether.

Quantitative restrictions on exports had to be abolished by the end of the first stage at the latest. Member-countries were nevertheless permitted to impose import, export, or transit restrictions or prohibitions which were justified for reasons of public morality, public order, public security, or on similar grounds, provided there was no arbitrary discrimination or any concealed restriction of trade. In fact, all quotas on industrial imports from member-countries were abolished on 31 December 1961.

As regards certain State monopolies in the member-countries which might have led to restrictions in intra-Community trade with effects similar to quota restrictions, the Treaty provided that all such monopolies had to be gradually changed so that at the end of the transitional period any discrimination between nationals of member-countries as regards both purchases and supplies ceased. If a certain product was subject to a commercial State monopoly in one or several member-countries, the Commission could then authorise the other member-states to take certain protective measures.

*Agriculture* Agricultural products are included in the Common Market (unlike such organisations as Efta) although the Treaty envisaged a special regime to apply in view of the different social structure of agriculture in the various member-countries, where it made it difficult to introduce a completely liberalised market.

*Labour, Settlement, Services and Capital* The free circulation of labour, services, and capital, as well as the right to settle, work and trade anywhere in the Community, was to be fully established by the end of the transitional period.

*Labour* As soon as the Treaty came into force, the Council of Ministers decided by simple majority voting what measures were necessary to ensure complete mobility of labour within the Community, including (i) the abolition of all discriminatory measures between nationals of member-countries; (ii) the right to apply for jobs anywhere within the six countries, and—on terminating any employment—to stay on in the country concerned under conditions to be fixed by the Commission. Measures taken by the Council of Ministers include provisions (i) for the dissemination of information about available jobs and labour, as well as other procedures to meet supply and demand under conditions which avoid serious danger to the standard of living and employment in the various areas and industries; (ii) for the removal of administrative difficulties; and (iii) for close collaboration between national labour organisations. Also the Council of Ministers have to decide on social security arrangements applicable to conditions of full mobility of labour.

*Right of Settlement* All restrictions on the right to settle freely in any member-country, or the right of nationals of any member-country to set up agencies, branches, or subsidiary companies in the territory of another, are to be gradually removed during the transitional period. The right of settlement includes the right to engage in any economic activity and to establish or manage companies and other enterprises.

The Treaty stated that before the end of the first stage of the transitional period the Council of Ministers would work out a general programme to remove from existing restrictions every kind of activity, and to determine the various stages of implementation. All decisions relating to the execution of this general programme, or for the abolition of restrictions on specific activities, would be taken by the Council of Ministers.

The Council are also drawing up rules for the mutual recognition of diplomas, certificates, and other qualifications, and for the co-ordination of existing regulations in the member-countries concerning the practice of professions.

*Services* All restrictions on the offering of services by insurance companies, banks, finance houses, the wholesale and retail trade, and by members of the professions will gradually be removed within the Community during the transitional period. Before the end of the first stage the Council of Ministers drew up a general programme to implement this principle.

*Capital* Existing restrictions on the movement of capital between the Community countries are planned to be progressively removed. As far as is necessary for the proper working of the Common Market, restrictions on current payments relating to the movement of capital (e.g. interest, dividends, rents, premiums) should have been completely abolished not later than the end of the first stage of the transitional period. The aim was that decisions by the Council of Ministers on the abolition of capital movement restrictions would be taken by unanimous vote during the first two stages, and by a qualified majority thereafter but progress has been slow in this field.

The only exceptions from the general rule of the eventual free movement of capital within the Community will apply in the following cases: (a) loans directly or indirectly intended to finance the Government, public institutions, or organs of local government of one member-country could be issued or sold in another member-country only with that country's consent: (b) member-countries while generally forbidden to introduce any new restrictions concerning capital movements, would be entitled to take protective measures within certain limits if such movements were likely to disturb their economies—the application of these protective measures being, however, supervised by the Commission.

As regards capital movements between member-countries and non-Community States, the Council of Ministers lay down all the measures required for controlling such movements and the foreign exchange policies connected with them, with the aim of achieving the highest possible degree of liberalisation. Council decisions in these matters will require unanimity. In the event of different degrees of liberalisation of capital movements and foreign exchange policies between one member-country and another leading to abuses of the regulations then existing, a member-country affected by such abuses is able to take suitable measures to stop them after consulting with the other member-countries and the Commission. Measures of this kind, however, might be subsequently amended or abolished altogether by decisions of the Council.

*Transport*   The Council of Ministers will establish a joint transport policy and common rules for international transport within or through the Community, covering rail, road, and inland water transport. It will also lay down the conditions under which transport undertakings of one member-country will be permitted to operate in another. These decisions will have to be taken unanimously in the first two transitional stages and by a qualified majority thereafter, but unanimity will still be required after the second transitional stage whenever the Council's decisions related to principles of transport policy and might seriously impair the standard of living and employment in certain areas.

The extension of suitable common rules to sea and air transport, and the procedure applying in these cases, will be a matter for the Council to decide and such decisions requiring unanimity.

The Treaty laid down that all freight rates which discriminated as to the national origin or destination of the goods transported would be suppressed by the end of the second stage of the transitional period, whilst all special rates or privileges granted by a member-country for the purpose of helping or protecting specific undertakings or industries would have to be ended at the beginning of the second stage, unless specially authorised by the Commission. Two years after the coming into force of the Treaty, and after hearing the views of the Economic and Social Committee, the Council issued general regulations so that the Commission could take the necessary individual decisions after hearing the views of all the member-countries concerned.

In taking its decisions, the Commission take into account not only the requirements of an adequate location of industry but also the needs of less developed areas; the problems of areas which have suffered greatly through political conditions; and the effects of the various rates and tariffs on the competitive position between various kinds of transport. West Germany is authorised, notwithstanding the provisions of the Treaty, to take any measures required to compensate the areas affected for economic disadvantages arising from the political division of Germany.

However, general agreement on Transport policy has not advanced at the pace envisaged in the Treaty.

A consultative committee of experts appointed by member-Governments was set up to advise the Commission on all transport questions.

ECONOMIC AND SOCIAL POLICY OF THE COMMUNITY

To ensure free and equal competition within the Community, common rules and policies were introduced in the member-countries as summarised below.

COMMON RULES

*Cartels and Monopolies*   Any agreement or association preventing, restraining or distorting competition within the Community is forbidden, e.g. agreements or associations directly or indirectly fixing prices; regulating or controlling production, investment or technical development; sharing markets; requiring the acceptance of additional goods besides those needed by the customer; or providing for discriminatory conditions of supply. Exceptions were only permissible if such agreements contribute to production, distribution, or technical or economic progress, and if (i) an adequate share of the benefits arising therefrom is passed on to the consumer; (ii) the restrictive effect is not greater than was necessary for the purpose; (iii) the agreements do not open the way to monopolistic practices. The abuse by any or a number of enterprises enjoying a dominant position in a given market within the Community is also forbidden.

The plan was that during the early period anti-monopoly rules would be enforced nationally on the basis of detailed reports by the Commission to member-governments. Within three years, however, international rules and directives having the force of law throughout the Community would be issued by the Council of Ministers; those decisions would require a unanimous vote. If no such rules and directives had been issued by the Council within the three-year period, it would be able to make them thereafter by a qualified majority, on a proposal of the Commission and after consulting the Assembly.

Although the member-countries themselves would initially enforce anti-cartel and anti-monopoly regulations, the Commission had certain supervisory functions immediately after the coming into force of the Treaty. Specifically, the Commission could note violations of anti-cartel or anti-monopoly rules and could authorise a member-country whose interests were affected to take the necessary protective measures.

These principles apply not only to private industry but also to public enterprises, as well as to enterprises enjoying special or exclusive rights and privileges. State monopolies of a fiscal character and similar undertakings will, in principle, also come under the Treaty. The rules governing competition are examined in more detail in Chapter 10.

*Dumping* Dumping practices by any member-country within the Common Market are prohibited. If, during the transitional period, the Commission find that a member-state has engaged in such practices, it can make 'suitable recommendations' to the country concerned with a view to ending them. If the country concerned nevertheless continues such practices, the Commission can authorise that the other member-country or countries affected take the necessary protective measures, details of which would be laid down by the Commission.

*State Subsidies* Unless otherwise provided by the Treaty, State subsidies, of whatever kind, which distort or threaten to distort competition are prohibited. Nevertheless, certain subsidies are permissible notably subsidies of a social character; relief after natural catastrophes; subsidies given to certain areas in West Germany as compensation for the economic disadvantages caused by the division of Germany; special aid for under-developed areas or for projects of common European importance; and aid for the development of certain branches of the economy, provided it does not affect trade conditions in a manner detrimental to the common interest.

The Commission also examine all existing subsidies falling under this provision, in co-operation with the member-countries. And where it found that they were incompatible with the principles laid down in the Treaty, or were abused, it has ordered their abolition or amendment. If the country concerned does not carry out the Commission's decision within the stipulated period, the Commission itself or any other member-country affected can immediately appeal to the Court of Justice.

All member-countries are obliged to inform the Commission in advance of any proposed introduction of amendment of such subsidies; if the Commission considers these measures incompatible with the Treaty it can apply the procedure mentioned above.

*Approximation of Laws* By unanimous vote, the Council of Ministers can issue rules for the approximating of such existing legislation in member-countries which directly affects the setting-up or working of the Common Market.

ECONOMIC POLICY

The aim of the Treaty is that member-countries will harmonise their general economic, foreign exchange, and foreign trade policies.

*General Economic Policy* The general economic policies of member-countries is regarded as a matter of joint interest, and the countries concerned consult each other as well as the Commission on the measures which should be taken to meet changing circumstances. Such measures can be laid down by a unanimous vote of the Council of Ministers.

*Balance of Payments* Although each member-country remains autonomous in currency matters and has sole responsibility for the maintenance of equilibrium in its balance of payments, combined with the maintenance of a high degree of employment and stable prices, all members co-ordinate their general economic and foreign exchange policies to the extent necessary for the efficient working of the Common Market. This co-ordination includes co-operation between their Economic Ministries and Central Banks. A Monetary Committee was set up with the task of supervising the exchange and financial positions of member-countries and of making regular reports to the organs of the Community.

Each member-country should conduct its foreign exchange policy in harmony with the common interest. All payments relating to the exchange of goods and services and the movement of capital, as well as the transfer of interest, dividends, rents, wages, salaries, etc., to other member-countries, should be permitted as far as such transactions were liberalised under the Treaty.

If a member-state is threatened with serious balance-of-payments difficulties the Commission is required to conduct an inquiry without delay. It can then propose to the Council of Ministers measures whereby the rest of the Community might help the member-state concerned, such 'mutual help' including the provision of limited credits by the other member-countries. If the latter refuse to give such aid, however, the organs of the Community will permit certain protective measures in favour of the country affected. Member-countries are, nevertheless, able to take the necessary protective measures on their own initiative, and without waiting for the Commission's decision, if they are threatened by a sudden balance-of-payments crisis; in such eventualities the Council might, however, subsequently demand that the country concerned should amend, suspend, or abolish the measures in question.

*External Trade Policy*  A common external trade policy will be established by the end of the transitional period; pending this, member-countries are required to co-ordinate their trade relations with non-Community countries. The Commission is working out proposals for the procedure to be applied during the transitional period with a view to the eventual unification of external trade policies, and will submit these proposals to the Council of Ministers for the latter's approval. In harmonising their trade policies during the transitional period, member-countries will endeavour to unify their liberalisation lists *vis-à-vis* non-Community countries at the highest possible level, on the basis of recommendations by the Commission. One of the biggest efforts to achieve these ends was E.E.C. negotiating as a group at the Kennedy Round discussions of G.A.T.T. As an important aspect of this process of co-ordination, the export subsidy policies of the member-states is to be harmonised before the end of the transitional period.

The common external trade policy after the end of the transitional period will cover the application of a common customs tariff; the joint conclusion of trade and customs agreements; the unification of trade liberalisation measures; the working-out of common export policies; and the joint application of protective measures, e.g. against dumping or subsidies by non-community countries.

For trade and customs negotiations with non-Community countries the task of the Commission is to initiate discussions with the consent of the Council of Ministers, and to be in continuous consultation with a special committee appointed by the Council for this purpose; any agreements reached would need confirmation by the Council, which would be the organ for officially concluding agreements on behalf of the Community. This procedure applied to all Customs negotiations from the coming into force of the Treaty, and to all trade negotiations from the end of the transitional period.

During the transitional period member-countries consult each other in all matters relating to international economic organisations, with a view to harmonising their actions, and attempt to pursue a common policy as far as possible. Thereafter they would act in agreement throughout.

In formulating their joint trade policy, member-countries take into account the favourable results which the abolition of customs duties within the Community are expected to produce in increasing the competitive power of their industries.

SOCIAL POLICY—CREATION OF EUROPEAN SOCIAL FUND

*General Provisions*  The Commission has promoted the co-ordination of the social policies of member-countries, with particular reference to employment, labour legislation, conditions of work, vocational training, social security, prevention of industrial accidents and occupational diseases, health protection, trade union rights, and collective bargaining between employers and employed. The Commission carries out this task by means of inquiries, recommendations, and consultations, and deals with both internal problems and questions raised by international organisations. Before making any recommendations, the Commission listens to the opinion of the Economic and Social Committee. The Commission also reports on social developments within the Community in its annual report to the Assembly. The latter body can request the Commission to make reports on special problems of a social nature.

*Wages and Social Insurance Contributions*   The Treaty laid down the principle of equal pay for equal work and that this should be generally applied during the first transitional stage (this, in fact, was not achieved). A special protocol annexed to the Treaty dealt with Social Security contributions in France.

*European Social Fund*   A European Social Fund was established to facilitate employment and the mobility of labour within the Community. This Fund refunds to any member-country 50 per cent of the cost incurred by that country, or its public bodies, for the following purposes: (a) re-training workers who had become unemployed as a result of the Common Market for another occupation, provided they had worked at least six months in their new jobs; (b) moving workers who had been compelled to change their residence (as a result of the setting-up of the Common Market) to other localities, provided they had been employed at their new places of residence for at least six months; (c) special subsidies paid to workers who were temporarily forced to work short time, or who had been temporarily thrown out of work, through changes in production by the undertaking employing them, and which had been paid to enable the workers concerned to maintain their standard of living pending the restoration of their full employment. The 50 per cent refund is dependent on (i) the workers affected having been fully employed again by the undertaking concerned for at least six months, and (ii) the Government concerned having previously submitted an approved reorganisation scheme to the Commission.

The Fund is administered by the Commission, assisted by a Committee consisting of representatives of member-Governments and trade unions. The Fund's budget is part of the Community's general budget, and is prepared by the Commission and needs the approval by the Council of Ministers. All regulations for the working of the European Social Fund, and for laying down in detail the terms on which it will aid member-countries, are issued by the Council of Ministers on proposals of the Commission, and after consulting the Economic and Social Committee and the Assembly. The Council of Ministers also lay down general principles for a joint policy in vocational training, designed to contribute to a harmonious economic development both in the individual member-countries and in the Common Market as a whole.

## THE EUROPEAN INVESTMENT BANK

The Treaty stated that the European Investment Bank would be set up as an independent legal entity, its members consisting of the countries signatory to the Treaty. The Bank would promote a common investment policy within the Community and would, on a non-profit basis, grant loans or guarantees for (i) projects in under-developed regions; (ii) the modernisation, reorganisation, or extension of industries which were difficult to finance on a purely national basis; and (iii) new industries of joint interest to several member-countries which, because of their size or special character, would be difficult to finance by a single member-country.

The Bank's initial capital would be 1,000,000,000 E.P.U. units ($1,000,000,000), of which France and West Germany would each contribute $300,000,000, Italy $240,000,000, Belgium $86,500,000, the Netherlands $71,500,000, and Luxembourg $2,000,000. Member-countries would be required to pay in 25 per cent of their capital shares, in five equal instalments, within $2\frac{1}{2}$ years after the Treaty entered into force; of each payment, 25 per cent would be in gold and the remainder in the national currency.

The Bank could also borrow in the capital market, but if this were not possible on reasonable terms, it could request member-countries to grant it special loans for financing specified projects. Such request could only be made, at the earliest, four years after the Treaty came into force, and the loans might not exceed a total of $400,000,000, or $100,000,000 borrowed in any one year. They would bear 4 per cent interest per annum unless the Board of Governors fixed another rate.

The Bank—the statutes of which were annexed to the Treaty— would have (a) a Board of Governors, consisting of the members of the Council of Ministers; (b) a Board of Directors, comprising 12 members and 12 alternate members who would be appointed by the Board of Governors for five years. The Board of Directors would be independent of the member-governments and would comprise 3 members and 3 alternate members nominated by France, 3 each by West Germany, 3 each by Italy, 2 each by the Benelux countries jointly, and one each by the Commission. There would also be a steering committee consisting of a chairman and 2 vice-chairmen, appointed by the Board of Governors on the recommendation of the Board of Directors.

Examples of the achievements of the Bank are given in Chapter 7.

ASSOCIATION OF OVERSEAS TERRITORIES WITH COMMON
MARKET—SPECIAL DEVELOPMENT FUND FOR OVERSEAS
TERRITORIES

The overseas territories of Belgium, France, Italy, and the Netherlands were allowed to be associated with the Community. A special
convention annexed to the Treaty laid down the details of this
association for the initial five-year period.

*The main principles of Association* were that the products of the
overseas territories would enter the Community on equal terms with
those of the member-states, and each territory would extend to all
the other member-countries any concessions applying to the country
with which it was specially connected. Whilst Customs duties between
the overseas territories and member-countries would, in general, be
gradually removed under the five-year convention, and quantitative
import restrictions progressively abolished, the overseas territories
would nevertheless be allowed to continue to impose Customs duties
required for the development of their industries and the financing of
their public expenditure. Such duties, however, would be progressively reduced *vis-à-vis* other member-countries to the same level
applicable to goods imported by the territory concerned from the
member-country with which it was specially connected—thus
abolishing any discrimination against the other member-countries.

As regards existing individual import quotas of the overseas
territories, these would be converted into global quotas for the benefit
of all those member-countries (and their overseas territories) with
whom the territory in question was not specially connected. (Thus, in
a French overseas territory there would be a global import quota for
imports from, e.g. Belgium, Germany, Italy, and the Netherlands, in
place of previously existing individual import quotas from each of
these countries.)

*Overseas Development Fund*  The five-year convention provided for
the setting-up of a special Development Fund for the overseas territories, with a total of $581,250,000. Of this sum, France and West
Germany would each contribute $200,000,000, Belgium and the
Netherlands each $70,000,000, Italy $40,000,000, and Luxembourg
$1,250,000. The Fund was allocated to the overseas territories of the
four member-countries concerned as follows: France $511,250,000;
Netherlands $35,000,000; Belgium $30,000,000; and Italy $5,000,000.

Details of the initial contributions and allocations for each of the
five years were agreed as follows:

CONTRIBUTIONS

| Years | First | Second | Third | Fourth | Fifth |
|---|---|---|---|---|---|
| Percentage | 10% | 12·5% | 16·5% | 22·5% | 38·5% |
| Countries: | | in million dollars (E.P.U. units) | | | |
| Belgium | 7 | 8·75 | 11·55 | 15·75 | 26·95 |
| W. Germany | 20 | 25 | 33 | 45 | 77 |
| France | 20 | 25 | 33 | 45 | 77 |
| Italy | 4 | 5 | 6·60 | 9 | 15·40 |
| Luxembourg | 0·125 | 0·15625 | 0·20625 | 0·28125 | 0·48125 |
| Netherlands | 7 | 8·75 | 11·55 | 15·75 | 26·95 |

ALLOCATIONS

| Years | First | Second | Third | Fourth | Fifth |
|---|---|---|---|---|---|
| Percentage | 10% | 12·5% | 16·5% | 22·5% | 38·5% |
| Overseas territories of: | | in million dollars (E.P.U. units) | | | |
| Belgium | 3 | 3·75 | 4·95 | 6·75 | 11·55 |
| France | 51·125 | 63·906 | 84·356 | 115·031 | 196·832 |
| Italy | 0·5 | 0·625 | 0·825 | 1·125 | 1·925 |
| Netherlands | 3·5 | 4·375 | 5·775 | 7·875 | 13·475 |

Applications for the financing of projects out of the Development Fund are made by the responsible authorities of the member-countries and overseas territories concerned. The Commission then draws up annually the general programme of proposed investments on which the Council of Ministers make the final decisions, on the principle of a rational geographical distribution of the projects to be financed. These projects comprise, in particular, hospitals, technical training and research institutions, institutions to increase employment, and investment projects connected with productive development.

*Association of Other Countries* It was also provided that member-countries might offer participation in the Community to certain independent countries such as Morocco, Tunisia, and Libya, and to the Autonomous territories of the Netherlands Antilles and Surinam.

GENERAL FINANCE

The member-states contribute to the Community budget in the following proportions: France, Italy and West Germany, each 28 per cent; Belgium and the Netherlands, each 7·9 per cent; Luxembourg 0·2 per cent.

The budget is prepared by the Commission, which also investigates the possibility of replacing the contributions of member-countries by independent resources, notably receipts from the common tariff. (The agricultural crisis of 1966 in which France partially withdrew from

E.E.C. working committees was caused by the problems of control of Community funds arising from the common external tariff.) The budget is submitted for approval first to the Council of Ministers and then to the Assembly. In the case of any modifications proposed by the Assembly, the Council of Ministers, in consultation with the Commission, makes the final decision.

GENERAL PROVISIONS AND SAFEGUARDS

*Safeguarding Clauses*  With the consent of the Commission, member-countries are able during a limited period to deviate from the provisions of the Treaty in order to meet special difficulties which are caused to some of their industries during the gradual introduction of the Common Market.

A member-country which is, for example, in serious and persistent difficulties is entitled during the transitional period to take special steps to safeguard its economy or the economy of certain areas; in such a case the Commission decides without delay about the measures which it considered necessary, and at the same time lays down the conditions of their implementation.

Member-states are also allowed to take special measures for the protection of their interests in the sphere of defence or in the event of war.

*Membership and Association*  The Treaty applies to Algeria and the French Overseas Departments under special conditions.

Any other European country can apply for membership of the Community; the terms of its admission, and any consequential amendments of the Treaty which might become necessary, would be agreed between the original member-countries and the applicant country.

Agreements can also be concluded with another country or group of countries for their association with the Community, based on certain mutual rights and obligations, joint action, and special procedures. Similar agreements of association could be entered into with international organisations.

ANNEXED PROTOCOLS

The following protocols were annexed to the Treaty:

(1) A protocol containing the statutes of the European Investment Bank.

(2) A protocol sanctioning the continuation of trade between West

and East Germany as a German internal matter. It laid down that each member-country would inform both the other members and the Commission of any agreements relating to its trade with East Germany; that member-countries would ensure that the implementation of such agreements were not contrary to the principles of the Common Market; and that they would accordingly take suitable measures to avoid any damage to the economies of the other member-countries. It was also laid down that member-countries would be prepared to take suitable measures to prevent difficulties for themselves arising from the trade of another member-country with East Germany.

(3) A protocol allowing France to maintain for the time being the system of export subsidies and import duties in the franc area. This system would, however, be reviewed annually by the Commission and the Council of Ministers.

(4) A protocol stipulating that the Italian 10-year plan for industrial expansion (the 'Vanoni Plan') would be taken into account in the policy of the Community.

(5) A protocol providing for certain protective measures for the agriculture of Luxembourg.

(6) A protocol allowing the continuation of special tariffs for imports by member-countries from certain other countries with which they maintained particularly close political or economic relations— e.g. imports into the Benelux countries from Surinam and the Netherlands Antilles; imports into France from Morocco, Tunisia, and the former Indo-Chinese States (Cambodia, Laos, and Vietnam); and imports into Italy from Libya and the former Italian Somaliland.

(7) A protocol providing that tariffs for imports from the other member-countries into Algeria and the French Overseas Departments would be regulated in due course.

(8) A protocol on oil products allowing member countries to maintain their Customs duties on such products *vis-à-vis* other member-countries for a period of six years.

(9) A protocol confirming that the Netherlands would ratify the Treaty only in respect of its European territory and Dutch New Guinea.

(10) A protocol allowing West Germany to import certain quantities of bananas below the common Customs tariff.

(11) A protocol containing special provisions for the import of coffee into Italy and the Benelux countries.

(12)   A special declaration on Berlin was annexed to the Treaty, reading as follows: 'The Governments of Belgium, West Germany, France, Italy, Luxembourg, and the Netherlands, having regard to the special position of Berlin and the need for the free world to support it, and wishing to reaffirm their association with the population of Berlin, will support within the Community all measures required to ease the economic and social situation of the city, to further its reconstruction, and to secure its economic stability.'

(13)   Seven lists covering the items for which special maximum levels would be provided in the common Customs tariff were also annexed to the Treaty, together with a list dealing with agricultural products.

### AGREEMENT ON COMMON INSTITUTIONS

Among the subsidiary conventions and protocols also signed at Rome on 25 March 1957 was an agreement laying down: (a) that there should be one Assembly common to the three European Communities (i.e. the Economic, Atomic Energy and Coal and Steel Communities); (b) that there should be a Common Court of Justice and (c) that the E.E.C. and Euratom should share a single Economic and Social Committee.

### SEAT OF INSTITUTIONS

A Treaty for the merger of the separate executives of the three Communities—the Commission of the E.E.C., the High Authority of the E.C.S.C., and the Commission of Euratom was signed by the member-countries on 8 April 1965 and this took place on 1 July 1967. The decision to merge the institutions was generally felt to be the prelude of the merger of the Communities themselves.

The main difficulty in agreeing on the merger had been to find a formula agreeable to Luxembourg which sought to maintain both its political status as a Capital of Europe and the material advantage of being the headquarters of the Coal and Steel Community. It was agreed, however, that Brussels, Luxembourg and Strasbourg would remain the working seats of the Community as long as no final choice of a single capital had been made. Brussels would be the seat of the new single Community Executive and the consultative bodies attached to it; meetings of the Council of Ministers would be held there except in April, June and October when Luxembourg would be the meeting-place.

Luxembourg would retain the Secretariat of the European Parliament and the Court of Justice and would also become the seat of other legal and quasi-legal bodies which might be set up including any body with legal jurisdiction in the patents field.

Strasbourg continued to be the meeting-place of the European Parliament.

Luxembourg became the seat of the financial institutions such as the European Investment Bank which was formerly in Brussels.

Under the Treaty certain other services would be transferred to or remain in Luxembourg such as the Community Statistical Offices which were divided between Brussels and Luxembourg, the joint publications office, services dealing with workers' health and the dissemination of scientific data from Euratom.

## THE TREATY OF BRUSSELS

The Treaty of Accession, which will become known as the Treaty of Brussels, was signed in Brussels on 22 January 1972 by the Six and the new member states.

The declaration of the Council of the Communities in favour of the admission of the new members required no further ratification. The Treaty of Rome empowers the Council acting by unanimous vote to admit other European States. On the other hand, the new members must submit the Treaty to their Parliaments for ratification. Denmark, Norway and Ireland are obliged, by their Constitutions, to hold referenda as well. The instruments of ratification must be deposited by the new member States by 31 December 1972 for the Treaty to enter into force on 1 January 1973.

The Treaty consists essentially of two parts:

(1) The Treaty concerning the accession of the new members to the European Economic Community and the European Atomic Energy Community; and the Decision of the Council of the Communities concerning the accession of the new members to the European Coal and Steel Community. (The need for a separate procedure lies in legalistic differences between the Treaty of Rome which established the European Economic Community and Euratom and the Treaty of Paris which established the European Coal and Steel Community.)

(2) The 'Act' concerning the conditions of accession and the adjustments and amendments to the treaties.

If Part 1 establishing the Treaty could be called the power house

of the Treaty, this 'Act' consisting of 161 Articles could be called its
workshop.

It sets out in detail all the amendments to and derogations from
the Treaty of Rome and its subsequent legislative instruments made
necessary by the agreements on the terms of entry of the new members (summarised for the United Kingdom in Chapter 2).

The Act provides, *inter alia*, for an increase in the number of
delegates to the Assembly from 142 to 208 to provide seats for the
new members; of the size of the Council from 6 to 10 and of the
Commission from 9 to 14. It provides also an increase in the number
of Judges in the Court of Justice and changes their rota.

The 161 Articles range from the stages of the transitional period
for the new members down to an amended definition of newsprint
for quota purposes; from adjustments to the Statute of the European
Investment Bank to the rights of the Channel Islands and the Isle of
Man. It includes, as Protocols, a full list of the Community treaties
and related instruments as at the date of the signature of the Treaty of
Accession, by which the new members will be bound.

One important Protocol provides for an interim committee for
consultation between the Four and the Six on matters which will
involve the Four after membership, including trade negotiations
with the rump of Efta.

*The European Communities Act, 1972*

The legislation in the United Kingdom consequential to the signing
of the Treaty of Accession will be the European Communities Act, 1972.

In essence its purposes are:

Part I.   To give the force of law in the United Kingdom to present
and future Community law in so far as that law will be directly
applicable in the member States and will supersede national law.

Part II.   To repeal and amend U.K. law

   (i)   to enable the United Kingdom to implement its Community
obligations and to exercise its rights as a member of the
European Communities.

  (ii)   to share in the finances of the Communities as to both payments and receipts

 (iii)   to conform to the Customs Duties of the Communities

 (iv)   to set up an Intervention Board to operate the Common
Agricultural Policy and to provide for the collection of
levies on agricultural imports.

    (v)   to harmonise the work of the Restrictive Practices Act 1956 with the United Kingdom obligations under the Rules of Competition of the Treaty of Rome.

   (vi)   to amend the law to comply with the Regulations issued by the Commission on companies, food, seed, cine films, transport, animal and plant health, fertilisers, etc.

  (vii)   to fulfil all other obligations accepted by signing the Treaty of Accession.

Breaches against Community Regulations will be treated in the national Courts of the member States in the same way as breaches against national laws; for example against Community Regulations on Restrictive Trade Practices (Rules of Competition) by the Restrictive Practices Court; against Regulations of Companies under the Companies Acts; against making false statements before the European Court under the Perjury Acts; against disclosure of 'classified' information in Euratom under the Official Secrets Act.

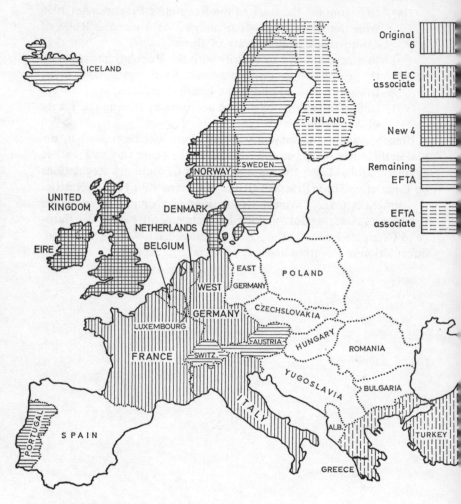

Other associate membership E E C
BURUNDI • CAMEROON • CENTRAL AFRICAN REPUBLIC
CHAD • CONGO-BRAZZAVILLE • DAHOMEY • GABON
IVORY COAST • KENYA • MADAGASCAR • MALI • MALTA
MAURITANIA • NIGER • RWANDA • SENEGAL • SOMALIA
TANZANIA • TOGO • UGANDA • UPPER VOLTA • ZAIRE

# CHAPTER 4

## The Institutions of the European Communities

We have mentioned earlier that in April 1965 the Six member-countries signed a Treaty providing for the merger of the three executives of the European Coal and Steel Community, the Common Market and Euratom into one Commission and also for a single Council of Ministers.

The Institutions of the European Community are as follows:

### THE ASSEMBLY OR EUROPEAN PARLIAMENT

This consists of 142 members elected by the national Parliaments of the member-countries: 36 members each from France, West Germany and Italy, 14 each from Belgium and the Netherlands and 6 from Luxembourg. The members are divided into four political groups: Christian Democrats, Socialists, Liberals and the European Democratic Union; the groups sit together in the Chamber irrespective of nationality. The election of members is determined by the national rules of each member-country, but it was agreed that the Assembly would later draft proposals providing for the introduction of a uniform electoral procedure in all member-countries. Plans were, in fact, drawn up in 1960 which envisaged members' direct election to the Assembly by universal suffrage.

The European Economic Community shares the Assembly with the European Coal and Steel Community and Euratom.

The Assembly meets in October each year to discuss the annual reports of the Committee of Communities. It has the power to enforce the resignation of the Commission, such decision requiring a two-thirds majority of the votes cast as well as an ordinary majority of its total membership. The Assembly also discusses the Communities' budgets and is empowered to propose amendments. It has to be consulted on certain proposals of the Commission and when the Council of Ministers wishes to implement essential principles of the Treaties. It is also entitled to meet in extraordinary session if a majority of members demand it, or at the request of the Commissions, High Authority or of the Council of Ministers.

THE COUNCIL OF MINISTERS

This is the only Community Institution whose members directly represent the member governments. Representatives of the national governments sit in the Council. The Foreign Ministers are generally present for major decisions, but the actual Minister of, say, Agriculture or Transport or Economic Affairs is generally present for the subject under discussion. The Council consists of one representative each from the governments of the member-countries and it takes decisions in one of three ways: either unanimously, by simple majority, or by a weighted majority according to the various circumstances laid down in the Treaties. The unanimity requirement applied particularly in the early stages of the Community's existence.

Decisions requiring a simple or a qualified majority are in most cases taken only on a proposal made by the Commission and any such proposal would not generally be amended by the Council except by unanimous vote. (This provision was aimed at conferring great responsibility upon the Commission and at safeguarding the stability of its activities; this method has met with some difficulty largely because France and the E.E.C. Commission clashed over the Common Agricultural Policy which is discussed in some detail in Chapter 8.)

THE COMMISSION

This consists of 9 members. There were 14 until the merging of the executives of the Communities in July 1970. It is the civil service of the Communities and its members must act throughout their period in office in full independence both of the member governments and of the Council. The Council cannot remove any member from office. The Assembly can, if it wishes, cause a vote of censure, which would compel the Commission to resign *en bloc*. Details of how conflict can arise between member-countries and the Commission is given in the chapter on Agriculture. (See page 86.)

ADMINISTRATIVE PROCEDURES

The various means by which the Council of Ministers, and the Commission guide the work of the Community are defined as follows:
(a) *regulations*, which are compulsory and directly applicable to any member-state;
(b) *directives*, which are binding on the recipient State in respect of the result to be attained, but allowing it to choose ways and means of achieving that end;

(c)   *decisions*, which are obligatory on the parties concerned; and

(d)   *recommendations and opinions*, which have no binding force.

(Of the millions of words that have been written and spoken about the Community considerable comment has been made, and sometimes banner headlines printed, concerning ideas put forward under 'recommendations and opinions' which have subsequently been ignored and forgotten. This has sometimes led to considerable public confusion.)

FINANCING THE COMMUNITY

On the Commission's proposal and following the political guidelines agreed upon at The Hague Conference in December 1969, the Council of Ministers gave their approval in 1970 for a system for granting the Community certain financial resources of its own. The six Parliaments of the member-states had to approve this decision, in accordance with the E.E.C. Treaty, before its entry into force on 1 January 1971.

This new system is being introduced gradually between 1971 and the end of 1977. During a first period, 1971 to the end of 1974, only a part of Community expenditure will be covered by revenue of its own. This revenue will consist of levies on imported agricultural products, which since the beginning of 1971 without exception have formed part of the Community's own resources, and of an increasing proportion of customs duties. The remaining amount of revenue necessary for a balanced budget is still met by national contributions calculated on the basis of an overall scale taking account of each country's gross national product.

From 1 January 1975, the budget will be financed entirely by Community resources. These will include the total amount of levies and customs duties, and also revenue corresponding to the product of a fraction of the value-added tax (V.A.T.) up to the equivalent of a one per cent rate of that tax.

A certain framework has been provided to enable this system to be introduced gradually. During the first period, 1971–74, each member-state's relative share in financing the budget may only fluctuate from one year to the next between +1 per cent and −1·5 per cent. This framework will be extended for a three-year period once the financing is entirely ensured by Community resources, but at this point the fluctuation from one year to the next may not exceed 2 per cent either way. From 1 January 1978 the system will be applied in its entirety without any restrictions.

THE COURT OF JUSTICE

Like the Assembly this is common to the three Communities and superseded the then existing Court of Justice of the European Coal and Steel Community. It consists of seven members jointly appointed by the member-Governments, holding office for six years and eligible for reappointment. There are also two Advocates-General.

The functions of the Court are to safeguard the law in the interpretation and application of the Treaties, to decide on the legality of decisions of the Council of Ministers or the Commission, and to determine violations of the Treaties. Actions can be brought before the Court either by a member-country, or by the Council of Ministers, or by the Commission, or by any person or legal entity affected by a decision of the Community. Action is based on the contention that the Council or the Commission were not empowered to take a decision; have violated essential rules of procedure; have violated a Treaty or any rule implementing it; or have abused their discretionary powers.

THE ECONOMIC AND SOCIAL COMMITTEE

This is also common to the Economic Community and Euratom and consists of representatives of all sections of economic and social life, such as employers' organisations, trade unions, and similar bodies. Its members, appointed for four years by a unanimous decision of the Council of Ministers, are drawn from the member-countries in the following numbers: 24 each from France, Italy, and West Germany; 12 each from Belgium and the Netherlands and 5 from Luxembourg, making a total of 101 members.

The Committee assists the Council of Ministers and the Commissions in an advisory capacity, and has to be consulted in those cases specifically laid down in the Treaty.

THE CONSULTATIVE COMMITTEE

With 51 members carries out similar tasks for the E.C.S.C.

THE SCIENTIFIC AND TECHNICAL COMMITTEE

This body assists the Euratom Commission in an advisory capacity and consists of 20 members. In addition there are a number of other consultative bodies which aid the Community's work such as the Monetary Committee, the Short and Medium-term Economic Policy Committees, the Committee of Central Bank Governors, the Budgetary Policy Committee, the Transport Committee, the Administrative Commission for the Social Security of Migrant Workers and the Nuclear Research Consultative Committee.

Enlargement of the Community through the entry of the four new member-states would not alter the structure of the Community's institutions and the rules governing their functioning, but would necessarily change their composition.

These adjustments to the institutions had not yet been decided by the conference negotiating the Community's enlargement. It seems likely that the Commission of the enlarged Community would contain 14 members instead of 9, representing the addition of two British members and one member from each of the other three applicant countries (Ireland, Denmark and Norway). Each of the new member countries would be represented on the Council of Ministers.

The number of Judges and Advocates-General in the Court of Justice would also be increased. The European Parliament and the Economic and Social Committee would contain delegates from the new members.

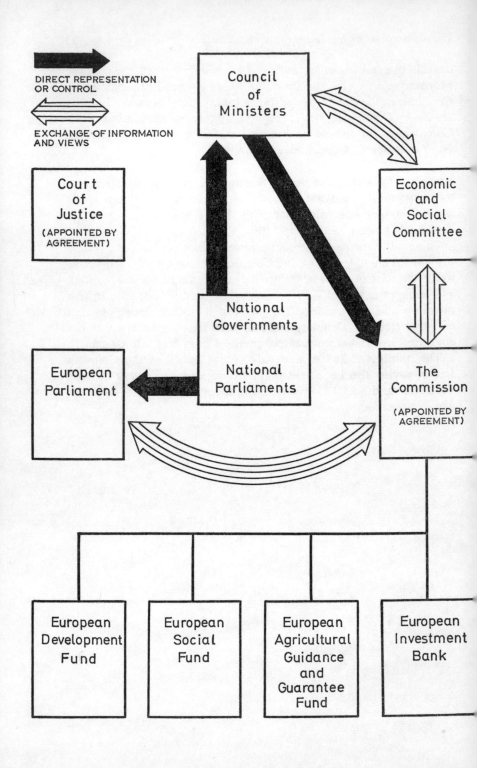

# CHAPTER 5

## The Tariff Structure of the Common Market

The first task of the Treaty of Rome was to set up the Customs Union. Its chapter on this lays down the principles, firstly, for the elimination of customs duties as between the member-states and, secondly, for the establishment of a common customs tariff for everything they buy from outside the Common Market.

For all practical purposes, 1968 can be regarded as the year for the final completion of the Customs Union of the Six members of the European Economic Community. Leaving aside the associate countries, Greece and Turkey, whose moves towards full participation in the Customs Union provisions of the Community are spread over a longer period, and the other Associated Territories, the European Economic Community, by mid-1968, achieved complete free trade within its own frontiers for all industrial goods and will be protected by the common external tariff against all countries which have not signed the Treaty of Rome or treaties of association.

The table on p. 56 shows the dates on which the progressive changes in both the internal and external tariffs were originally planned and the dates on which they were actually implemented by the accelerated stages of the transitional periods.

With the free trade within the Common Market fully established by mid-1968 the pre-Common Market tariffs of the Common Market countries towards one another became a matter for history rather than for economic research.

It is, therefore, with the common external tariff of the enlarged Community that we are concerned in this chapter.

The Treaty laid down that, with a few exceptions, the duties under the common customs tariff should be at the level of the arithmetical average of the individual duties applicable in the four customs territories covered by the Community (Germany, France, Italy and Benelux).

In practice, the common external tariff as originally fixed was higher and more restrictive than the average incidence of the 1957 tariffs. A weighted average would have been lower than an arithmetical

| | Moves in Internal Tariffs for Common Market Countries trading with one another. | | Moves towards Common External Tariffs for Common Market Countries trade with other countries. | |
|---|---|---|---|---|
| | Per cent of national tariffs laid down in the original planned transitional period. | Actual per cent of national tariffs applied under the accelerated timetable for the transitional period. | Per cent alignment of national tariffs towards the common external tariff—planned. | Per cent alignment of national tariffs—made. |
| **Treaty came into force 1 January 1958** | | | | |
| **Stage 1**  1959 1 January | 90% | 90% | | |
| 1960 1 July | 80% | 80% | | |
| 1961 1 January | — | 70% | | |
| **Stage 2**  1962 1 January | 70% | 60% | 30%* | 30%* |
| 1 July | — | 50% | | |
| 1963 1 July | 60% | 40% | | |
| 1964 — | — | — | | |
| 1965 1 January | 50% | 30% | | |
| **Stage 3†**  1966 1 January | 40% | 20% | 30% | 30% |
| 1967 1 July | — | 15% | Common external tariff effective | |
| 1968 1 July | — | nil | | |
| 1969 | | | | |
| 1970 | | | | |

† In Stage 3 remaining duties were due to be removed at the latest by 1 January 1970.

* Where the difference between the national and the common tariff was 15 per cent or less the common tariff was adopted at the end of Stage 1.

average because Germany and Benelux, both low tariff territories, accounted together for 60 per cent of the imports of the Six.

Moreover, the method used in fixing the levels of the common external tariff was deliberately weighted the other way by means of the device of using levels based upon the 'legal' or authorised import tariffs instead of the lower rates that were actually being applied for French import duties for certain items for the purpose of calculating the arithmetical averages. The items for which this device was used are those in List *A* of the Treaty. For example, France's import tariff for plastic materials on the basis of chemical derivatives of cellulose (ex B.N.39.03) was mainly 20 per cent. For the purpose of calculating the arithmetical average of the common external tariff for this item, List *A* fixed 30 per cent as the duty to be taken into account for France. For pianos the French import duty of 24·4 per cent became 30 per cent in List *A* for the purpose of increasing the average of the common external tariff. This device for inflating the arithmetical averages was used for some 50 items of chemical, paper, textile and engineering products.

A second device (Article 19 paragraph 3a) covered a wide range of chemical products which allowed the so-called average to be inflated by raising certain Benelux tariffs not exceeding 3 per cent to 12 per cent so as to allow an upper limit of 25 per cent for the common tariff on these items.

Most of the devices used originally for fixing the Common External Tariff are of less relevance than they were at the time because of the effects of the Kennedy Round of tariff negotiations in GATT.

The European Economic Community is, of course, a member of GATT (General Agreement on Tariffs and Trade) and in the twenty-four years of GATT's existence probably the most significant landmark was agreement on the 'Kennedy Round' in May 1967. GATT came into being 'to seek a world trading system based on non-discrimination and aimed at higher living standards to be achieved through fair, full and free exchange of goods and services'.

Forty-nine countries took part in the Kennedy Round negotiations and it is interesting to note that member-states of the E.E.C. negotiated as one. These countries represented 80 per cent of world trade and as a result of these protracted discussions which originated with the passing of the U.S. Trade Expansion Act 1962, tariff cuts averaging 35 per cent and in some cases reaching 50 per cent were agreed on industrial goods. The timing of the cuts varied between states but the rough plan was to reduce by five equal instalments ending on 1 January 1972. This procedure was adopted by the United States but the E.E.C., United Kingdom, Sweden and Switzerland reduced by two-fifths on 1 July 1968 followed by further instalments on 1 January 1970, 1971 and 1972.

Apart from the material advantages the real importance of the Kennedy Round to E.E.C. was that it demonstrated that the Community could negotiate as a single unit with the rest of the world on vital economic matters.

By January 1972, therefore, the tariff cuts agreed in the Kennedy Round had taken effect, although, in September 1971 for balance of payments reasons, the United States imposed a surcharge of 10 per cent on their imports over a wide area of commodities, a unilateral measure which diminished by a considerable proportion the Kennedy Round tariff cuts.

So to the Common External Tariff, as it is now in the Community and as it will be for Britain and the other new member-countries at the end of the transitional period on 1 July 1977.

How the tariff changes will be applied to Britain, Norway, Denmark and the Republic of Ireland between them and the Six for intra-Community trade and between the Ten and all non-member-countries is set out in the following table.

| | Tariffs between the Six and the four reduced by | Making a cumulative reduction of | Moves in adoption of C.E.T. by the Four | Cumulative effect of moves towards C.E.T. |
|---|---|---|---|---|
| | % | % | % | % |
| 1 April 1973 | 20 | 20 | — | — |
| 1 January 1974 | 20 | 40 | 40 | 40 |
| 1 January 1975 | 20 | 60 | 20 | 60 |
| 1 January 1976 | 20 | 80 | 20 | 80 |
| 1 July 1977 | 20 | 100 | 20 | 100 |
| | | (i.e. tariffs abolished) | | (i.e. full use of C.E.T. by U.K.) |

Britain will, therefore, by 1 July 1977, have duty-free access for industrial goods to the whole of the enlarged Community. Over the whole range of industrial products, the average of the Common External Tariff is lower than the average of U.K. tariffs, but there are some divisions in which the advantage to the U.K. will be considerable.

Special solutions have been agreed for the tariff treatment of certain industrial materials. These are briefly as follows:

| | |
|---|---|
| Woodpulp and Lead bullion | Common External Tariff suspended or other duty-free arrangements. |
| Phosphorus | Common External Tariff suspended until 1977. After that, U.K. can apply for further suspension or duty-free quota |
| Plywood | Largely duty-free. |
| Wattle extract | Common External Tariff reduced. |
| Alumina | Duty-free until 1976. Then 5·5 per cent with provision after entry for a duty-free quota. |
| Silicon carbide, ferro chrome, ferro silica, refined lead, zinc and aluminium | Adequate supplies should be available from domestic U.K. producers or suppliers in the enlarged Community. Provision made for application for duty-free quotas if the supply position changes. |

The following table shows for a representative list of industrial goods the Common External Tariff as it now is in the Six and as it will be reached by the new members in 1977.

Against each item is shown the total value of U.K. Imports in 1969 and the proportion of these which came in that year from countries which traded then or will trade in the future tariff-free and the proportion which came from countries whose products will be subject to the Common External Tariff.

The percentages are of interest in order to predict the patterns of trade in the years after 1977. Free trade will then be fully established in the enlarged Community while imports from non-member-countries will still be subject to tariffs, in some instances at relatively high levels.

It is interesting to note that during the twelve years which covered the abolition of internal tariffs, trade with the Community calculated in terms of the imports of principal industrial products increased by more than six times. Their imports from the U.K. in the same products and over the same period increased by $3\frac{1}{2}$ times.

| | Common External Tariff of E.E.C. after 1 Jan. 1972 | Total U.K. imports 1969 | Proportion of these imports from | | |
|---|---|---|---|---|---|
| | | | E.E.C. | Efta | Other |
| BASE METALS *Iron and Steel* | % | $ million | % | % | % |
| Blooms and Billets | 4–5 | 49·4 | 8 | $5\frac{1}{2}$ | $86\frac{1}{2}$ |
| Iron and Steel Coils for re-rolling | 5–6 | 10·8 | 11 | 26 | 63 |
| Iron and Steel Wire Rod | 5–7 | 11·7 | $9\frac{1}{2}$ | 80 | $10\frac{1}{2}$ |
| Iron and Steel Bars and Rods | 5–7 | 34·3 | 23 | 67 | 10 |
| Angles of Iron and Steel | 6–7 | 5·0 | 46 | 28 | 26 |
| Universals, Plates and Sheets of Iron and Steel | 6–8 | 101·4 | 56 | 20 | 24 |
| Iron and Steel Wire | 8 | 4·4 | 20 | 66 | 14 |
| Weldless Tubes and Pipes ⎫ Welded Tubes and Pipes ⎬ Tube and Pipe Fittings ⎭ | 9–10 | 58·9 | 45 | 18 | 37 |
| NON FERROUS METALS | | | | | |
| Copper, unwrought | Free | 650·0 | $2\frac{1}{2}$ | 4 | $93\frac{1}{2}$ |
| Nickel, unwrought | Free | 77·9 | 10 | 15 | 75 |
| Aluminium, unwrought | 7%* | 208·8 | 1 | 45 | 54 |
| Lead, unwrought | $1·32– 100 kg.* | 82·3 | | | 100 |
| Zinc, unwrought | $1·32– 100 kg* | 47·6 | 2 | 4 | 94 |

* Subject to duty-free quotas.

| | Common External Tariff of E.E.C. after 1 Jan. 1972 % | Total U.K. imports 1969 $ million | Proportion of these imports from | | |
|---|---|---|---|---|---|
| | | | E.E.C. % | Efta % | Other % |
| **CHEMICALS AND CHEMICAL PRODUCTS** | | | | | |
| *Mineral and Chemical Fertilizers* | | | | | |
| Nitrogenous | 8 | 10·6 | 79 | 15 | 6 |
| Phosphatic | nil–4·8 | 1·4 | 94 | 6 | — |
| Potassic | 2·4 | 26·3 | 30 | — | 70 |
| Paints and varnishes | 12 | 26·5 | 35 | 15 | 50 |
| Synthetic organic dyestuffs | 10 | 36·3 | 42 | 50 | 8 |
| Soaps, cleansing and polishing products | 12 | 12·3 | 40 | 26 | 34 |
| *Pharmaceutical products* | | | | | |
| Medicaments | 7·8–23·8 | 61·1 | 38 | 23 | 39 |
| Insecticides | 6·4–9·6 | 7·7 | 60 | 10 | 30 |
| **PULP AND PAPER** | | | | | |
| *Paper* | | | | | |
| Newsprint | 7* | 114·6 | — | 41 | 59 |
| Other printing and writing paper | 12 | 10·9 | 13½ | 80 | 6½ |
| Kraft paper and paperboard | 12 | 136·2 | 1 | 48 | 51 |
| Fibre and building boards | 11 | 27·9 | 3½ | 75 | 21½ |
| *Pulp* | | | | | |
| Mechanical wood pulp | 3* | 54·5 | — | 98 | 2 |
| Chemical wood pulp diss. grade | 3* | 65·7 | 4½ | 34½ | 61 |
| Sulphate wood pulp | 3* | 182·7 | 1 | 66 | 33 |
| Sulphite wood pulp | 3* | 86·4 | 1 | 90 | 9 |
| **FACTORY PLANT AND EQUIPMENT** | | | | | |
| *Industrial machinery* | | | | | |
| Power gen. m/c other than electric | 5·5 | 240·7 | 42 | 9 | 49 |
| Heating and cooling equipment | 4·5–9 | 63·5 | 36 | 40 | 24 |
| Pumps and centrifuges | 6–9 | 89·7 | 35 | 27 | 38 |
| *Production machinery* | | | | | |
| Paper and pulp machinery | 5–5·5 | 20·4 | 53 | 25 | 22 |
| Textile machinery | 4·5–7·5 | 122·4 | 50 | 27 | 23 |
| Machine tools for metal working | 2·5–8 | 100·3 | 50 | 20 | 30 |
| Printing and bookbinding m/c | 4·0–6·5 | 46·5 | 60 | 13 | 27 |
| Construction and mining m/c | 5·5–9 | 94·4 | 37 | 7 | 56 |
| Food processing m/c | 5 | 16·2 | 42 | 32 | 26 |
| *Engineering supplies* | | | | | |
| Grinding and polishing wheels and stones | 6·5–7·5 | 3·9 | n.a. | n.a. | n.a. |

\* Subject to duty-free quotas.

| | Common External Tariff of E.E.C. after 1 Jan. 1972 | Total U.K. imports 1969 | Proportion of these imports from | | |
|---|---|---|---|---|---|
| | | | E.E.C. | Efta | Other |
| | % | $ million | % | % | % |
| Abrasive cloths and paper | 4·5–5 | 6·7 | n.a. | n.a. | n.a. |
| Refractory products (not construction) | 9 | 2·2 | ,, | ,, | ,, |
| Manufactures of asbestos | 8–12 | 5·8 | ,, | ,, | ,, |
| Ball bearings | 9 | 32·0 | 31 | 20 | 49 |
| Rubber belting | 10 | 3·7 | n.a. | n.a. | n.a. |
| Leather belting | 5 | 0·3 | ,, | ,, | ,, |
| **ELECTRICAL PLANT** | | | | | |
| Electric power m/c | 5–8·5 | 56·1 | 31 | 18 | 51 |
| Apparatus for elec. circuits | 5–8 | 94·6 | 32 | 14 | 54 |
| *Electrical equipment* | | | | | |
| Insulated wire and cable | 11 | 13·8 | 30 | 8 | 62 |
| Electric lamps | 6–7·5 | 11·2 | 66 | 3 | 31 |
| Thermionic valves and tubes | 6·5–17 | 101·7 | 34 | 10 | 56 |
| Batteries | 20 | 6·7 | 50 | 9 | 41 |
| Accumulators | 4–10 | | | | |
| Electrical measuring and control instruments | 9–11 | 85·1 | 25 | 11 | 64 |
| Automotive elec. equipment | 7–10·5 | 11·9 | 35 | 2 | 63 |
| Electro-mech. hand tools | 7 | 5·0 | 42 | 20 | 38 |
| **TRANSPORT EQUIPMENT** | | | | | |
| Passenger motor cars over 2·8c³ | 22 | 131·6 | 81 | 14 | 5 |
| Lorries and Trucks other | 11 | 6·7 | 78 | 1 | 21 |
| Bodies and parts of motor vehicles | 7·12 | 126·9 | 72 | 6 | 22 |
| Motor cycles | 10·5 | 8·4 | 40 | 13 | 47 |
| Bicycles | 17 | 3·5 | 65 | 20 | 15 |
| Tractors, other than road | 6–20 | 7·5 | 48 | 3 | 49 |
| **MECHANICAL HANDLING EQUIPMENT** | 3·5–11 | 55·0 | 40 | 30 | 30 |
| **PHOTOGRAPHIC AND OPTICAL GOODS, SCIENTIFIC INSTRUMENTS AND SUPPLIES** | | | | | |
| Binoculars, microscopes, etc | 9 | 8·9 | 37 | 7 | 56 |
| Photographic cameras | 13 | 24·7 | 25 | 12 | 63 |
| Cine cameras and projectors | 10–11 | 10·3 | 30 | 23 | 47 |
| Medical instruments, n.e.s. | 5·5–10 | 12·7 | 24 | 14 | 62 |
| Electro-medical apparatus | 5·5–10 | 9·0 | 54 | 23 | 23 |
| **PLASTICS** | | | | | |
| Products of condensation | 10·4–17·6 | 72·7 | 58 | 8 | 34 |
| Products of polymerisation | 10·4–18·4 | 116·3 | 51 | 10 | 39 |
| Regen. and deriv. of cellulose | 10·4–18·4 | 29·3 | 22 | 6 | 72 |

| | Common External Tariff of E.E.C. after 1 Jan. 1972 | Total U.K. imports 1969 | Proportion of these imports from | | |
|---|---|---|---|---|---|
| | | | E.E.C. | Efta | Other |
| **OFFICE EQUIPMENT** | | | | | |
| Typewriters | 6·5 | 26·7 | 78 | 4 | 18 |
| Calculating and accounting machines (electronic) | 14 | 59·6 | 43 | 14 | 43 |
| Statistical machines, card or tape | 7 | 51·0 | 48 | 3 | 49 |
| Other office machines | 6–6·5 | 221·1 | 29 | 4 | 67 |
| **TOOLS AND IMPLEMENTS** | | | | | |
| Tools for hand and machine use (electric) | 7 | 49·0 | 37 | 25 | 38 |
| **TEXTILES AND CLOTHING** | | | | | |
| Cotton fabrics, woven grey not merc. | 13–15 | 79·7 | 1 | 7 | 92 |
| Cotton fabrics, woven other than grey | 13–15 | 59·4 | 30 | 23 | 47 |
| Woollen fabrics, woven | 13–18 | 18·1 | 56 | 12 | 32 |
| Linen fabrics, woven | 16 | 0·9 | 33 | 12 | 55 |
| Synthetic fibre fabrics, woven | 15–16 | 43·2 | 37 | 33 | 30 |
| Artificial silk fabrics, woven | 15–16 | 44·0 | 45 | 33 | 22 |
| Knitted fabrics | 13–14 | 23·1 | 18 | 39 | 43 |
| Lace, embroidery, ribbons | 9–13 | 13·4 | 14 | 63 | 23 |
| Clothing of textile fabrics not knitted | 10·5–17 | 146·8 | 12 | 15 | 73 |
| Clothing, knitted | 10·5–18 | 118·7 | 8 | 24 | 68 |
| Footwear, leather | 8 | 85·2 | 32 | 12 | 56 |
| **HOUSEHOLD AND CONSUMER DURABLES** | | | | | |
| Domestic electric appliances | 7–11·5 | 47·1 | 53 | 17 | 30 |
| Sewing machines | 6–12 | 22·8 | 38 | 12 | 50 |
| Glass tableware | 15·5 | 12·7 | 41 | 17 | 42 |
| Pottery | 7·5–14 | 8·0 | 39 | 12 | 49 |
| Furniture | 6–11 | 32·3 | 24 | 37 | 39 |
| **MISCELLANEOUS METAL MANUFACTURES** | | | | | |
| Cutlery | 6–10 | 12·0 | 23 | 8 | 69 |
| Nuts and bolts | 7–10 | 14·9 | 21 | 14 | 65 |
| **TELEVISION AND RADIO** | | | | | |
| Television receivers | 14 | 5·0 | 26 | 34 | 40 |
| Radio receivers | 14 | 24·5 | 25 | 15 | 60 |

| | Common External Tariff of E.F.C. after 1 Jan. 1972 | Total U.K. imports | Proportion of these imports from | | |
|---|---|---|---|---|---|
| | | | E.E.C. | Efta | Other |
| **MISCELLANEOUS MANUFACTURES** | | | | | |
| Watches and clocks | 7·5–10 | 84·1 | 31 | 1 | 68 |
| Gramophones, tape recorders | 7·5–9·5 | 43·2 | 26 | 27 | 47 |
| Gramophone records | 3·5–7 | 22·6 | 38 | 5 | 57 |
| Pianos and other string instruments | | | | | |
| Toys and games | 8·5–19 | 45·0 | 8 | 4 | 88 |
| Pens, pencils and fountain pens | 5–13 | 8·2 | 30 | 8 | 62 |

Sources: Common External Tariff of E.E.C.
Commodity Trade O.E.C.D.

# CHAPTER 6

## Community Law in the Member-States

Community law now constitutes an integral part of the member-countries' legal system. The courts in those countries must implement Community law in litigation within their own jurisdiction where Community law requires. A number of treaty provisions impose, in binding and self-sufficient terms, obligations on the member-states, the acceptance of which confers both rights and obligations on individuals which must be upheld by the municipal courts in those states.

Moreover, the Treaty rules impose on the member-states clear and unconditional obligations to refrain from certain acts (and there is no requirement that any steps need be taken by the Community or by the member-states before these obligations must be complied with).

There is, thus, no discretion allowed to the member-states in respect of certain Articles in the Treaty, for example Article 12, by which they must refrain from introducing any new customs duties on trade between themselves; Article 53 by which they allow freedom of establishment of nationals, of companies and other bodies; Article 37 which excludes discrimination by State monopolies; Article 95 which proscribes the imposition of internal tax changes which might afford indirect protection to like domestic productions; or Articles 31 and 32 which abolish quotas.

On the other hand, consultation rather than specific prohibition has been ruled with regard to Article 93 on existing forms of state aids; Article 102 on legislative disparities; and Article 97 on the averaging of turnover tax for the purpose of calculating the tax both for export and import, although with the wider use of tax on value added, it would seem that this item is no longer relevant.

The supremacy of Community law over Municipal law in the member-states is becoming increasingly established particularly in the field of 'Competition'. When the member-states signed the Treaty, they accepted a definite restriction of their sovereign rights which could not be undone by any subsequent unilateral act. France endeavoured to establish the principle that 'lex posterior' (in one particular case) should prevail irrespective of the meaning or scope of Community law, but the Court of Justice of the Community confirmed not only the supremacy of Community law but that individual decisions made by the Commission must override internal decisions in the member-states, in the application of the Community Rules of Competition.

Article 177 of the Treaty is the effective instrument to ensure the uniform application of Community law.

The nature of Community law, as an integral part of the law in the member-countries, is such that uniform interpretation of Community law must be guaranteed whichever national court is required to implement it. This is the purpose of Article 177 of the E.E.C. Treaty, which is of capital importance to the development of Community law, and gives the Community Court of Justice jurisdiction to give preliminary rulings concerning (a) the interpretation of the E.E.C. Treaty, (b) the validity and interpretation of measures taken by the institutions of the Community and (c) the interpretation of the statutes of bodies set up by a formal measure of the Council, where those statutes so provide.

To mid-1970, seventy-two cases concerning the interpretation of the Treaty (or its provisions) or the validity of acts of Community institutions had been submitted to the Court under Article 177. They include matters as important as the direct applicability of certain Treaty provisions, the supremacy of Community law and the interpretation of Article 85 as regards exclusive dealing agreements.

Article 177 is the procedural counterpart of the fundamental principle that Community law is of general application.

The essential feature of this procedure is co-operation between Municipal courts and the Community's Court of Justice. A request for a ruling under Article 177 can be made only by a national court and not by individual litigants. The Court confines itself to construing Community law: it refuses to consider the facts at issue in the national court.

Recourse to Article 177 has become more and more frequent over the years, not only by lower courts but also by a number of supreme courts. In some of the member-countries, however, the courts seem still to hesitate to use this procedure.

In this context, mention should also be made of the problem of the *acte clair*, that is the question how far supreme courts are entitled to refrain from submitting a matter of interpretation to the court on the ground that the provisions at issue are sufficiently clear.

In a resolution adopted on 8 October 1969 the European Parliament cautioned the supreme courts against excessive reliance on the theory of the *acte clair*. It suggested supplementing Article 177 by making provision for appeals 'in the interest of correct interpretation of the Treaty'. This would enable Community authorities, in cases where they considered that a decision handed down by a municipal court was inconsistent with Community law, to refer the matter to the Court of Justice without challenging the decision as such.

Another current problem is the extension of the Court's powers to interpret international conventions concluded by the member states, especially those based on Article 220 of the E.E.C. Treaty. The Council is now considering this in connection with the two conventions dated 29 February 1968 (on mutual recognition of bodies corporate) and 27 September 1968 (on jurisdiction and the enforcement of civil judgments). Considerable weight is being given to the Commission's view that these conventions should be interpreted solely with reference to Article 177.

The Court of Justice has clarified the different types of Community legislation by the Council and by the Commission.

The distinction between *regulations* and *decisions* is to be made by examining their form of address. Regulations are addressed to whole categories of persons in the abstract; decisions to a limited number of identifiable persons.

In addition to the above there are directives, which *bind* member-states as to results, while not specifying the means. Recommendations and opinions have no binding force.

## 'DERIVED' LAW

The gradual extension of 'derived' Community law has been occasioned by the increase in the tasks entrusted to the Commission by the Council. This phenomenon has raised a number of legal, technical and political problems which have been examined by the European Parliament. On 3 October 1968 the Parliament adopted an important resolution on Community procedures for implementing derived Community law (see *Official Gazette* No. C 108, 19 October 1968), covering both the principle of the exercise of executive powers (reserved to the Council and the Commission) and action by agencies (generally called 'committees') for which no provision is made in the Treaty. These committees, which do not have uniform functions and are not organised along uniform lines, are compatible with the

Treaty since they do not impair the distribution of responsibilities and the institutional equilibrium of the Community. (The agricultural management committees, for example, have consultative powers only, the effect of which when they vote against a Commission proposal is to transfer the power of decision from the Commission to the Council.)

It is claimed that the practice of delegation of authority within the Commission has proved indispensable as a result of the growth of the institution's administrative tasks; it is not unobjectionable provided it is confined to the measures involved in preparing and giving effect to Commission discussions.

As from the date of her membership of the Common Market, Britain will be accepting Community law and with it the whole body of legal rights and obligations deriving from the Treaty and all the instruments under the Treaty which have been subsequently decreed.

Thus, provision will have to be made for matters upon which the Treaty leaves the necessary legislation to be passed by member States, for example, customs duties, agriculture and transport. These will have to be enacted by Parliament or by delegated legislation issued under Parliamentary authority and covering both present and future Community instruments.

Legislation will also be necessary to give the force of law to those provisions of the Treaty and Community instruments, which are intended to take direct internal effect within the member-states.

Community law having direct effect is designed to take precedence over the domestic law of the member-states. Legislation will have to be provided to ensure that Community law will override national law in so far as the latter is inconsistent with it.

Of course, Community law operates only in the fields of economic activity covered by the Treaty, that is Customs Duties, Agriculture, Free Movement of Labour, Services and Capital, Monopolies and Restrictive Practices, State Aid for Industry and the Regulation of the Coal and Steel Industries.

Community provisions which have direct internal effect would fall to be considered by the U.K. courts which would have to judge individual cases but not on the applicability of the Treaty to the process in question if that were in doubt. Such decision is the prerogative of the Community Court of Justice. It is in the field on which Community law has direct internal effect that persons and undertakings in the U.K. will be subject to penalties imposed directly by the Community.

Most of the Community law which has direct internal effect does so in relation to industrial and commercial activities falling within the Rules of Competition as set out in Articles 85 to 90 of the Treaty. It does not touch citizens in their private capacity and the powers of enforcement are not applicable to such citizens even as directors or officers of a company held liable for breaches. In some cases the Treaty or Regulation requires the member-state to provide penalties under its own domestic legislation for breaches of Community law. These sanctions are recoverable by civil rather than criminal processes similar to the fines and penalties imposed under the U.K. Income Tax Acts. The enforcement of the Treaty regulations on restrictions of trade can be compared with the operation of Restrictive Trade Practices legislation enforced within the U.K. since that legislation came into force.

The enforcement procedure for Decisions of the Council or of the Commission is defined in Article 192 of the Treaty of Rome, which says:

Decisions of the Council or of the Commission which contain a pecuniary obligation on persons other than the State shall be enforceable.

Forced execution shall be governed by the rules of civil procedure in force in the State in whose territory it takes place. The writ of execution shall be served, without other formality than the verification of the authenticity of the written act, by the domestic authority which the Government of each member-state shall designate for this purpose, and of which it shall give notice to the Commission and to the Court of Justice.

After completion of these formalities at the request of the party concerned, the latter may, in accordance with Municipal law, proceed with such forced execution by applying directly to the authority which is competent.

Forced execution may only be suspended pursuant to a decision of the Court of Justice. Supervision as to the regularity of the measures of execution shall, however, be within the competence of the domestic courts or tribunals.

In November 1971, before the signature of the Treaty for the enlarged Community, consultation procedures were worked out between the Six and the four new member countries for reciprocal consultation before any new Community legislation is adopted and any new national legislation is enacted by the new members which might conflict with Community laws.

CHAPTER 7

# The Social and Development Funds and Investment Bank

## EUROPEAN SOCIAL FUND

The European Social Fund was established under Articles 123–127 of the Treaty, the aim of which is to 'increase the availability of employment and mobility of workers within the Community'. This is achieved by giving grants of up to 50 per cent of expenses incurred by member-countries in vocational and settlement projects. The Fund has now the power to start retraining, etc., and can act only at the request of the member-country although, of course, the Commission uses its powers to help persuade member-countries to take advantage of the Fund. In July 1970 the Council of Ministers agreed the outline of a reform of the Fund. Although it will continue to help to retrain workers because of structural unemployment, and these came mainly from the south of Italy, it will gradually devote considerably more money to helping workers who have become redundant because of the E.E.C.'s policies. In these cases the Commission will be able to take the initiative.

\*　　\*　　\*

The aim which the Treaty assigns for the association of the overseas countries with the European Economic Community is: '. . . to promote the economic and social development of the overseas countries and territories, and to establish close economic relations between them and the Community as a whole. . . . This association shall in the first place permit the furthering of the interests and prosperity of the inhabitants of these countries and territories in such a manner as to lead them to the economic, social and cultural development which they expect.' (Article 131.)

## EUROPEAN DEVELOPMENT FUND

One of the specific means to this end is the European Development Fund for which the Treaty and the Implementing Convention on the association provide.

The European Development Fund finances economic or social

development schemes in the associated overseas countries by means of outright grants. The Fund has three particular features: it is a Community Fund; its action is supplementary; and it is democratically operated.

It is a Community institution, maintained by contributions from the six member-states of the European Community which exercise no national control over the capital once contributed. It was never intended that contributions to the Fund should become, as it were, national credits offered to the associated countries in each of the national currencies concerned, and used only in that currency. Such an arrangement, which would have obliged the associated countries to use such credits in Francs, Marks, Florins or Lire only for purchases in the individual member states concerned, would have been contrary to the unity of purpose which the Fund represents.

The Fund is supplementary—one more of the many national and international agencies now concerned with spreading prosperity more equitably throughout the world. Its contributions supplement the investment efforts of the associated countries themselves and the aid they already receive bilaterally or multilaterally: they are also a part of a general policy of assistance to developing economies, in which commercial, legal, and technical aid is at least equally important.

The Fund is democratically operated because the choice, the working out and the implementation of the projects which it finances, rests with the Governments of the associated countries themselves. Development plans are not prepared elsewhere: it is the countries that benefit from the Fund which decide what projects to propose for financing, and this takes place through the agency of their own official bodies.

## The European Development Fund Finances

Social projects: improvements in equipment for public health, educational or scientific purposes, and in social services and living conditions; technical or scientific research affecting the people of the country concerned.

Economic projects for the improvement of the associated overseas countries' economy and their infrastructure. The Fund's aid forms part of the economic and social policy laid down by the responsible Governments and is implemented through the development programme of each Government, if possible in such a way as to stimulate further economic development. For example, it may be used to improve the infrastructure which makes possible private investment and enterprise; or for general and technical training, on which economic progress and social betterment very largely depend.

Priority is given to schemes that will have an almost immediate and direct effect on the standard of living.

The Fund leaves to the Governments the initiative in suggesting projects for which they want assistance. There are no conditions attaching to the grant of assistance.

## Consideration of the Requests

The formal request is submitted by the Government of the overseas associated country concerned.

It is received at the office of the Fund in Brussels. The various documents filed with the request are examined, and economists and overseas specialists are appointed to consider with the relevant technical services the set of projects concerned, and to work out arrangements for carrying them out. The Standing Committee of the Fund considers the request.

The Commission announces its decision. If an economic project is concerned, it is translated into the four official languages of the E.E.C. and referred to the Council of Ministers, which makes known its decision within a month. For social projects the Commission's decision is sufficient.

The financial agreement with the Government concerned is drawn up and signed.

## Carrying out the Projects

The country itself draws up the request for tenders. These papers are passed by the Technical Controller in the country concerned and sent to the Fund, which has them translated into the official languages of the Community and publishes notices of invitation to tender in the official gazette of the European Communities.

After a period of anything between one and four months—it depends on the scale of the project—tenders are sent in and their examination begun by the appropriate technical service of the country concerned, under the guidance of an adjudicating committee.

Once a firm tender has been accepted, the technical services draw up the contract and have it signed. The Commission is informed and takes the necessary steps to effect payment.

Payments are made in instalments as the work proceeds, to the order of the authority in the country concerned and through the bank at which the E.E.C. keeps its account. Payments are made very promptly. Provisional and final acceptance complete the process.

It is to be noted that as soon as the financial agreement has been signed, the project is carried out on the responsibility of the associated country itself, by its authorities and in its own way. The Commission intervenes only in order to assist through technical control in the drawing up of invitations to tender and in solving problems arising in the implementation of assisted projects.

By 31 December 1970, the Six had subscribed a total of over $1,306,000,000 multilateral aid in respect of 350 projects.

Aid from the Fund has been used for such purposes as building schools, improving medical facilities, modernisation of rural areas such as constructing wells, soil conservation and anti-erosion campaigns, improvement in transport and improvements in urban conditions.

66 per cent of the aid was allocated to modernisation of economic infrastructure and development of production and 23 per cent for social development.

## THE EUROPEAN INVESTMENT BANK

The aims of the European Investment Bank, as laid down in the Treaty, are to promote a common investment policy within the Community and grant loans, on a non-profit basis, or guarantees for (1) projects in under-developed regions; (2) the modernisation, reorganisation, or extension of industries which are difficult to finance on a purely national basis; (3) new industries of joint interest to several member-countries which, because of their size or special character, would be difficult to finance by a single member-country.

By 31 December 1970 the Bank had signed contracts for $1,813,000,000 for 317 loans for all member and associated member-countries and $1,449,000,000 was still outstanding.

Some of the projects in which the Bank has invested have been: (a) Development projects in regions of Apulia, Campania and Abruzzi and the modernisation of the important Mont Cenis railway line linking Paris and Genoa via Turin. The total amount provided was $50,000,000 divided between four projects in the iron and steel industries, engineering industries, clothing industries and the railway modernisation.

(b) A thermal power station built in West Berlin, financed by the bank to the extent of $2,400,000.

(c) Four loans for the construction of major roadworks: (i) a new road from Athens to Corinth in Greece $2,000,000; (ii) a new road from Corinth to Patras in Greece $6,200,000; (iii) modernisation of the road from Antirrion to Agrinion in Greece $2,600,000; (iv) a new road from Lamia to Larissa in Greece $6,200,000.

(d) Irrigation and development of the Metaponto Plain in Italy $24,000,000.

(e) Construction of a thermal power station at Salerno in Italy $15,000,000.

Several small loans have been made to Associated African States and several loans to Turkey including one for the construction of a dam on the Euphrates.

The capital structure of the Bank is given on page 39 and in addition to the capital subscribed by member-countries the Bank has successfully raised funds in the capital markets of Europe and U.S.A. totalling $1,081,000,000 by December 1970.

# CHAPTER 8

## Agriculture and Fisheries

### AGRICULTURE

The member-states have introduced by stages a common agricultural policy, as required by the Treaty of Rome. It is financed from a central fund and covers over 90 per cent of the Community's agricultural production. Free trade markets for beef and veal and milk products were introduced in 1964; for olive oil in 1966; for grain, pigmeat, eggs and poultry, oils and fats, rice and sugar in 1967; for plants and flowers and processed fruit and vegetables in 1968; for wine, flax and hemp, and tobacco in 1970; for fish in 1971, see page 97.

Each member-country had its own agricultural policy in 1958 and these varied considerably but the policy was, on the whole, for protection of the industry. It was not possible to remove the obstacles to trade by applying to agriculture the same procedures as with manufactured goods. The E.E.C. decided to abolish all existing national policies and to establish a Community policy with its own finance and with a decided policy towards non-E.E.C. countries.

### The Original Idea

*Policy Objectives*  The main objectives of the common policy for agriculture were outlined as follows:

(a)  to balance supply and demand within the Community and externally by influencing supply by such measures as more regional specialisation, stockpiling, and structural reforms, and increasing demand by improving the quality of products.

(b)  to provide farmers with a fair income by structural and regional improvements, the consolidation of holdings, electricity supplies, better transport and farming methods, information services, and education.

(c)  to stabilise the market by protecting farmers from speculative price fluctuations while not insulating them from the influence of long-term movements in world markets.

(d)  to ensure equitable supplies to consumers by enabling the processing industries to find external outlets at reasonable or competitive
prices, and by preventing prices from being fixed on the basis of
marginal production costs.

*Products*  The regulations adopted by the Ministers applied to
grain, pigmeat, eggs, poultry, fruit and vegetables, and wine. Fundamental decisions were also taken on the remaining major farm
products (rice, beef and veal, dairy produce, and sugar) and a time-
table was set for the publication of the full regulations on all these
items in 1962. The products which were covered constituted over 46
per cent of the total inter-Community trade in farm produce.

*Transition Period*  A seven-year transition period pending the full
implementation of the common policy was fixed from 1 July 1962 to
31 December 1969, but a decision to shorten this period to six years
could be taken in the third year.

*Quality Standards*  Common quality standards would be progressively applied to fruit and vegetables marketed within the producing
member-states. The exporting member-states would exercise a
quality control before products were exported to another member-
country. A quality and grading certificate would accompany the
goods, for checks by the importing country. Quantitative import
restrictions would be abolished for graded products as follows:
(i)    'Super' Grade by 1 July 1962;
(ii)   Grade I by 1 January 1964;
(iii)  Grade II by 1 January 1966.

*Harmonisation of Prices*  All prices, except for maize, were to be
harmonised between an upper limit based on present German prices
and a lower limit based on French price levels. Separate Community
marketing organisations would be set up for wheat, coarse grains,
sugar, and dairy produce, and there would be detailed intervention
in the internal markets of the Community and external protection in
the form of variable levies.

'Target' prices would be fixed annually for all these products, while
for grain there would also be 'intervention' prices at which the
marketing organisations would buy up supplies in order to guarantee
to producers sales at a price as close as possible to the target price.
Intervention prices would be target prices less a fixed percentage
determined by each country between a minimum of 5 per cent and a
maximum of 10 per cent. During the transition period adjustments
would also be made where prices varied between different regions of

member-states. 'Threshold' prices would be fixed as a sort of minimum import prices for grain, and would be the target price in the area of the greatest deficiency (i.e. with the largest imports) less the cost of transport from the point of entry.

For beef, pigmeat, poultry, and eggs there would be no target prices and no intervention prices and therefore no guaranteed prices and the system would be based on arrangements for protection from world markets. Minimum import prices would, however, be fixed as 'Sluice-gate' prices for pigmeat, eggs, and poultry—in the last two cases for trade with non-member-countries only, and in the case of pigmeat also for intra-Community trade.

Fruit, vegetables, and wine would be subject to supervision of quality. The common organisation would also introduce a minimum price system applicable to non-member-countries. Where the Community markets suffered from, or were threatened by, serious dislocation due to imports from non-member-countries, these imports might be suspended or subjected to a uniform compensatory levy charged on entry by all members.

*Safeguard Clause*   An escape clause covered all products subject to the agricultural policy. Under the clause a member-country might close its frontiers immediately if imports from other member-states jeopardised its home production, but it must then immediately inform the E.E.C. Commission, which would decide within four days whether the closure was justified; there would be no appeal against its decisions except to the Court of Justice. In the case of cereals the time-limit would be extended from four to ten days, while for vegetables and fruit no country could take unilateral action and imports must be continued while the countries concerned appealed to the Commission. This last decision was taken after a lengthy debate during which the Italian delegation pointed out that their fruit and vegetables might rot at the German frontier if they were stopped while high-level decisions were taken on import suspension.

*Management Committee*   Five Management Committees would be set up respectively for grain, pigmeat, eggs and poultry, fruit and vegetables, and wine. They would consist of representatives of the member-states presided over by a member of the Commission, who would have no vote.

Where appropriate, the Commission would consult the relevant committee on the draft of a proposed measure; decisions of the committee would be taken by qualified majority vote. The Commission would then decide on the measures to be taken and these would be immediately applicable. If they were at variance with the opinion given by the committee, the Commission might postpone their application for a maximum of one month, during which period the Council of Ministers, acting by qualified majority, could take a different decision. This procedure would apply to such matters as fixing the lump-sum figure which in effect determines the margin of Community preference, and to the arrangements to avoid diversion of trade in the grain sector.

*The Agricultural Fund* The common agricultural policy would be financed by a Guidance and Guarantee Fund whose revenue for the first three years would consist of financial contributions by member-states. The Fund's total revenues would be fixed annually by the Council and would consist in the first year as to 100 per cent from national budgets; in the second year as to 90 per cent would come from national budgets and 10 per cent from levies on imports from non-member countries; and in the third year as to 80 per cent from the national budgets and 20 per cent from such levies.

Before the end of the third year the Council would lay down rules to ensure gradual progress towards a common market system. When the common market stage was reached receipts from the levies on imports from non-member countries would go to the Community and be used to cover Community expenditure.

The Fund would be used for three main functions:
  (i)   the subsidising of export from high-cost producers;
  (ii)  market intervention to ensure stability of prices;
  (iii) to aid the modernisation of farms (e.g. by subsidising lower interest rates or by extending periods of credit), such help being exclusive of aid to farms from the Social Fund of the European Investment Bank.

*Levies* The system of levies (under which consumers in the importing country make up the difference between lower world prices of imports and those of the home agricultural market) would apply to the grain, pigmeat, eggs, and poultry sectors, for which it would supersede all national measures of protection at the frontier. During the preparatory stage a system of intra-Community levies would also be in force, but to maintain a preference for member-countries the amount of these levies for their products would be lower.

*Grain* The amount of the levies on soft wheat and coarse grains from non-member-countries would be equal to the difference between the most favourable c.i.f. price for the product and the threshold price of the importing member-state. For intra-Community trade the amount thus calculated would be reduced by a lump sum.

For hard wheat the member-countries producing such wheat would fix the levies for it in accordance with a similar procedure, the threshold price being fixed at a level at least 5 per cent higher than that for soft wheat. The amount of the intra-Community levy in the case of a member-state not providing hard wheat would be the same as that imposed upon imports from non-member countries.

For a number of products of grain processing such as malt, gluten, bran, feeding-stuffs, etc. the levy would contain a first element corresponding to the price difference for the basic products and a second element to allow for the need to protect the processing industry; this latter portion would, however, be progressively reduced in the case of the intra-Community levies.

*Animal Products*  For animal products such as pigmeat, poultry and eggs, the system of levies would be similar but not uniform because the present level of protection of the three products also differed, viz. the production of eggs was protected only by tariffs in all member-countries, pig breeding was often further protected by measures such as quotas, minimum prices etc. and the import of poultry was free except in France.

The levy for the three products would comprise three parts (1) an amount corresponding to the difference in the cost of feeding-stuffs; (2) an amount to replace the Customs duties in respect of both member and non-member countries (towards non-member-countries this amount would rise by 2 per cent annually until it reached a level of 7 per cent—the same duty therefore for the three products); (3) an amount to replace quota protection (this part could be applied anywhere for pigment but for the import of poultry only in France. It would take account of the difference between the average market prices in the importing and in the exporting member-country during a reference period.)

After intensive negotiations within the Council of Ministers on the detailed regulations implementing the common agricultural policy, it was announced in Brussels on 2 June 1962 that full agreement had been reached and that the first stage of the common farm policy involving the creation of common marketing organisations for cereals, pigmeat, eggs, poultry, fruit and vegetables, and wine would come into operation on 30 July 1962.

Dr. Sicco Mansholt, Vice-President of the E.E.C. Commission and the member in charge of agriculture, gave details of the new policy at a press conference on 27 July 1962. Describing the entry into force of the common agricultural policy as an event 'of great importance not only for Europe but for the whole world', Dr. Mansholt explained that the Commission would have to establish every day c.i.f. prices in the Community for the agricultural products involved, taking into account all the information coming in from the ports, from world markets, from the trade, and so on; it had to be able to take common decisions extremely quickly so that the policy could be put through. Although there would be unforeseen difficulties, Dr. Mansholt expressed confidence that in view of the co-operation already developed all problems could be solved. He added that he did not think there would be great changes in the first year because of the standstill of prices.

\* \* \*

The next important step in establishing the Common Agricultural Policy was to obtain agreement on common cereal prices. This was achieved on 15 December 1964 after much indecision and disagreement. One of the principal points of issue was the wide difference between the prices of wheat in France and in West Germany, the official price payable to French farmers being much lower than that which German farmers were guaranteed by their Government; while the French Government was unwilling to agree to a marked upward revision of the wheat price for fear of possible inflationary effect, the West German Government objected to a sizeable reduction in the receipts of German farmers, which might have cost them the electoral support of the agricultural community.

France, moreover, having a substantial grain surplus, was concerned about finding additional export markets in other member-countries, especially West Germany, which hitherto had obtained a large part of her import requirements from overseas.

An important step towards a solution to the cereal price problem was a set of proposals presented by the E.E.C. Commission to the Council of Ministers in November 1963. These had been worked out by Dr. Mansholt and subsequently became known as the 'Mansholt Plan'. It was a modification of these proposals that was adopted by the Council of Ministers in December 1964.

*The Mansholt Plan*   The Council of Ministers would fix basic target prices for the whole Community for soft and hard wheat, rye, barley

and maize, starting with the 1964–65 selling season. The target price
for soft wheat (the most important single product) would be DM425
(approximately £38·62½ per ton. Subsequently the Council would set
the basic prices for each year's harvest by 1 August of the previous
year.

During the Common Market's transition period the unfavourable
effects of this once for all move on the income of farmers in certain
member-countries would be fully compensated by appropriate financial aid from the Community. Starting in 1966, however, this aid
would gradually be replaced by Community measures to improve
farming efficiency and living standards. In addition to the basic target
price, the proposals included a series of intervention or support
prices based on selling prices in the main consuming areas after
allowances had been made for transport costs. The plan also provided for the setting up of quality standards, rules for estimating
monthly price variations and rules for fixing the threshold price in
areas having no target prices.

The Commission's proposals meant a reduction of all grain prices
in Germany by between 11 and 15 per cent; in Italy of wheat and rye
prices by 11 per cent; and in Luxembourg by 16 per cent for wheat
and 8 per cent for rye. Thus a loss of farm income would result in
these countries.

For France there would be a rise in most grain prices—8 per cent
for wheat, 16 per cent for barley, 1 per cent for maize; for Italy an
increase of 23 per cent for maize and 15 per cent for barley; and for
the Netherlands one of 6 per cent for wheat and 8 per cent for barley.
It was emphasised that, whereas change in prices would be fully
reflected in farmers' incomes, any calculation of their incidence on
consumer prices would have to take into account processing and distribution costs; on this basis prices would only fall or rise by one-
third or one-quarter of the actual increase or decrease in grain prices.
Thus the overall rise in consumer prices for bread, pasta, pigmeat,
eggs and poultry might reach 3 per cent in France, 5 per cent in the
Netherlands and 1–2 per cent in Italy.

The estimated losses to farmers arising from the price changes
would be as follows: Italy $65m.; Luxembourg $900,000; West
Germany $140m.

The aim of the Commission's proposals for wheat prices was to
maintain the Common Market's import needs at about their 1956–57
to 1958–59 volume of 10,000,000 tons annually. It was specifically

expected that the proposed increase in French prices would not encourage a serious increase in the amount of land under wheat. Discussions on the 'Mansholt Plan' took place from May 1964 onwards and it was not until after a meeting of the West German Cabinet in late November that Herr Schmücker, the West German Minister of Economic Affairs was able to inform the Council of Ministers on 1 December that his Government would accept a unified grain price, proposing DM440 a ton for soft wheat against the DM460 originally demanded by West Germany and the DM425 envisaged in the Mansholt Plan. These proposals became the basis of the eventual agreement.

At the December 1964 meeting of the Council of Ministers it was also requested that the E.E.C. Commission should present proposals on how the common agricultural policy should be financed for the period 1965–1967 and that these proposals should be presented by 1 April 1965.

## The Commission's Proposals

The Commission accordingly submitted its proposals to the Council. These covered not only the renewal of levies on agricultural goods but also proposed that both these levies and industrial import duties should be paid into the E.E.C. fund. *As these receipts represented enormous amounts and constituted the E.E.C.'s financial resources, the Commission proposed that the European Parliament should be strengthened by being given powers to determine the Community's revenue, and that it should also receive wider powers over the Community's budget.*

The Commission's proposals were grouped as follows:

(1) A new regulation on the financing of the common agricultural policy;

(2) Arrangements for replacing the financial contributions of member-countries by the Community's own resources;

(3) Amendments to Articles 201 and 203 of the Treaty.

The Commission considered that these proposals which were not confined to agricultural matters and were intended to make the Community financially autonomous, would mark an important and decisive step forward towards European integration, inasmuch as the Community would then have financial resources of its own and its expenditure would be governed by decisions taken at Community level, in which the European Parliament would play an important part.

*Proposed New Agricultural Regulation*   The Commission considered
that the introduction of the single market system on 1 July 1967,
would involve the common financing of refunds on agricultural
exports to non-member-countries and of measures to regulate
markets under the common organisation, since such expenditure
would be the financial consequence of agricultural policy decisions
taken by the E.E.C. as a whole. Arrangements should therefore be
made to enable the Guarantee Section of the Fund to finance
measures other than those already provided for, should such
measures be decided upon under the common organisation of
markets.

The Commission also considered that, if they were to be regarded
as the responsibility of the Community as a whole, the measures to be
financed should be based, at the single market stage, on precise and
comprehensive rules, particularly as regards commercial policy.
Because refunds on exports to non-member-countries, measures
taken to regulate markets, and other measures would be financed in
their entirety by the E.E.C., methods would have to be worked out of
checking that expenditure conformed to Community rules.

According to the Commission's proposals, financing of the common agricultural policy through the European Agricultural Guidance
and Guarantee Fund would be built up after 1 July 1965, in two
stages:
(i)   from 1 July 1965 to 30 June 1967 the transitional system provided
for would be maintained; and
(ii)  from 1 July 1967 the single market system would be in
operation.

During the transitional period (i above) the contribution of the
Fund (Guarantee Section) would be fixed for 1965–66 at four-sixths
of the eligible expenditures, and for 1966–67 at five-sixths.

The expenditure of the Fund would be covered by contributions
determined according to the following scale:

|              | 1965–66  | 1966–67  |
|--------------|----------|----------|
|              | Per cent | Per cent |
| Belgium      | 7·96     | 7·96     |
| Germany      | 32·35    | 30·59    |
| France       | 32·35    | 30·59    |
| Italy        | 18       | 22       |
| Luxembourg   | 0·22     | 0·22     |
| Netherlands  | 9·12     | 8·64     |

At the single market state (ii above) the Fund (Guarantee Sections acting in accordance with Community rules), would finance refund on exports to non-member-countries, measures taken to regulate markets, and other measures decided by the Council by a qualified majority on a proposal from the Commission. When the single agricultural market became effective, the proceeds of agricultural levies would automatically accrue to the Community. The Commission considered, however, that, in view of the degree of market integration attained by 1 July 1967, *it would be important that, with effect from that date, the proceeds from agricultural levies as well as duties on imports from non-member countries should accrue to the Community as revenue in its own right, since the place where the levies and duties would be collected and the place where imports would be consumed would be less likely to lie within the same member-country, The replacement of member-countries' financial contributions by the Community's own resources appeared desirable because, if the Community was to develop smoothly, the removal of obstacles to intra-Community trade could not be confined to agricultural produce. If there was to be a coherent economic policy, not only agricultural levies but also Customs duties on industrial products would have to be abolished on 1 July 1967.*

The Commission pointed out that a problem which confronted all Customs unions would arise in the Community: the place where levies and customs duties were collected would correspond less and less with the place at which the imported goods would be consumed, and the Commission had therefore made its proposals for financing of the common agricultural policy part of the whole financial and institutional balance of the E.E.C.

The Commission recalled that different scales were used to calculate the financial contributions of member-countries to the Community budget—there being one scale for the operation budget, another for the Social Fund, and another for the Agricultural Fund. The Commission made estimates of the percentages of total expenditure for 1967 which each country would have to pay according to these different scales. These percentages or weighted scales were estimated to be: for Belgium 8·14 per cent; for Germany 29·88 per cent; for France 29·79 per cent; for Italy 22·88 per cent; for Luxembourg 0·21 per cent; and for the Netherlands 9·10 per cent.

*Contributions for 1967* For the year 1967 the Commission proposed

maintaining the weighted scale. The budget would be reckoned in
two equal parts:
(i)   During the first half-year on the basis of financial contributions
from  member-countries;
(ii)  During the second half-year on the basis of the Community's
own resources.

Member-countries would pay to the Community the agricultural
levies and a part of the customs duties collected in their respective
territories, the total amount of such payments being equal for each
country to its contributions in the first half-year. The Commission
would then note the percentage of the proceeds of levies and Customs
duties left to each member-country.

*Contributions in 1968–71*   During the following four years (1968–71)
the percentage of receipts remaining with the member-country would
be reduced by one-fifth each year. In this way all the revenue from
levies and Customs duties would accrue to the Community after
1 January 1972.

(If in 1967, for example, a country had to allocate 60 per cent of its
total receipts from Customs and levies to the Community, that
country would have to pay 68 per cent in 1968 (60 plus one-fifth of
40), 76 per cent in 1969, etc.)

*Total Revenue and Expenditure, 1967 and Expenditure 1967 and 1968.*
Total revenue from levies and Customs duties was estimated at
$2,300,000,000 per annum. The total expenditure that the Commun-
ity would have to meet, if the Commission's proposals were adopted,
was estimated at $1,237,000,000 for 1967 and $1,758,000,000 for 1968.

*The Commission proposed a limited increase in the European
Parliament's powers under Article 201 of the Treaty of Rome so that
wider powers of control over the budget would be accompanied by
wider powers to determine the Community's revenues.*

Taking into account the ideas put forward by the Parliament
itself on 12 May 1964, the Commission sought to introduce an
arrangement effecting a certain balance between the powers of the
Parliament, the Council of Ministers, and the Commission. It therefore proposed certain amendments to Article 203 of the Treaty
dealing with Budget procedure, as follows:
(i)   Any amendments made by the Parliament to the draft budget
prepared by the Council would be deemed to have been approved
unless the Council, within twenty days, modified them by a majority
of five-sixths; if, however, the Council and the Commission agreed on

changes to the Parliament's proposals, they could be adopted by a smaller majority of four-sixths.

(ii)   The Commission 'shall study the conditions under which the financial contributions of member-states provided for in Article 200 may be replaced by Independent Community revenue.'

(iii)   The Commission would submit proposals to the Council, which would refer them to the Assembly. The Council would take its decisions by unanimous vote, but a qualified majority would be sufficient if the Assembly had rendered an opinion supporting the Commission's proposals by a two-thirds majority of the votes cast constituting an absolute majority of its members. The provisions adopted by the Council would have to be approved by the member-countries according to their respective constitutional rules, until such time as the members of the Assembly were elected by direct universal suffrage.

(iv)   The financial year should run from 1 January to 31 December, and the preliminary draft budget should be laid before the Council by the Commission not later than 15 September of the year preceding that to which it referred. The Commission would at the same time send the preliminary draft to the Assembly, and the draft budget would be laid before the Assembly not later than 15 October.

*The Commission considered that the new budget procedure would be a step towards full budgetary powers for the European Parliament, which it would exercise when elected by direct universal suffrage.*

Dr. Hallstein, the President of the Commission, had informed the European Parliament, at its session of 22–26 March 1965, that the Commission intended to submit to the Council proposals on financing the Common Agricultural policy and the provision of independent revenue for the E.E.C. The Parliament adopted a resolution approving the principle that the proceeds of agricultural levies and duties on imports from non-member-countries should accrue to the Community, but urged that the burdens should be fairly shared; it also expressed the view that the creation of independent revenue for the Community should be conditional upon transfer to the Parliament of power to fix revenue and expenditure.

The Netherlands States-General (Parliament) adopted on 16 June 1965, by an overwhelming majority, a resolution which emphasised: (a) the need for the common agricultural market and the common industrial market to come into effect at the same time; (b) the essential condition that, as the creation of the Common Market's own

D

revenue resources necessitated a change in the Community's budgetary procedure, an effective sharing of the powers of decision and control with the European Parliament should be simultaneously introduced; (c) the desirability of a beginning being made in granting legislative powers and the right of veto to the Parliament; (d) that, to strengthen parliamentary democracy in the E.E.C., the holding of direct elections to the Parliament was urgent.

The E.E.C. Commission's scheme was considered by the Council of Ministers at a meeting in Brussels which opened on 28 June 1965, under the chairmanship of M. Couve de Murville, the French Foreign Minister.

M. Couve de Murville immediately rejected the Commission's proposals, maintaining that political conditions had been imposed by the Commission which were totally unacceptable to France, and that the sole question to be settled was the renewal of levies after the expiry of the existing agricultural finance regulations on 30 June.

## The Constitutional Crisis

Dr. Luns, the Netherlands Foreign Minister, on the other hand strongly urged the adoption of the Commission's proposals, being supported by Dr. Schröder and Signor Fanfani, the West German and Italian Foreign Ministers. M. Spaak, however, expressed the view that the renewal of the agricultural finance regulations must be decided by 30 June as demanded by France, while the other points raised by the Commission could be dealt with at a later date.

Professor Hallstein, on behalf of the Commission, defended its proposals by reason of its authority to pursue economic integration under the Treaty and under subsequent Council regulations on agriculture. He nevertheless indicated the Commission's willingness to reconsider its proposals, but M. Couve de Murville refused to agree, although the other Foreign Ministers were in favour of continuing the debate.

Discussions of the Agriculture Ministers on 21 June, under the chairmanship of M. Pisani (France), on farm finance questions likewise remained indecisive; and after further talks by the Foreign Ministers on 30 June Herr Lahr (West German State Secretary for Foreign Affairs) stressed that the German delegation continued to insist on all the three aspects of the Community's policies—finance for the Agricultural Fund, direct revenues for the Community, and increased budgetary powers for the European Parliament—being decided together. M. Couve de Murville, in reply, gave a warning that if the 30 June deadline for deciding on the renewal of the financial regulations were not met, France would consider that formal commitments were no longer respected, and this would have serious consequences.

Although Dr. Hallstein, Signor Fanfani, Dr. Schröder, and Dr. Luns stressed their willingness to reach agreement and to continue the talks, another serious disagreement arose subsequently during discussions on the extent of the national contributions of member-countries to the financing of the common farm policy—the French delegation demanding a firm commitment for the period 1965–70, while the Italian delegation refused to accept such a commitment without obtaining a clearer picture of the burdens which it would involve for all the countries concerned.

Shortly after midnight on 1 July M. Couve de Murville declared that agreement was impossible and proposed that the Council should adjourn. In spite of suggestions that the clock be 'stopped' and that the Commission be asked to work out immediately a compromise proposal for further consideration, the discussion ended without result in the early hours of 2 July.

Following the temporary breakdown of the talks, the French Government announced on 5 July 1965 the withdrawal of its representatives from the Commission's working committees on agriculture, foreign relations, and the association agreement with Nigeria then under negotiation; the chief French Representative to the European Communities (M. Jean-Marc Boegner) was recalled to Paris on 6 July, and France boycotted a meeting of the Common Market representatives in Geneva on 6 July called to co-ordinate the tactics of the Six in the 'Kennedy Round' trade negotiations. M. Giscard d'Estaing failed to attend a meeting of Finance Ministers in Stresa in July and at the next meeting of the Council of Ministers on July 26–27 France was not represented—officials at the Quai d'Orsay defining the French boycott as the 'policy of the empty chair'.

Prior to this Council meeting, and in an effort to help solve the crisis, the Commission had published a memorandum on 22 July 1965, dealing with the problems which had caused the crisis. The Commission proposed in this memorandum that:

(a)  Independent revenue for the E.E.C. should be postponed until 1970, as 1967 was not acceptable to all member-countries;

(b)  Between 1967 and 1970 a compensation fund should be created to redistribute, among member-countries, the duties collected at points of entry. The common external tariff would become effective from 1967 and redistribution of duties would be essential because the points of entry would not always be in the country of use or consumption;

(c)   The existing system of financing farm policy would remain in effect until the time that the Agriculture Fund progressively took over the financing from member-countries;

(d)   A decision on these proposals should be made by 1 November 1965;

(e)   The new finance regulations should be linked to enforcement of common policies for sugar, fats and oils, fruit and vegetables, on which no agreement had so far been reached;

(f)   A ceiling should be placed on the financial cost to Italy;

(g)   when agreeing the final stages of the agricultural policy as from 1 July 1967, the complete elimination of Customs duties between member-countries and the introduction of the common external tariff on all goods entering the E.E.C. should be introduced on the same date.

The memorandum was discussed by the Council after M. Spaak had raised the question whether in France's absence the meeting was legally constituted. The Council decided that it would discuss the memorandum but left open the question whether it was to take material decisions.

During the autumn of 1965 much diplomatic activity took place in an effort to encourage France to return and take a full part in the Community's proceedings. On 30 November a further request by the 'Five' led to discussions between Signor Colombo, President of the Council, and M. Couve de Murville in Rome. Two days following the second ballot in the French presidential election the French Government accepted an invitation to meet the Council of Ministers in Luxembourg in January 1966 to try to reach a settlement.

The Council's Luxembourg meetings were devoted almost entirely to the discussion of the French requests concerning the non-application of majority decisions and the role of the Commission, a satisfactory solution of which the French Government had made a condition for resuming its active participation in the E.E.C.

It will be seen that 'procedures' and aspects of politics play a greater part in the Luxembourg Agreement than the subject of Agriculture but it was on the question of Agriculture that France took her political stand and therefore the subject must be included here.

Explaining the French objections to the principle of majority decisions, M. Couve de Murville said that in questions of vital interest only unanimous agreement was politically conceivable. Without pressing for an amendment of the Treaty the French Government therefore suggested a political agreement among the member-countries whereby the Council would abstain from deciding by majority vote if any member should so request it because of the vital importance of the question for his country.

The other members refused any formal settlement which would involve giving a member-country a permanent right to veto; they felt, however, that this was in practice largely a false problem, since unanimity would always be sought on major issues.

The solution eventually agreed upon was announced in a communiqué at the end of the second session on 29 January 1966, as follows:

(a) 'When issues very important to one or more member-countries are at stake, the members of the Council will try, within a reasonable time, to reach solutions which can be adopted by all members of the Council while respecting their mutual interests, and those of the Community, in accordance with Article 2 of the Treaty. (This article aims at approximating the economic policies of E.E.C. members to create a common market.)

(b) 'The French delegation considers that, when very important issues are at stake, discussion must be continued until unanimous agreement is reached.

(c) 'The six delegations note that there is a divergence of views on what should be done in the event of a failure to reach complete agreement.

(d) 'They consider that this divergence does not prevent the Community's work being resumed in accordance with normal procedure.'

Dealing with the role of the Commission and its relations with the Council, M. Couve de Murville put forward a list of ten points as a suggestion to assist subsequent discussion:

(1) The Commission should consult the member-Governments at the appropriate level before submitting proposals for Community action of particular importance to the Council.

(2) Commission proposals should not be made known to the European Parliament or the public before their submission to the Council.

(3)  The executive powers granted to the Commission in any policy field should be precisely formulated, leaving no room for its discretion.

(4)  Commission directives for Community policy should not specify the detailed manner of their application by the member-states.

(5)  The Council should reassert its prerogatives in diplomatic relations, particularly as regards accepting letters of credence.

(6)  Approaches to the Commission by non-member-countries should be brought to the early attention of the Council.

(7)  The Council should decide the nature and extent of the Community's relations with international organisations.

(8)  Commission members should observe political neutrality in public statements.

(9)  Community information policy should be a joint Council-Commission responsibility.

(10)  The Council should exercise a closer control over the Commission's budget.

Following discussion of the French aide-memoire it was found that there were possibilities of agreement and, according to the communiqué, the Council adopted seven points for improving its relationship with the Commission. These were:

(1)  It was desirable that the Commission, before adopting a proposal of particular importance, should, through the Permanent Representatives, make appropriate contacts with the Governments of the member-states, without this procedure affecting the right of initiative which the Commission derived from the Treaty.

(2)  Proposals and all other official acts which the Commission addressed to the Council and the member-states should only be made public after the latter had formally taken cognisance of them and had the texts in their possession.

The *Official Gazette* should be arranged so that legislative acts having a binding force were published distinctly as such.

(3)  The credentials of Head of Mission of non-member States accredited to the Community should be presented to the President of the Council and the President of the Commission, meeting together for this purpose.

(4)  The Council and the Commission would inform each other rapidly and fully of any approaches relating to fundamental questions made to either institution by non-member-states.

(5)  Within the scope of the application of Article 162, the Council and the Commission would consult together on the advisability of, the procedure for, and the nature of any links which the Commission might establish, under Article 229 of the Treaty, with international organisations.

(6)  Co-operation between the Council and the Commission on the Community's information policy, which had been examined by the Council on 24 September 1963, would be strengthened so that the programme of the Press and Information Service should be drawn up and carried out jointly, in accordance with procedures to be defined later and which might include an *ad hoc* body.

(7)  Within the framework of the financial regulations for drawing up and putting into effect the Communities' budgets, the Council and the Commission would define methods of increasing the efficiency of control over the acceptance, authorisation, and execution of the Communities' expenditures.

It was provided that these points would be discussed between the Council of Ministers and the Commission under Article 162 of the Treaty.

At the last sitting on 29 January 1966 M. Couve de Murville put forward a tentative programme of work comprising, on the one hand, certain outstanding problems such as the budget, agricultural finance regulation, and the second alignment towards a common Customs tariff, and on the other hand the entry into force of the Treaty on the merger of the Executives and decisions on the composition of the new single Commission. During the discussion, reservations were expressed by other members on the principle of such a time-table, no decision being taken.

At a press conference after the end of the Council meeting on 29 January, Signor Colombo and M. Spaak made statements which indicated that the most drastic effects of the crisis within the Community had been overcome, and that the way had been opened for a resumption of French co-operation.

Signor Colombo said: 'We can say that the European Community is starting work again, and that is what is most important from the political point of view. We have reached some agreement, come to some understanding, and have defined certain practices, but the Treaty, with its rules and institutions remains intact. And it is according to these rules and through these institutions that the life of the Community will start again. We can only express the hope that

crises like that which we have lived through in the second half of
1965 and the opening weeks of 1966 will not recur. . . .'

M. Spaak declared: 'One cannot say that all the difficulties have
been overcome by any means, but we have succeeded in what we had
to do. . . . As for majority voting, we are obliged to recognise that
we are not entirely in agreement. But what is essential is that we
recognise that the disagreement which continues does not hinder
France from coming back to Brussels, nor, therefore, the Community from resuming its activities.'

The E.E.C. Commission itself issued the following communiqué on
2 February 1966:

'The Commission is pleased that, after the Council meeting in
Luxembourg, the Community can now resume its normal activities,
both internal and external. There is a great deal of work to be done in
the coming months, and many decisions must be taken, to make real
progress towards economic union. The Commission is ready to hold
consultations with the Council, in due course, in a spirit of co-
operation and in accordance with Article 162 of the Treaty in order
to make even closer the collaboration between itself and the Council.'

## The Final Breakthrough

After intense and closely argued negotiations extending over five
months, from 28 February until dawn on 24 July 1966, the Ministers
of Agriculture of the six E.E.C. member-countries, who were joined
in the closing stages by the Foreign Ministers, agreed on the final
details of the Community's common agricultural policy, thereby
culminating six years of difficult discussions.

The crisis in the E.E.C. had seriously retarded the implementation
of the programme agreed in December 1964 but more rapid progress
was made following the Luxembourg meetings of the Council of
Ministers and the resumption of active participation by France in
E.E.C. affairs.

At the first meeting of the Council of Ministers after the decision of
France to return to the conference table all member-countries agreed
that the target date for achieving a common agricultural policy would
be 1 July 1967. This implied the fixing of common prices for all farm
products, a free circulation of goods within the E.E.C., and the
establishment of a common external tariff.

Six further meetings of the Council of Ministers took place between
7 March and 5 May, in an effort to agree on the proposals of the

E.E.C. Commission for common price levels for milk, other dairy produce, beef and veal, sugar, rice, oilseeds and olive oil, which were presented to the Council by the Commission for consideration on 7 March 1966.

The Commission proposed the following prices as from the date of implementation of the establishment of a common price level and for the ensuing 12 months (in units of account, each unit being equivalent to one U.S. dollar):

|  | $ per 100 kg. |
|---|---|
| Milk (3·7 per cent fat content)—Target price | 9·50 |
| Butter—Intervention price | 176·25 |
| Butter—Threshold price | 191·25 |
| Cattle (on hoof, medium quality)—Guide price | 66·25 |
| Calves (on hoof, medium quality)—Guide price | 89·50 |
| Rice—Basic target price | 18·12 |
|     Intervention price—France | 12·30 |
|     Intervention price—Italy | 12·00 |
|     Threshold price | 17·78 |
| Sugar—Common target price for white sugar | 21·94 |
|     Intervention price for white sugar | 20·84 |
|     Minimum price for sugar beet (per ton) | 16·50 |
| Oilseeds—Common norm price | 18·60 |
| Oilseeds—Intervention price | 17·40 |
| Olive oil—Common norm price | 111·00 |

The *target price* is the basic price determined in the Community region with the least adequate domestic supplies, i.e. that needing the largest imports; basic target prices apply to foodstuffs, produced in only some member-countries, and common target prices to foodstuffs produced in all member-countries.

The *intervention price*, which should be as close as possible to the target price, is the one guaranteed to the producer.

The *threshold price*, fixed as a minimum import price, is the target price less the transport cost from the point of entry and that used for calculating the levy on imported supplies.

The *guide price*, applied to cattle, beef and veal, is a varying price according to standards, with minimum and maximum limits, and forms the basis for the calculation of Customs duties.

The *Common norm price* is the measure used for calculating deficiency payments for certain products.

It was pointed out that the effect of applying common prices would render superfluous any levies or other duties on trade between member-countries and would achieve complete free trade in agricultural goods on the same date as for industrial goods. In making its proposals the Commission said that it took into account the relationship between the price of grain—already fixed—and those of other foodstuffs, the foreseeable trends of consumption and supply, and the need to encourage certain forms of food production, e.g. beef rather than milk, and also beef in preference to veal because of the world shortage of beef. The Commission estimated that the foreseeable effect of the shift from national price levels to common prices on the cost-of-living index would be as follows:

|             | per cent |
|-------------|----------|
| Belgium     | +0·4     |
| Germany     | −0·2     |
| France      | +0·67    |
| Italy       | −0·4     |
| Netherlands | +1·0     |

As no comprehensive agreement on all the points involved in a common agricultural policy could be reached by the beginning of May the Ministers agreed at its meeting that it would be impossible to achieve the target date of 1 July 1967. The reason for the postponement was primarily that France declared that she could not accept the final removal of tariffs on industrial goods until the common agricultural market was completed. West Germany and the Netherlands thereupon proposed that 1 January 1968 should be the target date, but France then suggested that the end of 1968 would be early enough for the removal of industrial tariffs, pointing out that this would still be in advance of the dates laid down in the Treaty of Rome for achieving a common market.

It was finally agreed at the meeting of Ministers that 1 July 1968 would be the date for the bringing into operation of the full common market in respect of both agricultural and industrial goods, that is eighteen months earlier than envisaged in the Treaty of Rome.

By December 1970 the member-states had passed on to the E.E.C. a large proportion of the levies on agricultural imports entering the E.E.C. held by the European Agricultural Fund. Since 1 January 1971 all levies have been paid into the fund. Until December 1977 the balance of the cost of the policy is shared out among them on an agreed ratio. In 1969 the member-states themselves spent about $2,000,000,000 and the Community $285,000,000, on agricultural improvement; the Community spent $2,300,000,000 on market support and export refunds.

In March 1971, the Council of Ministers agreed to carry out, over a four-year initial stage of the Mansholt Plan, the principles of the Commission's proposals. Farmers between fifty-five and sixty-five who give up farming will receive annual pensions of not less than $600. Lump sums will be paid for land placed at the disposal of the authorities for afforestation or recreation, or made available for modernisation, by farmers of any age. For those remaining in farming, the member governments will offer grants, loan guarantees and interest rebates on submission of adequate farm-development plans; they will also provide improved training facilities for younger farmers and agricultural advisory services, and encourage the formation of producer groups.

25 per cent of the cost of most of these measures, except for the cost of pensions in Italy where it will repay up to 65 per cent, will be repaid by the Farm Fund.

Thus, the E.E.C. have accepted the principle of joint responsibility for the reform of farming. The impact of this programme, added to the existing national farm-reform measures, is expected to be considerable and will reduce the numbers of poor farmers and will increase the efficiency of the farmers who remain on the land.

## E.E.C. Agricultural Prices

| Commodity | Type of price | 1971–72 | 1972–73 proposed |
|---|---|---|---|
| | | £ | £ |
| Wheat | Target, per cwt | 2·32 | 2·37 |
| | Basic intervention | 2·13 | 2·18 |
| Barley | Target, per cwt | 2·12 | 2·18 |
| | Basic intervention | 1·95 | 1·99 |
| Maize | Target, per cwt | 2·05 | 2·12 |
| Sugar beet | Minimum per ton | 7·20 | 7·28 |
| Fat cattle | Guide, per live cwt | 15·24 | 16·35 |
| Milk | Target, per gall | 21·26 | 21·69 |
| Butter | Intervention, per ton | 753·57 | 753·57 |
| Skim milk powder | Intervention, per ton | 198·98 | 209·22 |

The British Government has said that 'agriculture is the largest single industry in the E.E.C. Together with forestry and fishing it employs 14 per cent of the work force and produces almost 8 per cent of the gross domestic product, compared with 3 per cent in Britain produced by 3 per cent of the work force. The farming population has been decreasing both here and in the Community. But productivity is greater in Britain and farms are larger (about eighty acres on average compared with thirty acres). About 15 per cent of farms in the Community are of more than fifty acres compared with nearly 50 per cent in Britain.

'The Six together produce about 90 per cent of all their food and virtually all they need of the main foodstuffs that can be grown in western Europe. In Britain we produce just over 50 per cent of our food and we import more food than most other developed countries. If we joined the Community more of these imports would tend to come from the other members. Denmark and Ireland who are also applying for membership are among our traditional suppliers. There would also be more incentive for British farmers to expand production. So the enlarged Community would produce nearly as much of its food as the Six do now.

'Both in Britain and in the Community the aim of agricultural policy is to maintain a stable and efficient agricultural industry, in the interests of consumer and of the economy as a whole, and also to safeguard the standard of living of those working in agriculture. But there are differences in the methods of achieving this aim.

'In general, imports have come into Britain freely, so that the market prices here have in many cases been the world prices. But British farmers receive direct financial support to give them an adequate return for their produce. In general, if the average return from the market is less than the guaranteed price the difference is made good by a deficiency payment. For milk and sugar beet there are no subsidies and the market is managed so that the consumer bears the full cost of the guarantee. The Government has announced its intention to move over to a system of levies, and to introduce interim schemes covering cereals, beef, lamb, and milk products other than butter and cheese. The Government also gives direct grants to farmers to help certain types of production and to encourage efficiency and investment. In some parts of Britain, especially the hill areas, farming is particularly difficult and special assistance is given. Horticulture is not covered by the guarantee system and is supported mainly through tariffs or quotas on imports.

'For many commodities, though not all, market prices are higher in the Community than in Britain, so that British farmers could expect higher returns under E.E.C. conditions for several important commodities, particularly cereals, beef and milk, though feed costs would be higher. The Community system of support would be introduced at the start of the transitional period. But market prices would be raised gradually over the following five years, during which deficiency payments would be phased out. Special transitional arrangements would apply to horticulture to help growers to adjust to conditions of equal competition with those in the Community.'

*Self-Sufficiency in E.E.C. plus Britain, Denmark, Ireland and Norway*

|  | E.E.C. | 6+4 |
|---|---|---|
|  | % | % |
| Wheat, incl. flour | 110 | 94 |
| Barley | 102 | 100 |
| Total cereals | 94 | 87 |
| Potatoes | 100 | 100 |
| Sugar | 103 | 83 |
| Beef and veal | 88 | 90 |
| Mutton and lamb | 75 | 53 |
| Pigmeat | 99 | 99 |
| Poultrymeat | 99 | 101 |
| Butter | 112 | 92 |
| Cheese | 102 | 99 |
| Eggs | 99 | 100 |

FISHERIES

At a meeting of the Council of Ministers held in Luxembourg on 19–20 October 1970 agreement was reached by the Ministers of Agriculture on a common fisheries policy which came into force on 1 February 1971. The decisions, which covered the common organisation of fish markets and a common structural policy, were taken despite protests from Britain, Norway, Denmark and the Republic of Ireland who wished to participate in formulating the policy.

*Market Organisation*

This would cover both fresh fish and frozen and preserved products, and involves *inter alia* the application of common marketing standards to eliminate products of unsatisfactory quality and to facilitate trading relations. Producers' organisations would be responsible for the market organisation. Arrangements were laid down to simplify the establishment and functioning of such organisations, for which purpose member-countries might grant aid, to be financed in part by the Community's European Agricultural Guidance and Guarantee Fund, but to be of a temporary and declining nature.

Guide prices would be fixed for products of special importance to the income of producers (certain fresh fish such as herring, cod, black pollack, northern hog-fish, etc., as well as shrimps) in order to determine price levels for market interventions; the guide prices would be based on prices noted over the previous three seasons in representative Community markets.

Market intervention would normally be carried out by the producer groups, excepting sardines and anchovies, for which public buying was planned, particularly in order to allow for the virtually complete absence of producer groups in the Italian anchovy industry. Intervention would be in the form of withdrawal of members' produce from the markets if prices should fall below a level set at 60 to 90 per cent of guide prices; as compensation producers would receive grants from the Community equal to 60 per cent of the guide price, or 55 per cent if the withdrawal price was 60 to 65 per cent of the guide price.

The arrangements also included measures to assist stocking by producers in case of a distinct fall in the prices of certain frozen products (sardines, sea-bream, squid, cuttle fish and octopus); in the case of tunny fish compensatory indemnities would be granted to Community producers if their income was threatened by a fall in import prices of tunny earmarked for canning.

Foreign exporters to the E.E.C. of the more important fresh fishes and of frozen fillets of certain fish of everyday consumption would have to respect reference prices laid down by the Community, but in principle all quantitative import restrictions would be abolished for the majority of products, which would be subject only to the common external tariff. The exceptions were a number of 'sensitive' products, such as imports covered by GATT rules of fresh trout from Denmark, fresh carp from Yugoslavia, tinned tunny fish from Japan and tinned sardines from Portugal, for which further negotiations on minimum prices with the countries concerned would be required.

Complete suspension of the common external tariff was planned (a) for herring, sprats and tunny fish, where Community production is insufficient, in order to ensure supply conditions for processing industries within the Community comparable to those from which these industries benefited in non-member exporting countries; (b) to maintain traditional imports of basic foodstuffs such as salted and dried cod.

As a basic principle, member-states must make the necessary arrangements to ensure equal rights of entry into ports and initial marketing facilities for fishing vessels flying the flag of any member-state. A safety clause, however, permitted the rapid implementation of all necessary measures to prevent the Community from being threatened by disturbances from outside.

*Common Structural Policy*

This was based on the principle that, subject to certain conditions, fishermen from the Community countries must have equal access to fishing grounds and to their exploitation in all waters within the sovereignty of member-states.

For certain kinds of fish, however, offshore fishing within the three-mile limit would be protected for a five-year period for the benefit of communities whose industry was closely related to fishing on an artisan basis, the boundaries of these areas to be fixed by the Council of Ministers. The Community would also take measures to safeguard existing fish resources, including restrictions on the capture of certain types of fish, boundaries, open and closed seasons, fishing methods and tackle.

The Commission would submit annually to the European Parliament and the Council of Ministers a report on the structure of the fishing industry, based on reports by member-countries, and the Council of Ministers would decide on any measures to be taken. Member-states would be authorised to grant financial help, in accordance with Community regulations still to be agreed, in order to meet the object of the common structural policy, and joint action might be decided upon and financed by the Community.

A Standing Commission on Fisheries Structures would be set up to help in the elaboration and implementation of the common policy, to co-ordinate the policies of member-states, and to ensure continuous co-operation between these states and the European Commission.

# CHAPTER 9

## *Sales and Turnover Taxation*

In broad terms, there are two forms of taxation, direct and indirect.

Direct taxes, like Corporation Tax and Income Tax, come into play at the end of the sequence of industrial operations or personal activities. They are based either on the profits of industrial or professional enterprise at the end of a year's activity or on wages and salaries when tasks have been performed and payment made. They are intended to play no significant part in the price of the merchandise or services on whose profits they are levied.

Indirect taxes, on the other hand, are taxes on consumption and as such they determine, together with the cost of production and distribution, the price of the merchandise.

Article 99 of the Treaty of Rome requires the harmonisation of indirect taxes, the most important of which are turnover taxes and excise duties. This harmonisation is regarded as of primary importance in the Community, because without it frontier controls would still be needed to equalise the cost of the product imported from other Common Market countries with that of the domestic product carrying turnover tax.

The first task of the Community in the field of indirect tax harmonisation has been, first, for each member country to abandon its particular form of turnover taxation in favour of the principle of the Value-Added Tax and then to adopt a level of Value-Added Tax common to all the member countries.

The following table shows the distribution of the different headings of taxation as a percentage of the Gross National Product at market prices in 1968 in eleven countries.

It is now mainly of historical interest to note the different forms of turnover tax which existed in the countries of the Community before the general adoption of the Value-Added Tax. They were of three kinds, first, the cumulative multi-stage cascade system used in Germany (until the end of 1967), Luxembourg (until the end of 1969) and the Netherlands (until the end of 1968). Under this system, tax was

*Total taxes (including social security contributions) as a % of GNP at market prices in 1968*

| | Total taxes and contributions | Taxes on income on households | on corporations | total | Taxes on expenditure | Social security contributions | of which paid by employers |
|---|---|---|---|---|---|---|---|
| Belgium | 33·0 | 8·1 | 2·1 | 10·2 | 13·3 | 9·5 | *6·0* |
| France | 36·9 | 4·7 | 1·8 | 6·5 | 15·9 | 14·5 | *10·8* |
| Germany | 34·2 | 8·1 | 2·1 | 10·2 | 12·9 | 11·1 | *n.a.* |
| Italy | 30·4 | 5·0 | 1·7 | 6·7 | 12·5 | 11·2 | *n.a.* |
| Netherlands | 37·8 | 10·4 | 2·8 | 13·2 | 11·2 | 13·4 | *9.9* |
| E.E.C. average | 34·4 | 7·3 | 2·1 | 9·4 | 13·2 | 14·9 | *n.a.* |
| United Kingdom | 34·4 | 10·6 | 2·5 | 13·1 | 16·2 | 5·1 | *2·6* |
| Norway | 38·2 | 12·3 | 1·5 | 13·8 | 15·2 | 9·2 | *4·7* |
| Denmark | 34·7 | 15·3 | 1·0 | 16·3 | 16·5 | 1·9 | *n.a.* |
| Sweden | 42·3 | 18·6 | 1·6 | 20·2 | 13·9 | 8·2 | *4·3* |
| U.S.A. | 30·0 | 10·9 | 4·7 | 13·7 | 9·1 | 5·3 | *2·8* |
| Japan | 18·9 | 3·9 | 4·0 | 7·9 | 7·5 | 3·5 | *2·2* |

Source: ECSO and OECD

levied on the gross value of the output at each stage of production, with no rebate on taxes paid at earlier stages.

Secondly, the tax on value added, a non-cumulative multi-stage system which has been applied in France since 1954 when T.V.A. (*Taxe sur la Valeur Ajoutée*) replaced earlier forms of production-to-distribution taxes.

Thirdly, there were the mixed systems which were cumulative multi-stage systems applied down to the wholesale stage but incorporating taxes applied at a single point for some goods. These mixed systems have been used in Belgium and Italy.

In contrast to these diverse systems in the Community countries, Britain has used her Purchase Tax system which is a single stage tax normally charged at the wholesale stage of distribution by registered manufacturers or wholesalers. All such undertakings can trade with one another without attracting tax, but taxes payable when the goods pass to an unregistered buyer (for example a retailer) or when the goods are otherwise put to taxable use.

A registered business may import goods under representation, in accordance with its certificate. This clears the goods free of purchase tax through the Customs control at the port of entry. They are taken into the importer's untaxed stock and will attract tax in due course when they pass into the hands of an unregistered buyer either as a straight re-sale or as part of the price if they are used in a manu-facturing or assembling operation.

All these systems of turnover taxation have had one characteristic in common. No tax is payable on exports. Each importing country has levied its own turnover taxes at the frontier or port of entry according to its own system and at the same time (unless the imports are brought in 'under representation') as the appropriate import duty.

## HARMONISATION IN THE COMMON MARKET

The Common Market is now tariff-free for intra-Community trade industrial goods. The maintenance of frontier posts for the levying of sales or turnover tax conflicts with the whole principle of the Treaty for the abolition of all border checks. The Council of Ministers decided in April 1967 that to implement the need for the eventual abolition of all border tax adjustments (which had created endless technical problems and new distortions of competition), it was necessary, as a first stage, that all member-countries should institute a common tax system based on the value-added principle; secondly, that by 1 January 1972 comparable products in each Community country will be subject to the same system of turnover tax (even if the rates varied) and exact compensatory measures will be possible for both intra-Community trade and trade with the rest of the world. (Italy obtained a postponement of six months from January 1972).

Thus, compensatory import taxes (and export rebates) will still exist after 1 January 1972 in trade between the member-countries because the first stage of harmonisation merely introduces a common system of Value-Added Tax and within this common system each country will determine its own tax rates and tax exemptions.

These tax frontiers will be removed during the second stage for which, however, no time limit has yet been fixed.

Many of the problems involved in applying compensatory measures at the frontier on intra-Community trade will disappear when all the member-countries have come into line with a common Value-Added Tax applied at the same levels and on the same transactions in all the countries.

It will then be possible for a supplier in country A to add V.A.T. at the appropriate Community rate to his invoice for goods consigned to country B and for the merchandise to pass unchecked across the frontier. Entrepreneurs in country B would then only be responsible for operating V.A.T. for value added in their own country and, indeed, if the goods then went to another Community country at some stage in their processing, the same method would apply.

Thus, V.A.T. on goods and services destined for the Community as well as for domestic use will be payable in the country of origin and, it is assumed, the proceeds, except for the proportion of V.A.T. payable to the Community Budget, will be retained in that country. There will be no accounting between one country and another of the amount they have collected in goods sent to each other.

Imports from non-member countries will be taxed at the point of entry and the tax paid on imports will be allowable as a deduction at subsequent stages just as if the goods had been bought in the home market and the tax paid by a domestic supplier.

Exports to non-member countries are relieved of V.A.T.

The arguments for adopting V.A.T. as the common system of turnover taxation in the Common Market have been stated by the Commission of the European Economic Community as follows:

(1)  V.A.T. is competitively neutral. At equal prices the same kind of goods carry the same amount of tax.

(2)  The fiscal burden is not affected by the number of intermediate stages or intermediaries involved in the production and marketing of the goods. Integrated businesses are, in spite of their apparent suppression of one or several stages, put on the same footing as non-integrated businesses.

(3)  V.A.T. encourages productivity and modernisation, tax already paid on investment goods being deductible.

(4)  V.A.T. encourages specialisation, since an increase in the number of stages to achieve greater specialisation does not lead to an increase in the tax burden.

(5)  V.A.T. permits the application of a precise tax refund on exportation and a precise basis of taxation on importation and so eliminates discrimination between home produced and foreign goods.

(6)  It adapts to the pursuit of the economic and social objectives of the Community, in particular because it allows the application of reduced rates at any stage.

The characteristics of V.A.T. as a method of imposing a general tax on the use of goods and services by the final consumer lies firstly in the fact that it is charged at each stage in production and distribution on the value that has been added to the product, by processing costs and profit in the case of manufacture or by profit in the case of re-sale and secondly that tax paid at earlier stages is deductible at each stage so that it is only at the final stage, that of the final consumption, that the tax becomes an actual fiscal charge which is no longer deductible.

The common system of value-added taxation is designed to extend

## Example I

| (1) Stage | (2) Value added at that stage | (3) Total value at end of this stage | (4) Tax on sale | (5) Deduction of tax borne at previous stage | Tax 10 per cent (6) V.A.T. payable at this stage |
|---|---|---|---|---|---|
| Manufacturer produces fibre and sells to | 25p | 25p | 2½p | | 2½p |
| Processor who crimps and weaves into fabric and sells to | 25p | 50p | 5p | 2½p | 2½p |
| Garment manufacturer who makes a shirt and sells to | 50p | £1 | 10p | 5p | 5p |
| Retailer who adds his gross margin | 50p | £1·50 | 15p | 10p | 5p |
| | | | | | 15p |

## Example II

*On 75,000 shirts*

| (1) Stage | (2) Value added | (3) Prior Ta paid |
|---|---|---|
| 1. Manufacturer produces fibre for 75,000 shirts. During the same accounting period he buys a new machine at £500 plus £50 tax (at 10 per cent) | 18,250  500 + | 50 (ta |
| | 18,750 + | 50 (ta |
| 2. Processor weaves material for 75,000 shirts. Buys dye and machinery at £200 plus £20 tax (at 10 per cent) | 18,550 + 1,875 (t  200 + | 20 (t |
| | 18,750 + 1,895 (t | |
| 3. Garment manufacturer makes 75,000 shirts. Buys buttons and thread at £500 plus £25 tax (at 5 per cent) and dye at £100 plus £10 tax (at 10 per cent) | 36,900 + 3,750 (t  500 +  100 + | 25 (t  10 (t |
| | 37,500 + 3,785 (t | |
| 4. Retailer sells 75,000 shirts. Buys new van at £500 plus £100 tax (at 20 per cent) | 37,000 + 7,500 (t  500 + | 100 (t |
| | 37,500 + 7,600 (t | |

to the retail trade just as does the French V.A.T. but member-states will be free to apply the system only to stages up to and including the wholesale trade and to levy, where necessary, a supplementary tax of their own on retail sales. Such permissive application of V.A.T. is being adopted by Italy for a transitional period pending the time when fiscal frontiers are abolished.

In parenthesis, it is of some interest that a value-added tax at any given rate is tantamount to a tax on the full price of the product because the tax is applicable on every item from the crude raw material onwards. As the crude raw material in its original state has been provided free by nature everything that is done to it is value added.

Examples must inevitably entail the simplification of the problem; firstly because too many stages are generally involved to make the example representative of what happens in practice and secondly because one has to select a point of time in a process which is continuous.

Example I illustrates the impact of the value-added tax on one nylon shirt, in a highly simplified form with costings, margins and profits all imaginary.

| al value nd of e | (5) Tax on sale | (6) Prior tax paid now deducted | (7) V.A.T. payable |
|---|---|---|---|
| | 1,875 50 | | |
| 50 + 50 (tax) | 1,925 3,750 20 | 50 1,875 20 | £ 1,875 |
| 00 + 1,895 (tax) | 3,770 7,500 35 | 1,895 3,750 35 | £ 1,875 |
| 00 + 3,785 (tax) | 7,535 11,250 100 | 3,785 7,500 100 | £ 3,750 |
| 500 + 7,600 (tax) | 11,350 | 7,600 | £ 3,750 |
| | | Total tax paid = £11,250 = 15p per shirt | |

Moreover, it is assumed that the manufacturer who produces the fibre starts from the extraction of the natural crude material which he uses, and is therefore at the first stage of adding value to that crude material.

Example II elaborates the process because it introduces an element of bought-in materials on which tax has been paid and is therefore deductible at the next stages and an element of the purchase of capital equipment. Of course, the purchase by the processor of £200 worth of machinery would not in practice be allied specifically to the manufacture of these 75,000 shirts. It would take place during a given accounting period during which these particular shirts are probably made and sold. Nevertheless, allowing for the simplification, this is a fair example of the operation of V.A.T. through a series of manufacturing and selling stages from the processor of the crude materials to the consumers who finally buys the shirts.

The following diagram (Example III) illustrates the way in which the value-added is determined by the deduction of tax previously paid. As the value added is the difference between purchases and sales, and the tax previously paid on purchases is deducted for the tax due on sales, the taxation of the value added is calculated by means of the deduction of previous tax.

It is not necessary to wait for the sale of an individual article to deduct the tax paid on purchases. The total value of purchases or taxes previously paid and the total value of sales or tax on sales must be determined for a tax period and settlement made at the end of that period.

The earlier tax on purchases which is deductible includes all tax shown in the accounts which is borne, for example, by goods or raw materials, services, investment goods or general expenses. As tax paid earlier is deductible at the end of each tax period and tax on sales is due at the same time the corresponding goods, including longer term stocks and investment goods, are carried in the accounts at net prices. All earlier fiscal elements are thus eliminated and taxation of the disposal of goods starts afresh at each stage.

THE EFFECT OF REDUCED RATES IN V.A.T.

The deduction of tax already paid is also possible when reduced rates apply to certain transactions. However, it should be noted that when the normal rate is applied to the following stage, there is a compensatory effect since the goods are taxed again as if they had never benefited from a fiscal concession. As the following example shows, the tax payable decreases or, as in the diagram (Example IV), disappears at the stage where the reduced rate is applied, but the compensatory effect at the following stage leads to a corresponding

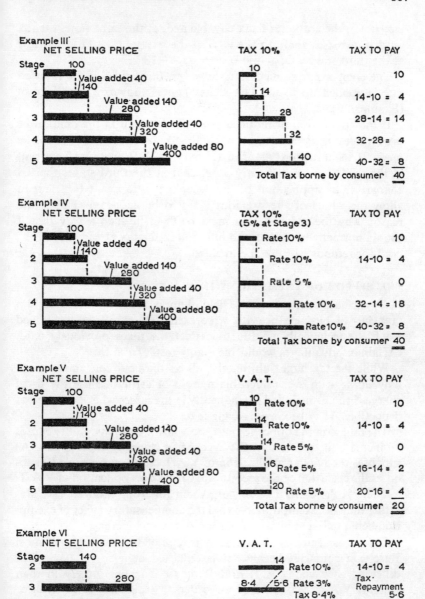

**Example III**

NET SELLING PRICE

| Stage | | TAX 10% | TAX TO PAY |
|---|---|---|---|
| 1 | 100 | 10 | 10 |
| | Value added 40 / 140 | | |
| 2 | | 14 | 14-10 = 4 |
| | Value added 140 / 280 | | |
| 3 | | 28 | 28-14 = 14 |
| | Value added 40 / 320 | | |
| 4 | | 32 | 32-28 = 4 |
| | Value added 80 / 400 | | |
| 5 | | 40 | 40-32 = 8 |

Total Tax borne by consumer 40

**Example IV**

NET SELLING PRICE

| Stage | | TAX 10% (5% at Stage 3) | TAX TO PAY |
|---|---|---|---|
| 1 | 100 | Rate 10% | 10 |
| | Value added 40 / 140 | | |
| 2 | | Rate 10% | 14-10 = 4 |
| | Value added 140 / 280 | | |
| 3 | | Rate 5% | 0 |
| | Value added 40 / 320 | | |
| 4 | | Rate 10% | 32-14 = 18 |
| | Value added 80 / 400 | | |
| 5 | | Rate 10% | 40-32 = 8 |

Total Tax borne by consumer 40

**Example V**

NET SELLING PRICE

| Stage | | V. A. T. | TAX TO PAY |
|---|---|---|---|
| 1 | 100 | 10 Rate 10% | 10 |
| | Value added 40 / 140 | | |
| 2 | | 14 Rate 10% | 14-10 = 4 |
| | Value added 140 / 280 | | |
| 3 | | 14 Rate 5% | 0 |
| | Value added 40 / 320 | | |
| 4 | | 16 Rate 5% | 16-14 = 2 |
| | Value added 80 / 400 | | |
| 5 | | 20 Rate 5% | 20-16 = 4 |

Total Tax borne by consumer 20

**Example VI**

NET SELLING PRICE

| Stage | | V. A. T. | TAX TO PAY |
|---|---|---|---|
| 2 | 140 | 14 Rate 10% | 14-10 = 4 |
| 3 | 280 | 8·4 / 5·6 Rate 3% Tax 8·4% | Tax Repayment 5·6 |

increase in the amount of tax payable and, at the same time, the tax burden increases again to the level of the normal rate. (Tax payable at the third stage $= O$, at the fourth stage $= 18$.)

The compensatory effect can, however, be avoided if the reduced rate is applied up to the last stage. This is shown in the diagram (Example V).

If the application of reduced rates would result in the amount of tax on sales being less than the tax already paid, a refund should be made. If, as in the next diagram (Example VI), the rate is 10 per cent at the second stage and only 3 per cent at the third stage, the tax chargeable by application of the 3 per cent rate is not sufficient to allow the whole of the previous taxes to be deducted. This is the reason why the reduced rate must be fixed in such a way that it should normally be possible to offset all of the tax already paid. The need for refunds will thus be avoided.

THE EFFECT OF EXEMPTIONS IN V.A.T.

If, by excluding them from the field of application of V.A.T., certain branches of business activity were exempted, the firms concerned would be technically unable to deduct the taxes previously paid. Certain disadvantages would inevitably result from this.

While the tax might ultimately fall on the final consumer, it can only do so with a considerable margin of error because the fiscal charges become included permanently in the prices when they are not deductible. They become cascade taxes.

The tables on the opposite page show how non-deductibility causes an increase in the price at the succeeding stage. In these tables (A) supposes the regular application of V.A.T. at all stages and (B) supposes the exclusion of the second stage from the application of V.A.T.

There is therefore a strong argument for using reduced tax rates rather than tax exemption to avoid the compensatory effect of exemption being reflected in accumulation of tax and increases in price.

The British Purchase Tax system is reputed to be the envy of most European countries because it is collected at a single stage. The difference between V.A.T. and Purchase Tax lies largely in their history. V.A.T. was evolved in order to transform a generalised production tax which has previously fallen on investment and certain other business costs (as well as on consumer goods) into a tax falling on consumer goods only. Purchase Tax from its inception was designed as a tax on consumer goods.

The multi-stage design of V.A.T. involves a much larger and more complicated structure for administration and collection than Purchase Tax, as can be seen by the fact that the collection of the three elements of V.A.T. in France (T.V.A., T.P.S. and Taxe Locale) involves two million firms, whereas Purchase Tax involves only 65,000 firms. The average tax per V.A.T. taxpayer in France is about £1,000 compared with £10,000 per Purchase Taxpayer in the United Kingdom.

It is the fractional method of payment which has set the pattern of V.A.T. as the method of taxing consumers for all time. No tax administration could face the problem of compressing the collection of one-quarter of its total tax revenue into 10 per cent of the proportion of the population who pay it now. Purchase Tax will have to change to V.A.T. V.A.T. will never change to Purchase Tax.

TABLE A

| | I<br>Production from<br>raw materials | II<br><br>Processing | III<br><br>Manufacture |
|---|---|---|---|
| Purchase price | — | 100(a) | 140 |
| Added value | 100 | 40 | 140 |
| Tax base | 100 | 140 | 280 |
| Rate | 10% | 10% | 10% |
| Tax | | 14 | 28 |
| Calculation of selling price | 100 + 10 | 140 + 14 | 280 + 28 |
| Selling price | 110 | 154 | 308 |

(a) When the goods are subject to V.A.T., the previous taxes are deducted.

TABLE B

| | I<br>Production from<br>raw materials | II<br><br>Processing | III<br><br>Manufacture |
|---|---|---|---|
| Purchase price | — | 110(a) | 150 |
| Added value | 100 | 40 | 140 |
| Tax base | 100 | — | 290 |
| | 10% | 0% | 10% |
| Tax | 10 | 0 | 29 |
| Calculation of selling price | 100 + 10 | 150 + 0 | 290 + 29 |
| Selling price | 110 | 150 | 319(b) |

(a) When the goods are not subject to V.A.T., taxes already paid are not deducted.
(b) The price increase by comparison with Table A is 319 − 308 = 11, including the non-deductible tax at the first stage ( + 10) and the tax charged on the latter at the third stage ( = 1).

There is, however, one important point common to both systems. In themselves, neither V.A.T. nor Purchase Tax stimulates or impedes exports. It is sometimes held that V.A.T. favours exports. Earlier French taxes from which V.A.T. evolved created certain difficulties for export. The removal of these difficulties caused some misunderstanding of the situation.

Almost all French exports are carried on under suspension of tax at all stages; just in the same way as British exports never enter into the Purchase Tax system.

Eventually, all sales from one Community country to another will be regarded as domestic sales for V.A.T. purposes. The tax will only be rebated on exports to non-member countries.

The tax base for V.A.T. includes the delivery of goods and services and the eventual standard rate of V.A.T. will be the same for the delivery of goods as for the performance of services.

The Community lists the following as services subject to V.A.T.

(1)   The assignment of patents, trade marks and similar rights and the granting of licences concerning those rights.

(2)   Work done to tangible goods and on behalf of a taxpayer, which constitute repairs, cleaning etc. but not any form of manufacture.

(3)   Architectural and similar services connected with construction.

(4)   Advertising.

(5)   Transport and storage.

(6)   Leasing of movable tangible goods to a payer of V.A.T.

(7)   Employment agencies.

(8)   Banking transactions on behalf of a taxpayer.

(9)   Services of consultants, engineer and similar technical, economic and scientific services.

(10)   The fulfilment of an obligation not to exercise a professional activity enumerated in this list.

(11)   The services of brokers, independent intermediaries, agents and others in connection with transactions involving goods or services.

When harmonisation of Turnover Taxation has been achieved there will remain the problem of Excise Duties, some of which are of no particular importance either as part of the budgets of the member-states or as influences on trade and competition. Others, of some importance, are regarded as capable of being brought into the future common V.A.T. system of the Community. A third category of Excise Duties, that which concerns alcohol, petroleum products and tobacco will prove the most difficult but even these will yield in the end to inclusion in the common system of V.A.T. and to adjustments affecting monopolies in the member-states to conform to the letter and spirit of the Treaty. These problems were all known when the Treaty was drafted.

The next stage, after the harmonisation of indirect taxation, is the harmonisation of direct taxes. Complete co-ordination is probably impossible because direct taxes are an inseparable part of the economic and social life of each country.

The aim of the Community is, therefore, to harmonise the effects of the tax laws rather than the laws themselves, so as to remove all incentives for enterprises to enter into mergers, to move their factories or headquarters or to invest or otherwise formulate their trading policy in so far as their policy might be influenced solely by tax considerations or advantages.

In company taxation, this broad front of co-ordination affects a range of taxes on distributed and undistributed profits, on allowances for depreciation, on the valuation of stocks, on the taxation of dividends and the problems of the international company.

A balance will be sought between restriction on movements which could distort competition on the one hand and a sufficient degree of flexibility on the other hand to allow the development of plans which are economically desirable; in particular where investment could assist to solve the problem of areas with continuing difficulties for creating new industries and employment.

The following table shows the V.A.T. Rates applicable in the Community countries, U.K., Denmark, Norway and Ireland.

Rates as a percentage of prices, before V.A.T.

|  | Standard rate | Reduced rates (foodstuffs and other essential goods) | Increased rates (luxury goods) |
|---|---|---|---|
| France | 23·46 | 7·53–17·65 | 33·33 |
| Germany | 11 | 5·5 | — |
| Netherlands | 14 | 4 | 15† |
| Luxembourg | 10 | 2–5 | — |
| Belgium* | 18 | 6–14 | 25 |
| Italy* | 12 | 6 | 18 |
| Denmark | 15 | — | — |
| Norway | 20 | — | — |
| Ireland* | 16·37 | 5·26 | 30·26 |
| U.K. | 10 | — | † |

\* Proposed.     † Supplementary rate for private cars (not deductible).

# CHAPTER 10

## *The Rules of Competition*

The Treaty of Rome imposed on the member-countries of the Common Market a task of unprecedented complexity. It decreed that the Six should unify their economies behind a protectionist tariff wall under conditions which if they are not to be described as *planification* on a European scale must be regarded as wiping out the last vestiges of *laissez-faire*.

Having made sure that no part of the Common Market has any advantage over another, in the price of its foodstuffs, in the cost of its raw materials, and eventually in wages (by means of the free movement of workers), in social charges, in taxation, in transport and all the other elements of the economy, the Treaty lays down Rules which are described as the 'Equalisation of Competition'.

It is impossible not to spare a thought for Adam Smith.

A market so large, so effectively integrated and so completely equalised is a producer's dream. In theory it affords all the opportunity for economies of scale for both production and distribution. In practice it is open to every conceivable activity for market sharing and monopoly.

Monopoly in our modern civilisation has been countered in different ways in different countries. The United States use their anti-trust laws; Britain has her Monopolies and Restrictive Practices legislation and the abolition of Retail Price Maintenance.

The Treaty approaches the problem from three directions. In order to ensure the complete fusion of the markets of the Six, it proscribes all agreements between enterprises or associations of enterprises which have as their object or result the prevention, restriction or distortion of competition. It controls aids granted by member-states unless justified by particular economic or regional considerations. It limits the powers of the member-states to enact fiscal provisions which could distort competition in their trade with other Common Market countries.

In some ways, the articles of the Treaty are less stringent than the Sherman Act and the Clayton Act in the United States. Monopolies and mergers are not effectively subject to legal scrutiny unless they aim at or result in the abuse of a dominant trade position. Then they fall within the provision for the banning of agreements between enterprises or associates of enterprises which have as their object or result the prevention, restriction or distortion of competition within the Common Market in Articles 85 and 86 of the Treaty. These are more far-reaching than any country in the world has attempted to enact. They cite, in particular, as incompatible with the Common Market.

(a)   the direct or indirect fixing of purchase or selling prices or other trading conditions.

(b)   the limitation or control of production, markets, technical development or investment.

(c)   market-sharing or the sharing of sources of supply.

(d)   the application to parties to transactions of unequal terms in respect of equivalent supplies thereby placing them at a competitive disadvantage.

(e)   the subjecting of a contract to conditions which have no connection with the subject of the contract.

(f)   any agreement which allows one or more enterprises to take improper advantage of a dominant position in the Common Market.

For the purposes of the present work, it is desirable to examine closely the effect of the Rules Governing Competition upon the kind of trade practices that are normally encountered by management in industry. The present chapter covers the activities of the European Economic Community in this field with particular reference to the efforts which have been made to interpret the Rules and to implement the Treaty's chapter which defines them.

The actions of the Commission of the European Economic Community have been concentrated in the early stages upon a general category of so-called exclusive dealing agreements between businesses rather upon cartels of a more general nature.

It has always been accepted as normal trade practice for a manufacturer in one country to confer the selling rights for his productions in a part or the whole of a second country on a distributor if the second country who confines his activities in the particular production to the territory for which he has been granted the sole selling rights; and refrains from selling the product back to traders either in the country of its origin or to traders in any third or additional territory. Occasionally this practice is reinforced by agreements which involve patents or trade marks. All this is the normal basis for sole distribution rights with which everyone in business has become familiar over the years.

The restrictions are designed mainly to enable a manufacturer to protect his distributor from interference from third parties which might arise, *inter alia*, from price differentials between one area of distribution and another, and to allow the distributor to reap the fruits of his activities.

Articles 85 and 86 of the Treaty strike at the roots of these practices on the grounds that the Six are now economically one and that the national frontiers which have been abolished between the Common Market countries must not be replaced by artificial frontiers maintained or enacted by commercial agreements which could prevent the free flow of goods in all directions within the Common Market and whether those goods are produced inside the Common Market or are imported from countries outside.

Article 85 (1) of the Treaty lays down that certain practices in the form of agreements between enterprises which are likely to prevent, restrict or distort competition in the Common Market are incompatible with the Common Market and are prohibited.

Article 85 (3) then enumerates certain classes of agreements to which Article 85 (1) does not apply.

The considerations laid down for obtaining a declaration that the prohibition of Article 85 (1) is inapplicable are that agreements must fulfil *both* of two positive and two negative requirements. The positive requirements are:

(1)   The agreement must contribute to the improvement of production or distribution of the products or must promote technical or economic progress (e.g. agreements for rationalisation or standardisation).

(2)   The agreement must provide, at the same time, to users an equitable share of the benefits which result from such contribution (e.g. that a reduction in price or an improvement in quality or in service had directly resulted).

The two negative requirements are:

(1)   The agreement must not impose upon the parties any restrictive which is not essential to these objectives.

(2)   The agreement must not enable the parties to eliminate competition in a substantial proportion of the goods covered.

Article 86 sets out certain 'improper practices' connected with contracts in which improper advantage is taken of a dominant industrial position in the Common Market.

To enable them to implement the provisions of Articles 85 and 86 of the Treaty, the Commission under the authority of the Council of the Community issued their first Regulation—Regulation No. 17 of 6 February 1962. This regulation sets the pattern for the whole process involved in carrying out the provisions of Articles 85 and 86. In it, the Commission elaborated the considerations which demanded the uniform and balanced application of Articles 85 and 86, claiming that it was necessary to establish a system which ensured that competition would not be distorted in the Common Market. The preamble to the Regulation underlined the need for effective supervision and made it, in principle, obligatory for all enterprises wishing to invoke the exclusion effect contained in Article 85 (3) to register all their 'agreements, decisions and concerted practices' with the Commission.

Thus, the Commission approached the problem by the unusual method of declaring virtually illegal any 'agreement, decision or concerted practice' within a wide area of commercial arrangements which are quite normal practice in trade (without being in any way monopolistic) and by making it incumbent on the parties to such arrangements to submit the agreement to the Commission to get it cleared.

Regulation No. 17 gave two methods for clearing agreements which appeared likely to be caught by Articles 85 and 86 of the Treaty:

(1) 'Negative Clearance' which, if it is granted, ensures that the agreement will be immune from attack by the Commission for being incompatible with the Treaty.

(2) A form of registration called 'Notification' which, if it is accepted by the Commission, ensures that the agreement will stand as of legal validity within the Common Market and should, other things being equal, be so regarded in the courts of the individual member countries as well as being immune from attack by the Commission.

Regulation No. 27 of 10 May 1962 set out the precise procedure for the registration of agreements.

It became evident very soon after the issue of Regulations Nos. 17 and 27 that the Commission had extended its net too wide. Their Regulation No. 153 of 24 December 1962 went part of the way towards putting things right. This new regulation laid down two revised principles excluding certain agreements from being caught by Article 85 (1).

These exclusions concerned:

(1)  Contracts with Commercial Agents, i.e. agreements between principals and agents by which the agent does not engage in activities proper to an independent trader; does not buy and sell the principals' goods on his own account; does not ever own the goods and does not (apart from the occasional 'del credere' guarantee) assume any risk resulting from the transactions.

In practice this exception covers the long-established function of the manufacturers' representative or agent working on a commission basis. The agent may be a sole agent in so far as he is the only representative of the principal in a given territory, and is paid commission on all the business that comes from that territory; but the restrictions which this relationship represents are held not to create any restraint or distortion of commission. Such contracts with Commercial Agents do not have to be submitted to the Commission.

(2)  Patent Licence Contracts, in which obligations are imposed on certain forms of exploitation of an invention provided by the patent laws of the member countries, even though such obligations involve limitations

(a) of time (e.g. a licence shorter than the life of the patent), (b) of space (e.g. a licence granted for a part of the Common Market or to one place of exploitation or to a specific factory), and (c) of persons, (e.g. prohibitions against the licensee assigning his licence or granting sub-licences).

In general terms, this means that a patentee may, without finding his agreements caught by Article 85 (1), grant licences in which the period and area of exploitation within the Common Market are defined and exclusive, but not exceeding the period of the validity of the patent. Regulation No. 153 states that, providing the contract falls within a range of obligations of which the foregoing is a brief summary, there is no need to register such contracts or agreements with the Commission.

In the same Regulation (No. 153) the Commission provided for a simplified method for the registration of certain exclusive dealing agreements. The clause in question added a paragraph to Regulation No. 17.

The use of this simplified form of notification was, under Regulation

No. 153, limited to agreements between two parties by which one party gives an undertaking to the other party to supply certain products only to the latter for the purpose of re-sale within a defined part of the territory of the Common Market; or one party gives an undertaking to the other party to buy certain specified products only from him for the purpose of trade in those products. In the notification of such agreements it was necessary to certify that reciprocal exclusive concessions for the distribution of competing products made by the grantor and the grantee had not been set up and that the grant of the exclusive concession did not limit the power of intermediaries to obtain the products from another grantee or other intermediary within the Common Market or for the grantee to sell equally to customers outside the contractual territories; and that the agreement did not include any obligation on the grantee to observe a minimum re-sale price fixed by the grantor.

The general principles covered by the simplified form of registration laid down in Regulation No. 153 have been consolidated in Regulation No. 66/67/CEE issued on 25 March 1967 which gives a block exemption from Article 85 (1) to a wide range of exclusive dealing agreements of a purely bilateral character until 31 December 1972.

Regulation No. 66/67/CEE lays down that, up to 31 December 1972, the ban on exclusive dealing agreements, Article 85 (1) of the Treaty, will not apply where the agreements apply on two parties and where

(a)   One undertakes, with regard to the other, to supply certain products to the other alone with a view to their resale within a specified part of the Common Market territory, or

(b)   one undertakes, with regard to the other, to purchase from the other alone certain products with a view to their resale, or

(c)   sole supply and purchase commitments, with a view to resale, of the type envisaged in the two preceding sub-paragraphs, have been entered into by the two undertakings.

Providing that there is no restriction on the sole concessions other than

(a)   the obligation not to manufacture or distribute, during the period of the contract or until the end of one year after its expiry, products competing with the products covered by the contract;

(b)   the obligation not to advertise products covered by the contract, not to establish a branch and not to maintain a warehouse for distribution, outside the territory covered by the contract.

E

But the concessions enumerated above do not apply where

(a) manufacturers of competing products entrust each other reciprocally with the sole distribution of those products;

(b) the contracting parties restrict intermediaries' or users' possibility of obtaining the products covered by the contract from other resellers with the Common Market, in particular where the contracting parties

(i) exercise industrial property rights with a view to interfering with the supplying to resellers or users in other parts of the Common Market of products covered by the contract, properly marked and put into circulation, or with the sale of the said products by those resellers or users in the territories covered by the contract;

(ii) exercise other rights or adopt measures with a view to interfering with the supplying to resellers or users of products covered by the contract elsewhere in the Common Market, or with the sale of the said products by those resellers or users in the territory covered by the contract

The Commission of the European Economic Community, after examining the agreements which were submitted to them when the first Regulation was published, have come to recognise that a large proportion of the arrangements that are made between a manufacturer on the one hand and a distributor on the other have not the implications of restricting, distorting or preventing competition in such a way as to undermine the unity of the Community. They are, in fact, normal, common sense and workable trade practices.

The phases by which they have reached their conclusions have been complicated and tortuous. The philosophical analysis of what makes industry tick makes strange reading to the ordinary man, but under the conditions of the study and drafting of the regulations, this was perhaps inevitable.

The E.E.C. Commission has given considerable publicity to the cases which they selected from thousands of agreements submitted to them which they decided were caught by Article 85 (1) and on which they have taken action.

The first case resulted in the specific prohibition of an agreement between the Grundig Sales Company in West Germany and the Consten Company in France. The purpose of the agreement was to make Consten the sole distributor of Grundig products in France for which purpose Grundig had imposed a ban on all their dealers in other countries so that French purchasers could buy Grundig products only from Consten. In addition, Grundig and Consten had signed a supplementary agreement on the use of a special trade mark ('Gint') the purpose of which was to hinder the importation by firms other than Consten of Grundig products into France.

Consten sought to uphold its claim to exclusive dealership by taking action against a rival importer, Unef, of Paris, which was importing Grundig products from German wholesalers. Consten contended that Unef had not respected the established sales organisation and were introducing unfair competition. This case came before the Paris Courts and was adjourned pending a decision by the Commission on the compatibility of the exclusive distribution agreement between Grundig and Consten with the cartel rules of the Treaty.

The Commission decided that the agreement in question offended against the ban in Article 85 (1) of the Treaty and that it could not be approved under the provisions of Article 85 (3). In addition, the Commission forbade Grundig to obstruct rival imports of their products into France. The Commission held that the agreement in question constituted a restraint of competition, because the freedom of business activity of the parties to the agreement was restricted and that of firms outside the agreement was impaired. Customers for Grundig products were denied the possibility of making their purchases from other suppliers.

The Commission argued that, in the class of goods concerned, competition even at retail level is essential. The sales arrangement between Grundig and Consten was 'liable to affect trade between member-states'. The agreement was signed between two firms established in different member-states and regulated trade between those member-states in such a way that such trade was wholly in the hands of Grundig and Consten. Here was clearly a case where two commercial undertakings had set up for their own purposes trade frontiers which coincided with the national frontiers and had thereby rendered integration of the national markets into a common market more difficult. It was considered that the protection which the agreement gave Consten and consequently the obstruction of rival imports into France went beyond any restraint of competition which might conceivably be necessary for the improvement of production and distribution.

The two companies involved in this case exercised their right to challenge the legality of the decision by the Commission and they appealed to the Court of Justice of the Community. Except for a technicality that the inclusion of certain provisions in the agreement were irrelevant in the case submitted to the Court, the Court upheld the Commission's interpretation of the Regulations and the exclusive dealing agreement between the two firms remains 'incompatible with the Common Market' and illegal in terms of the Treaty.

The E.E.C. Commission has also made public its decisions to give 'Negative Clearance' to a number of so-called Exclusive Dealing Agreements.

One of such agreements was between an American firm and its distributor in Belgium, which was nothing more than a straightforward contract between a manufacturer of motor car accessories in the United States and its distributor. The contract had no limitations of marketing area, no restrictions on the suppliers not to sell direct if they wished to do so and none on the distributor not to deal in competing products.

Another such agreement concerned the grant by a French manufacturer of synthetic fibres of exclusive distribution rights to a Swiss importer with a restriction on the Swiss firm not to re-export to the Common Market. The Swiss firm would be hard put to do this anyway, because the product would bear double customs burden, and it was stated by the Commission that the contract involved no perceptible restraint of competition affecting trade in the Common Market.

A third agreement concerned the relations between a French company and a British company engaged in manufacturing and selling hairdressing preparations. In this case, the only restrictions consisted in that, the French firm having sold certain trade mark interests outside the Common Market, but retained those interests for operations within the Common Market, the British firm was not expected to compete with the French firm in the Common Market area.

Other cases include the grant of negative clearance to Kodak who revised their conditions for the resale of their products abroad and for the fixing of resale prices and whose new conditions are described as exemplary from the Commission's point of view in as much as any purchaser, at no matter what point in the distribution chain, is free to export to the other Common Market countries by selling to whom he likes at whatever price he likes, subject to the wholesaler or retailer satisfying certain required professional standards.

The effect of this type of arrangement is said to be that wholesalers and retailers are free to benefit from any abnormal difference in price in a neighbouring country by marketing their goods there at a lower price since it will no longer be possible for prices to be maintained at different levels from one Common Market country to another.

Article 86 of the Treaty has also been invoked, for the first time, against an industrial merger which involved the takeover by Continental Can of America of the Dutch firm Thomassen & Drijver-Verblifa NV and which the Commission considers creates a dominant trade situation in food packaging materials.

The Commission has already been successful in taking action under the same article of the Treaty against G.E.M.A., the German performing rights society (parallel societies in the other Community countries having already given up their restrictive practices in this field), to enable authors and other members to enter into direct arrangements in any country and not, as hitherto, to be restricted to granting licences through the society of their own country.

These and similar cases appear to be of the nature of test cases. Such a view is borne out by the phraseology in one of the paragraphs of the preamble to Regulation No. 17. This says 'considering the such agreements, decisions and concerted practices are probably very numerous and cannot therefore all be examined at the same time and that a number of them have special features which may make them less of a threat to the development of the Common Market'.

The kinds of agreement exempted in the later regulations are the obvious exemptions. The concept of Articles 85 and 86 is so wide that the Commission were bound to regard almost every agreement between manufacturer and distributor as a potential menace to the Common Market, and to start from there to sort out the wheat from the chaff.

The Regulations made by the E.E.C. Commission to implement the provisions of Articles 85 and 86 of the Treaty apply, within the Common Market to all exclusive dealing agreements whether the parties to the agreement are domiciled in the Common Market or whether one or all parties are domiciled in countries outside the Common Market. Of course, the jurisdiction of the Commission and the Court of Justice is restricted to the Common Market and agreements where one or all parties were outside could only be attacked in so far as they had some vulnerable spot inside the area. One party to an agreement, inside the Common Market playing a secondary part and following the instructions of the other party outside the Common Market, might well be exposed to action by the Commission in respect of any practice which they considered was perceptibly affecting competition within the Common Market area.

Membership of the Common Market brings all parties to agreements within these supranational powers of the Community. It is part of the price of the Treaty.

# CHAPTER 11

## Industrial Property: Patents and Trade Marks

The term 'Industrial Property' is used in this chapter in its proper context of patents, trade marks and design. International law on patents is a field of activity in which, strictly speaking, a layman in such matters can only comment with some reserve. Nevertheless, it cannot be avoided altogether if one is to do justice in an examination of the provisions of the Treaty of Rome to the changes which are taking place in the Common Market, and which must vitally affect industry in Britain in its production, licensing, and marketing plans for Europe in the future.

*     *     *

Industrial Property in the European Economic Community comes within the provisions of the Treaty under two headings. Firstly, under the general theme of the Common Market that conditions now existing or measures to be taken in the future in member-states and by industry in those countries must not constitute anything by which one State is artificially favoured or handicapped in relation to another State. This is part of the concept of the Rules of Competition. Secondly, in order to achieve this ideal concept of equality, there must be an eventual approximation of the laws of the individual member-states. This concept is provided for, partly in Article 36, but mainly in Article 100. It is important to note, however, that the Treaty does not change existing individual national systems of Industrial Property protection.

Article 100 of the Treaty of Rome falls under the chapter dealing with the Approximation of Laws and reads as follows:

The council, acting by means of a unanimous vote on a proposal of the Commission, shall issue directives for the approximation of such legislative and administrative provisions of the member-states as have a direct incidence on the establishment or functioning of the Common Market.

The Assembly and the Economic and Social Committee shall be consulted concerning any directives whose implementation in one or more of the member-states would involve amendment of legislative provisions.

Three conclusions can be drawn in the interpretation of Article 100. They are:

(1)   A free flow of goods in the whole of the Common Market must be achieved.

(2)   There must be uniformity in conditions of competition; for example, uniformity would not exist in such conditions as the case of an inventor who is free to exploit a patent in country A, while the same patent is protected for X in country B and for Y in country C.

(3)   Therefore, uniformity in the exercise of economic activity must be unimpeded by differences in the scope of protection given by, or in the obligations to exploit, an invention or trade mark.

In late 1959, the governments of the European Economic Community countries decided, in conjunction with the E.E.C. Commission, to set up three groups to study and prepare a programme for the harmonisation and unification of the Industrial Property laws in the Common Market countries, one group for each of the three categories of Industrial Property—patents, trade marks and design— and a further group to co-ordinate the findings of the three specialised groups. All this with particular regard for the concept of equality expressed and implied in the Treaty in relation to Industrial Property.

It was established at the outset that the kind of European Patent Law that must emerge from the process of unification should coexist with the existing national patent laws of the member countries, but, on the other hand, that all rights under a European patent should be autonomous and to that degree independent of national patent laws.

The co-ordinating committee on Industrial Property set up by the member-states of the Community and the E.E.C. Commission produced in 1962 their 'Draft Convention relating to a European Patent Law'.

The original Draft Convention of 1962 has been followed by two Draft Conventions drawn up by the Inter-Governmental Conference for the setting up of a European System for the Grant of Patents, the first in January 1970 in which 17 countries took part and the second in April 1971 in which 19* countries took part.

* France, Belgium, Netherlands, Germany, Luxembourg, Italy; Britain, Norway, Sweden, Denmark, Austria, Switzerland, Portugal, Greece, Ireland, Spain, Turkey, Monaco, Yugoslavia.

Under the provisions of the Draft Conventions relating to a European Patent any State which is a party to the Paris Convention for the Protection of Industrial Property (1883, last revised at Lisbon 1958) may ask to accede to the Convention, which will then apply to the territories of the Contracting States which the latter designate on signing or ratifying their accession. There are also provisions for a form of association by special agreement involving reciprocal rights and obligations.

The principle is that the Convention will create a European Patent valid in all the Contracting States, with a European Patent Office and Courts with power to deal with European Industrial Property matters which will fall under its jurisdiction. The latter will consist, *inter alia*, of an Examining Division and Boards of Cancellation and Appeal. The procedure which it is proposed to lay down will be the same whatever the nationality of the patentee.

A European Patent will be available for any one or more members of the Convention, but the Community will have to be designated as one country for the purpose of a European Patent. National patents will still be available, however, as at present in the individual countries, Community and non-Community alike.

The Convention proposes to establish a system of law, common to all the Contracting States, for the purpose of the grant of patents for invention.

Patents granted under the Convention will be called 'European Patents' and will have the effect of and be subject to the same conditions as a national patent granted by the Member State of the Convention.

The first essential feature of the preliminary draft is the creation of a European Patent Office which will have the power to grant a patent valid in one or more of or in all the Contracting States (the Common Market Countries being regarded as one State for this purpose).

A European Patent will confer on its proprietor, in each Contracting State for which it is granted, the same rights as are conferred by a national patent granted in that State. Such patents will co-exist with the national systems of patents.

Any infringement of a European Patent will be dealt with under the laws of a Contracting State in the same way as apply to infringement of a national patent.

The following is a summary of the main aspects of the procedure proposed for obtaining a European Patent:

I. *Filing of the Application*   (*1*) An application will be filed either at the European Patent Office or at the Patent Office or other competent authority of the Contracting State (in which case it will have the same effect as if it had been filed at the European Patent Office. There are time limits for the forwarding of the latter applications); (*2*) The application will contain, in addition to the request for a grant of a European Patent, the usual description, claims, drawings and require payment of the necessary fees; (*3*) Applications for a European Patent must designate the Contracting State or States in which protection for the invention is desired.

II. *Priority*   (*1*) Right of priority will be given for twelve months from the date of the filing of the first application (with provision for claiming priority for previous filings).

III. *Examination*   (*1*) Prior to the introduction of the inventor's request for examination, the *Examining Section* of the European Patent Office will determine whether the application is valid and whether or not the invention is obviously patentable. If the examination reveals deficiencies, the applicant will be invited to remedy them; (*2*) If the application meets the requirements, it is then passed by the *Examining Section* to the International Patent Institute at The Hague for a report on the state of the art. When this report is received, the European Patent Office will transmit it to the applicant, who, on the basis of the report, may abandon one or more of his original claims or submit new ones; (*3*) European Patent applications will be published as soon as possible after the expiry of a period of eighteen months from the filing of the application, or, if priority has been claimed, as from the earliest date of priority. At the request of the applicant, the application may be published earlier. The publication will contain the description, claims, drawings and the report on the state of the art.
Following publication, any third person may present his observations on the patentability of the invention. These will be communicated to the applicant; (*4*) The next stage is a formal request, this time to an *Examining Division*, for a European Patent which may be made by the applicant up to the end of six months after the date of the publication of the state of the art.
   If no request is made by the end of the period, the European Patent application will be deemed to have been withdrawn. The

request can be made by the applicant or by any other person.

If the request is made by the applicant, he will be required to comment on the report on the state of the art and to amend, if necessary, the description, claims and drawings.

It will be open to any other person to request the examination of a patent. The request for examination will be published. The applicant will then be given the option himself of proceeding further with the application or amending or withdrawing it.

IV. *Grant or Refusal*   (*1*) If the Examining Division is of the opinion that the application and the invention have met all the requirements of the Convention, it will inform the applicant and, where applicable, the third party who requested examination, of the form in which it intends to grant a European Patent and the patent will be entered into the Register of European Patents and published in the European Patent Bulletin.

A European Patent certificate will be issued, designating the Contracting States for which application was made.

The Examining Division may refuse a European Patent application if the inventor does not meet the requirements of the Convention, but the grounds of refusal must first be communicated to the applicant and to any third party, and when the refusal has become final it will be entered into the Register and published in the Bulletin.

V. *Opposition*   Within a period of nine months from the date of publication, any person may give notice of opposition. The Examining Division may, after giving the applicant the opportunity of amending the claims (but not extending the protection), then either revoke or maintain the European Patent and the decision will be entered in the Register and published in the Bulletin.

An appeal to a Board of Appeal will lie for decisions of both the Examining Sections and Examining Division and will have a suspensive effect.

It is important to note:

(1)   that all applications for a European Patent are to be published and that a third person will be able, even at this preliminary stage, to present his observations concerning the patentability of the invention.

(2)   that a request for examination may be presented, in addition to

the patentee by a third person if that person desires, for any reason, to expedite the grant or refusal of the patent.

(3)   that before the final grant of the patent, any person may, within a period of twelve months, give notice of opposition.

In the draft Convention there are provisions for the payment of fees for applications and examination and of fees and renewal fees for patents granted, and some provision is planned for the conversion of a European Patent application into a national application in certain circumstances.

The bundle of patents represented by a European Patent will be a cheaper and easier way of obtaining protection over a wide spread of European countries without depriving inventors from obtaining national patents separately in the different countries.

The question of simultaneous protection in any country under a European Patent designated for that country and under a national patent for an invention originating from the same inventor will be a matter for each Contracting State.

The duration of a European Patent is proposed at 20 years from the publication of the provisional patent. There will be compulsory licensing provisions effective in the entire territory of the Convention, or these may only be applied in one particular interested State.

Proceedings for infringement will be enforceable only through the courts of the Contracting States. A Board of Cancellation will deal with cancellation of Patents and Patent Licences with retroactive effect on certain defined grounds. Pending the signing of a Convention, measures are proposed for a '*dépôt commun*' so that rights to a European Patent can be established in the transitional period.

All decisions of the Examining Board and the Board of Cancellation will be subject to appeal to the Board constituted for that purpose.

The preliminary Convention is still only in draft form and it leaves many fundamental problems still to be solved. None the less, it is a notable step towards a consistent and unified system for a European Patent.

The Conference intends to hold a final session when a completed text will be agreed for presentation later to a Diplomatic Conference.

On Trade Marks, the procedure is not yet so clearly defined because of wider differences in the member states of the Common Market on the basis on which Trade Mark rights can be established. On the whole the trend is towards the German system with the right of a claimant to prior rights to be advised so that he can oppose the registration of the trade mark.

The European Patent is but one of the developments in Europe which are setting the pattern for future relationships between the countries and for devising means for their working together for which there are no precedents.

# CHAPTER 12

## Industrial Standards

With the completion of the customs union and tariff-free movement of industrial goods across the frontiers of the Common Market, the next stage is the removal of what have been called the invisible trade barriers.

These barriers consist of the industrial standards used by the different countries for a wide range of products.

The differences between the standards of different countries distort competitive conditions by denying an exporter access to a market which requires any variation from a basic specification. These differences can only be overcome by the harmonisation of national standards one with another.

The work of harmonisation falls under two headings, voluntary and mandatory, and is being carried out at several levels, world wide, in western Europe and the European Economic Community.

In western Europe, the national standards institutions of all E.E.C. and Efta countries came together in 1960 to form the European Standards Co-operating Committee (CEN) and an equivalent body in the electro-technical field called CENEL In addition, an organisation known as CENELCON exists for co-operation between the electrical standards bodies in the Community countries.

In 1967, a tripartite procedure called CEN-TRI was devised allowing representatives of the standards bodies of France, West Germany and Britain to reach preliminary agreement for CEN to endorse.

In addition to these and a number of other voluntary measures to harmonise standards in western Europe, there has been international collaboration among governments through the Food and Agriculture organisation (FAO), and the World Health Organisation (WHO) while the Organisation for Economic Co-operation and Development (OECD) has undertaken research and action in several areas, notably agricultural machinery and tractors as well as agricultural produce.

Under Article 100 of the Rome Treaty, the E.E.C. Commission may issue directives authorised by the Council to deal with situations where the free movement of goods is restricted by differences in member states' legislation. Under these directives, member countries are obliged to amend their domestic laws to meet the agreed specifications laid down and to open their frontiers within a given period, to goods manufactured to such specifications.

The programme of the Community provides for harmonisation by four methods:

(1)  Total harmonisation by which detailed Community rules replace disparate domestic regulations.

(2)  Optional harmonisation by which Community rules can exist in parallel with national regulations so that manufacturers can obtain access to Community markets if they so desire by using Community standards.

(3)  Harmonisation by reference to compliance with recognised voluntary standards agreed by national standards bodies particularly applicable in specifications to ensure safety.

(4)  Reciprocal recognition of legislation from one country to another.

Amongst the products for which directives have been issued or are being considered are: textiles, including labelling; motor vehicles and tractors, including safety and pollution; crystal glassware; electrical machinery; measuring instruments and weighing machinery; oil pipelines; material in contact with foodstuffs; plaster tanks and pressure vessels; pharmaceutical products; together with other commodities for which different standards exist in different countries, including a wide range of foodstuffs.

Industrial property rights (patents and trade marks) also constitute an invisible barrier which must be removed to give complete freedom of movement of industrial goods across frontiers.

Industrial property in the European Economic Community comes within the provisions of the Treaty of Rome under two headings: first, under the general theme of the Common Market that conditions now existing or measures to be taken in the future in member-states or by industry in those countries must not constitute anything by which one state is artificially favoured or handicapped in relation to another (in the way in which patent rights can be used to create restrictive conditions). Secondly, in order to achieve this ideal concept of equality, there must be an eventual approximation of the laws of the individual member states and in the manner in which those approximated laws are individually interpreted.

The European Patent is fully described in Chapter 11.

# CHAPTER 13

## Social Security

The obligations regarding workers and Social Security imposed by the Treaty setting up the European Coal and Steel Community on the High Authority (the executive body of the E.C.S.C.) and those imposed by the Treaty setting up the European Economic Community on the Commission (the executive body of the E.E.C.) are different one from the other.

The member states of the E.C.S.C. are bound to renounce all restrictions based on nationality in the employment of workers in their coal and steel industries and their Social Security Convention co-ordinates their Social Security schemes and extends their benefits to all migrant workers.

On the other hand, Article 118 of the Treaty of Rome stipulates that it shall be the aim of the Commission to promote close collaboration between member-states in the social field, particularly in matters relating to employment, labour legislation and working conditions, occupational training, Social Security and protection against occupational disease and accidents.

Some of the earliest regulations issued by the countries of the E.E.C. under the Treaty laid down rules for ensuring equal treatment for workers moving from one country to another so that insured persons taking up employment in another country should retain the rights they had already acquired at the time of moving from one country to another.

An agreement drafted by the Council of Europe in Strasbourg on the 16 April 1964 to establish a European Code of Social Security extending two agreements of the 11 December 1953 called the European Interim Agreements on Social Security Schemes relating to Old Age, Invalidity and Survivors and on Social Security other than schemes for Old Age, Invalidity and Survivors was designed to secure reciprocal treatment for workers from one country moving to another. Very little of this agreement has been ratified or implemented. In any case reciprocity in matters of Social Security is not, of course, the same process as unification which is the ultimate aim of the member-countries of the Common Market.

The Treaty formula for approaching a common system of Social Security throughout the European Economic Community was obviously designed to have regard for the wide differences in the national systems of the member-countries and, of course, for the strongly political bias in each country for its own system.

Moreover, Social Security plays a large part in the budget of all the European countries inside and outside the Common Market and in the level of taxation.

There could be no greater challenge to the minds of men than the task of bringing all the different systems together.

There is no exact definition of the phrase 'Social Security'. It applies generally to a heterogeneous range of state and institutional activities designed in the main to secure the population, whether by insurance or direct state contributions against sickness, disability, un-employment, old age, poverty, the burden of the large family and many of the ills and problems to which man and his dependants are subject in the sophisticated society of the modern state, and for which organised assistance is their right.

Ever since the 18th and markedly during the 19th century, fragmen-tary pieces of legislation were enacted in Europe to aid certain cate-gories of indigent members of the community and workers in the coal mining industry in recognition of the obligations of the community towards its under-privileged members and those who suffered sick-ness and injury in their work.

The need was recognised in different ways and at different times in the six future member countries of the European Economic Com-munity.

The problem created by the ever-widening scope of the industrial revolution speeded the movement to recognise some form of collec-tive responsibility for the increasing mass of industrial workers. As far back as 1854 the Prussian Government introduced legislation for the protection of certain categories of workers, notably apprentices, miners and railway workers. In 1881 Bismarck announced a plan to add to existing safeguards specific measures for the betterment of the necessitous members of the community.

The plan was put in action by a law on sickness insurance in 1883, on industrial accident insurance in 1884, on disability and old age in 1889. These measures were consolidated into a disability and old age insurance system for employees and for widows and orphans in 1911. The financial burden of these insurance systems was shared between employer and employee with state subsidies where necessary.

The system introduced in Germany in 1911 had a considerable influence on the first scheme which was introduced in Britain by Lloyd George in 1911 just as later schemes in Europe were influenced by the Beveridge Plan thirty years later in Britain.

The problem of harmonising the various systems of Social Security in the Six countries of the European Economic Community is extremely complex; it will be even more so if and when those systems have to be reconciled with the interpretation of Social Security in Britain and in the Scandinavian countries.

The essential difficulty lies in the fact that each country's system of Social Security is inextricably bound up with a different philosophy of what Social Security means and what it has to achieve. Each system has been developed empirically from complicated historical, political, economic and demographic origins.

As different trees root and grow in different climates and different layers of the earth's surface, so the diverse systems have grown to meet the varying needs of the different populations.

Each system has the same broad objectives but its growth has been rapid and many retain their early basis of operation through friendly societies or other co-operative organisations with strongly regional or craft characteristics. Reform has followed reform rapidly in systems which have barely had time to take root.

All the member countries of the Common Market are moving towards unification of their own fragmented systems. These movements and the changes which they involve give to the whole field of Social Security a degree of instability which renders comparison difficult and unification a long process only to be achieved by gradual stages.

Article 117 of the Rome Treaty requires that the member-states promote the improvement and working conditions of labour so as to permit the equalisation of such conditions in an upward direction.

Articles 117 and 118 state the essential need. How is it to be put into effect in the area of Social Security?

In the first instance, it is easier to harmonise those elements in the different systems which present the least divergences, and a start has been made with the interchange of information based on national experience; in the handling of Social Security for migrant workers in the Community and in consultation between the member-states to ensure that such changes as are contemplated in the national systems will tend to make harmonisation easier in the future.

Behind the essential sociological and demographic considerations, there exist all the basic common criteria.

Freedom of movement of workers within the Community as it grows demands equality of all Social Security measures. The issue, cannot be forced. Rather will the solution be found in the gradual changes in national legislation on Social Security which tend to be of such a nature as to fit the pattern for the future.

All the other measures which the Common Market countries take to make them one Community will lead to the evolution of measures to unify their complex systems of Social Security. The freedom of movement of persons and capital is amongst its cardinal purposes. Time is needed and a common purpose. The Community has both. Unification of Social Security is essential to the realisation of the immediate aims of the Community.

This description outlines the different systems without attempting to do more than pick out the salient features of each system so that the reader may judge the extent of changes which will be needed to move towards harmonising them all.

Firstly, which members of the population come under Social Security provisions?

## I. *Dependent workers; wage- and salary-earners*

In general terms, this category of worker enjoys wider protection in the countries of the Community than workers who earn their livelihood in other ways. It was the wage-earner who originally needed the most help and it was upon him that most of the early systems were concentrated. Independently of considerations of history, economics and politics a system which covers groups of workers whose contributions can be deducted at the source of their wages is much easier to administer.

*France* In France, under the law of 4 October 1945, all wage-earners employed by another person or enterprise fall under a single plan for social insurance, workmen's compensation, health insurance, family allowances etc., whatever the level of their remuneration or their terms of service; but the deductions can only be made in respect of their earnings up to the equivalent of about £1,300 per annum, except for unemployment insurance where the ceiling is at a higher level.

Sickness, maternity, invalidity, old age and survivors insurance is levied at the rate of 24·5 per cent on wages of which 18 per cent is payable by the employer and 6·5 per cent by the employee.

Contributions for family allowances require 10·5 per cent of wages, all paid by the employer. Accidents at work and occupational illness rates depend on the trade and the risks of that trade. Unemployment requires 0·4 per cent of which 0·32 per cent is paid by the employer and 0·08 per cent by the employee. Taken together these add up to about 35 per cent of which about 29 per cent is paid by the employer and 6 per cent by the employee.

In terms of total wage cost of the employed person in France, it is estimated that the cost to the employer is 71 per cent in direct wages and 29 per cent in social charges.

*West Germany* In West Germany, social security insurance is compulsory only up to certain wage levels. These levels have been increased over the past few years. They start at present at the equivalent of about £1,700 for sickness, £2,600 for pension insurance, miners and unemployment, with additions for dependants.

Contributions for sickness and maternity are at the average rate of about 8 per cent on wages. Invalidity, old age, pension and survivors takes 17 per cent, unemployment takes 1·3 per cent. Accidents at work and occupational disease vary again according to the trade and are regulated by collective agreements.

In total, these contributions add up to about 26 per cent of wages of which half is paid by the employer and half by the employee.

In terms of total wage cost of the employed person in Germany, it is estimated that cost to the employer is 84 per cent in direct wages and 16 per cent in social charges.

*Italy* In Italy, insurance for invalidity, old age, survivors, sickness and maternity, accidents at work, social sickness and tuberculosis and unemployment is compulsory for all employed persons. Except for insurance contributions for family allowances, there is no limit on the wage level on which contributions are levied.

Contributions for sickness and maternity benefits are at the rate of 14·61 per cent on wages of which almost the entire amount falls on the employer; invalidity, old age and survivors is at the rate of 20·80 per cent payable as to about two-thirds by the employer and one-third by the employee. Family allowances take 17·5 per cent, unemployment insurance over 2·3 per cent, all payable by the employer and accidents at work average 3·9 per cent according to trade agreements, plus 20 per cent based on total salaries according to risk.

The total contributions in Italy amount to about 57 per cent on wages, 50 per cent of which fall on the employer and 7 per cent on the employee.

In terms of total wage cost of the employed person in Italy, it is estimated that the cost to the employer is 68 per cent in direct wages and 32 per cent in social charges.

*The Netherlands* In the Netherlands, social security provisions embrace all employed persons, regardless of the nature of their employment but limited to those earning less than £1,500 for sickness benefits in kind; £2,850 for sickness benefits in cash, invalidity and unemployment; £2,100 for old age-survivors and unemployed.

Sickness and maternity benefits take up to 15·25 per cent of wages (employer 10·50 per cent, worker 4·75 per cent); invalidity 5·30 per cent (employer 4 per cent, worker 1·30 per cent); old age-survivor 11·40 per cent paid by the worker; family allowances 5·45 per cent paid by the employer. Unemployment at 1 per cent is shared equally.

Together the contributions add up to about 38·40 per cent on wages of which 20·45 per cent is paid by the employer and 17·95 per cent by the worker.

In terms of total wage cost of the employed worker in the Netherlands, it is estimated that the cost to the employer is 80 per cent in direct wages and 20 per cent in social charges.

*Belgium* In Belgium, sickness, maternity and invalidity insurance takes 8·65 per cent of wages (employer 4·80 per cent, worker 3·85 per cent). Old age-survivors takes 14 per cent (employer 8 per cent, worker 6 per cent); family allowances takes 10·50 per cent paid by the employer. Unemployment at 2·40 per cent is shared equally.

The ceiling of renumeration is approximately £1,550 except for sickness benefits in kind where it is higher.

Together, the contributions add up to about 35·55 per cent (employer 24·5 per cent, worker 11·05 per cent).

In terms of total wage cost of the employed person in Belgium, it is estimated that the cost to the employer is 75 per cent in direct wages and 25 per cent in social charges.

*Luxembourg* In Luxembourg, social security contributions are compulsory for all employed persons.

Sickness and maternity benefits take 6 per cent of wages (employer 2 per cent, worker 4 per cent); invalidity and old age-survivors takes

*The Principal Social Security Contributions in the Common Market Coun*

|  | W. Germany | | Belgium | |
|---|---|---|---|---|
|  | Contributions % of wages | Ceiling | Contributions % of wages | Ceilin |
| Sickness, maternity | Average 8% W. 50% E. 50% | 14,400 DM | (a) 2·90% + (b) 2·90 | 204,60 174,6( |
| Invalidity | 17% | | W. $\begin{cases} 2\cdot65\% \\ + \\ 1\cdot20\% \end{cases}$ E. $\begin{cases} 3\cdot10\% \\ + \\ 1\cdot70\% \end{cases}$ | |
| Old age—survivors | W. 50% E. 50% | 21,600 DM | 14% W. 6% E. 8% | — |
| Accidents at work Occupational illness | Group rates fixed according to risks in different occupations. Contributions are fixed by trade bodies on an average basis. Ceiling 36,000 DM or higher. | | Mainly by contri· butions to Emplo Associations' Fur for Accidents. | |
| Family allowances | Paid from Federal Budget | — | E. 10·50% | 174,90 |
| Unemployment | 1·3% W. 50% E. 50% | 21,600 DM | 2·40% W. 50% E. 50% | 174,9( |
| Notes: W. Worker (Employee) E. Employer | Sickness contributions vary with different Funds | | (a) benefits in ki (b) benefits in ca | |

There are minor variations to the tables applicable to certain classes of workers in Belgium, Italy and Luxembourg.

| ce | Italy | Luxembourg | Netherlands |
|---|---|---|---|
| ributions wages  Ceiling | Contributions % of wages  Ceiling | Contributions % of wages  Ceiling | Contributions % of wages  Ceiling |
| %  18,000 F  50  ·25 | 14·61%  W. 0·15% —  E. 14·46% | 6%  W. 4%  219,000Fl.  E. 2% | 7·5% (a)  12,480 Fl.  1·25% (b) 17,450 Fl.  6.5% (c)  23,140 Fl.  W. 4·75%  E. 10·50% |
|  | 20·80% | 14% | 5·30%  23,140 Fl.  W. 1·30%  E. 4·0% |
| %  18,000 F  %  5% | W. 6·90%  E. 13·90% | W. 50%  E. 50% | W. 9·9%  17,450 Fl.  Old age  1·5%  Survivors |
| rates ling to risks. ibutions on total es, with a of 18,000 F. | 3·9% average  +20% based on  total salaries  according  to risks | Fixed by  collective scale  on total salaries | Covered under  sickness rates |
| 50%18,000 F | E. 17·5% 750,000  lires | E. 3·30 — | E. 5·45% 17,450 Fl. |
| 75,600 F.  )8%  2% | E. 2·30% | — — | 1·0%  W. 50%  23,140 Fl.  E. 50% |
| this bution 3% V. 2% E.) ated without for ceiling. | Sickness includes  3·8% for pen-  sioners' insurance.  2% Tuberculosis | | |

Tableaux Comparatifs des Régimes de Securité Sociale (Commission des Communautés ennes, 1970).

14 per cent (shared equally); family allowance 3·30 per cent (paid by the employer); insurance for accidents at work and occupational illness depends on the trade.

In total, the social security contributions are 23·3 per cent on wages of which about 11 per cent is paid by the employer and 12·3 per cent by the employee.

In terms of total wage cost of the employed worker in Luxembourg, it is estimated that the cost to the employer is 83 per cent in direct wages and 17 per cent in social charges.

Thus, out of the six members of the Common Market, only two, West Germany and the Netherlands, retain a wage or salary limit over which certain Health contributions are not compulsory. Apart from these two exceptions, the systems are similar in principle and different only in the levels of contributions and of benefits.

In almost all the countries, contributions are not payable on the amount of the wages over a specified upper limit. The exceptions are: Italy (all social security contributions except family allowances), Belgium (old age insurance for workers), Luxembourg (sickness insurance for workers).

BENEFITS

*Benefits in cash*   In the Common Market countries sickness and other benefits in cash are almost invariably geared to the wage or income of the insured person, ranging from 50 per cent to 80 per cent without hospitalisation and from 20 per cent to 50 per cent with hospitalisation and depending on the size of family. The duration of payment of benefits in cash ranges from 78 weeks in 3 years in West Germany to a maximum of one year in other countries. Inside and outside these limits there are numerous special criteria and conditions.

*Benefits in kind*   In view of the particular nature of benefits in kind which characterise the National Health Service in the United Kingdom, it is important to note the methods for providing these benefits in the Common Market countries.

In West Germany, Belgium, France, Luxembourg and the Netherlands, there is virtually a free choice of doctor and the patient pays the doctors fees and claims reimbursement. In West Germany and the Netherlands the insured person recovers the full amount. In Belgium the insured person (with certain exceptions) recovers 75 per cent, in France 80 per cent. In Italy, there are limited provisions for the insured person to pay part of the doctors' fees. In Luxembourg the proportion varies from one insurance fund to another, except for industrial workers who recover the full amount.

The fees for dental care are for the most part recovered in full by insured persons in all the Common Market countries.

For medicines, in general terms, in Germany the patient pays the equivalent of 5p per prescription for the first 11 days of illness. In Belgium 25 per cent. In France 10 per cent to 30 per cent. In Italy practically nil. In Luxembourg up to 25 per cent. In the Netherlands nil.

All the Common Market countries provide for a state of invalidity. Entitlement to benefits in cash and in kind to invalidity depends mostly upon the inability of the insured person by reason of illness or infirmity to earn more than one-third to one-half of the normal rate of pay for the job.

State aid towards the financing of social security is given in varying degrees in the different countries.

| | |
|---|---|
| *Germany* | Federal aid provides 400 DM for each maternity-benefit. |
| | Variable subsidies are paid for invalidity. Family allowances are paid from the Federal budget. |
| | Unemployment: the Federal budget covers deficiencies. |
| *Belgium* | From 27 to 95 per cent for specific State subsidies in all sectors. |
| *France* | Nil, except for unemployment. |
| *Italy* | Annual subsidies required in all sectors except industrial illness and accidents. |
| *Netherlands* | 475 million Florins annually for sickness, 202 million Florins annually for old age. The state contributes an amount equal to the amount collected in contributions. |
| *Luxembourg* | Participation in administrative charges for health insurance, and share of invalidity, family allowances, unemployment benefits. |

*II. Workers in occupations other than dependent wage-earners*

There is no unemployment insurance or benefit for self-employed persons in any of the Common Market countries.

The following table shows how the other services are covered in each country by *compulsory* contributions.

|                                          | West Germany | Belgium | France | Italy | Luxembourg | Netherlands |
|------------------------------------------|:---:|:---:|:---:|:---:|:---:|:---:|
| Sickness                                 | * |    | * | * | * |       |
| Maternity                                | * |    | * | * | * |       |
| Invalidity                               | * |    | * | * | * |       |
| Old Age                                  | * | ** | ** | * | * | **    |
| Survivors                                | * | ** | ** | * | * | **    |
| Accidents at work and occupational illness | * | * |  |  | * |       |
| Family Allowance                         | ** | ** | ** |  | * | **(i) |

*limited to one or more specified categories of self-employed persons.
**all categories of independent self-employed persons including the liberal professions, heads of commercial enterprises, agricultural and similar and artisans.
(i) depends on salary or wage level.

Thus in the Common Market, except Italy, self-employed persons benefit from family allowances. In all the countries there are provisions for voluntary membership for all services available to employed workers.

For old age, there is general coverage in Belgium, France and Luxembourg (except for the liberal professions) and in the Netherlands where the entire population is covered.

For sickness, protection is wider in Luxembourg and in Italy than in the four other countries. In France sickness insurance has been extended to self-employed agriculturists.

Within the general category of self-employed persons there are several sub-divisions made up of artisans, people working in commerce and industry, members of the liberal professions and the self-employed in agriculture.

(a) *Artisans*  The word is interpreted as craftsmen who sell the products of their own craftsmanship, but not the products made by others.

In *West Germany*, they participate in invalidity-old age-death insurance if they are registered with the appropriate guild or association. They are insured for accidents and occupational illness if their trade or professional body so provides in its statutes. They are entitled to family allowances and can contribute voluntarily to sickness insurance.

In *Belgium*, they contribute and are entitled to old age and family allowance insurance and they can be voluntary contributors to sickness, maternity, invalidity and in certain cases they can insure for occupational illness.

In *France*, artisans are only entitled to old age and family allowance insurance and, for survivors, to a reversion of pension and death benefits. Other risks have to be covered by voluntary insurance.

In *Italy*, independent non-wage earning artisans and members of their families working for them are entitled to benefits in kind for sickness and some rights in invalidity and old age.

In *Luxembourg*, there are special provisions for the insurance of independent non-wage earning workers.

In the *Netherlands*, these classes of persons are covered for old age, widows and orphans, and family allowances up to a limit of earnings as well as for family allowances for the third and subsequent child.

(b) *Self-employed persons in business* In general terms, this category of self-employed person enjoys more favourable conditions in Social Security than the artisan.

In *West Germany*, they are entitled to family allowance. If their guild or association so provides in its statutes, they contribute for benefit for insurance against accidents at work and occupational illness. Voluntary schemes only are available for sickness and maternity for themselves and their families, although such insurance is compulsory for certain heads of businesses.

In *Belgium*, this category have rights only to old age pension and Social Security services for their families. They can join voluntary schemes for sickness insurance. Widows and orphans have the right to pensions.

In *France*, self-employed persons in business have rights only to old age pension with reversion to widow, and family allowance. Under certain conditions, they can insure their families for sickness, maternity, old age and death benefits and accidents at work.

In *Italy*, Social Security for the self-employed in business is limited to owners of small businesses. These and members of their families who work for them as well as their commercial agents and representatives, are entitled to Social Security in respect of services in kind for sickness. Agents working on commission are also insured for old age-invalidity.

In *Luxembourg*, self-employed persons in business participate in sickness and maternity, pensions for invalidity and old age, family allowance and birth payments. They can participate voluntarily in insurance for accidents at work and occupational illness.

In the *Netherlands*, the whole population participate in old age pension insurance, the heads of a business included. These can draw family allowance with three children and low income. Voluntary participation is available for sick benefits in kind; and for medical care if the income is low.

Thus the method of fixing the contributions for self-employed persons varies greatly from one country to another.

In France in certain sectors of Social Security, there are fixed annual rates and in other sectors rates which vary according to the remuneration or the level of the benefits which the person chooses, subject to a minimum contribution.

In the other countries, contributions depend mainly upon the income of the insured self-employed person, with the State contributing the balance. The level of contribution mostly carries a ceiling and insurance beyond that is not subject to assessment for contribution.

(c) *Self-employed persons in Agriculture.*

Self-employed persons in Agriculture (Agriculturists or Cultivators) are subject to special regimes in the Common Market countries.

In *West Germany*, this category excludes persons whose agricultural activities are subsidiary to their other interests and who do not depend for their livelihood upon their agricultural activities, and the classification is based upon the extent of those activities.

Those who fall within the category of cultivators participate in old age-assistance insurance for themselves and their widow or widower; and accidents at work. They can, under specified conditions, become voluntary members of old age pension and sickness insurance in which event their dependants can receive sick benefits in cash for illness and maternity; widows receive benefits from the old age-assistance scheme and pension after the death of the insured person.

In *France*, agriculturists are recognised as self-employed if their income is above a certain minimum level. If not, they are regarded as wage-earners and fall under the Social Security regime for sickness-invalidity, old age, widows pension and family allowance.

In *Italy*, *bona fide* self-employed agriculturists fall under compulsory insurance for sickness and maternity benefits in kind, for old age, death, accidents at work and occupational illness. They are excluded from family allowance.

In *Luxembourg*, agriculturists are later to be included in benefits in kind and cash for sickness and maternity. They are entitled to retirement pension and are the only class of self-employed persons under compulsory insurance for accidents at work and occupational illness. They are entitled to family allowance similar to other categories of workers. Survivors are entitled to certain Social Security services.

(d) *Members of the Liberal Professions.*

In *West Germany*, the legislation of the Lander makes it compulsory for certain groups of the liberal professions to join insurance schemes for retirement pensions. They can also voluntarily take part in state insurance for sickness and old age pensions. Certain independent professions (midwives, nurses, musicians, actors, etc.) are regarded as employed persons for sickness benefits and pensions.

In *Belgium*, the position of persons in the liberal professions is similar to that of artisans.

In *France*, too, they are treated in the same way as other independent self-employed persons for family allowance and old age. Only doctors and pharmacists are entitled to invalidity benefits in cash.

In *Italy*, members of the liberal professions have no rights to family allowance, but they are entitled to certain benefits in kind for sickness, invalidity and old age.

In *Luxembourg*, they are included in benefits in cash and certain benefits in kind for sickness, maternity and family allowance. Their families are entitled to insurance for sickness and maternity.

Each of the Common Market countries is engaged in revising its Social Security services in more or less degree.

Belgium is concerned with establishing a uniform basis for old age insurance for the entire population and in re-classifying the categories of occupation with particular regard for encouraging the setting up of new industrial enterprises and in co-ordinating the different administrative branches.

France is concerned with the reform of the system of family allowance and unification of those concerned with old age.

Italy, too, is moving towards functional unification and simplification.

The Netherlands are engaged upon the reform of Social Security services so that benefits can be related to lost earnings and the degree of incapacity. It has been suggested that the ceiling on earnings should be abolished and there are moves to make family allowance available to all.

In an area so complex as Social Security, harmonisation is a vague term which can be interpreted in many ways and the Treaty confines its definition of the requirements for improving Social Security more to a statement of intent rather than to any fixed purpose. The intergovernmental Committees working within the Community have made progress largely because their method is one of exploration and consultation which allows time for a basis of collaboration to evolve from widely different systems.

Because the Common Market is an *economic* union it implies that workers must be able to move over national boundaries without difficulties. It is therefore essential that a degree of harmonisation of payments and benefits wherever they are paid or received should be achieved.

# CHAPTER 14

## Mobility of People and Capital

### PEOPLE

It has been said that the Common Market's social policy does not lend itself to systematic treatment; but the 'upward harmonisation' of living and working conditions is a fundamental principle of the Treaty. An *economic* union implies freedom of movement for labour. Therefore such aspects of social policy as the achievement of equal pay for men and women, the alignments of social security benefits and payments, and the equating of relative values of national professional qualifications are essential contributions in attempting to achieve the aims of the Treaty. Further aspects of this are the process of allowing freedom of establishment and freedom to supply services together with retraining schemes.

In fulfilment of the principle of equal remuneration for equal work between men and women as laid down in Article 119 of the Treaty, the Commission sent a formal recommendation to member-countries on 20 July 1960 summarising its interpretation of the Article and suggested ways of applying it from 30 June 1961, the date laid down in the Treaty. It was also proposed and subsequently approved by the Council, that the maximum differences should be reduced by 15 per cent by 30 June 1962 and to 10 per cent by 30 June 1963 and that all discrimination should be eliminated by 31 December 1964. However the translation of this policy from principle to practice has met with many obstacles. In June 1970 the Commission noted that, although equal pay for men and women had not yet been fully achieved, considerable progress has been made in all the member-states and the overall increase in wages has been accompanied by a gradual alignment of women's wages with those of men.

\*　　　\*　　　\*

It is essential to differentiate between 'mobility' of labour and 'migration' of labour. At a Conference on Regional Economics held in Brussels in 1961, Robert Marjolin, vice-president of the Commission said that migration of labour from region to region or country to country is sometimes necessary but such movements are generally accompanied by sociological, psychological and political difficulties and he stressed that wherever possible the aim should be for industry to move to the worker. When the worker moves to the work it generally means movement from rural areas to congested central areas. The large investments and contributions by the European investment Bank and European Development Fund, in Southern Italy are an indication of the E.E.C.'s concern in this matter.

However, in an economic union the *right* to freedom of movement is there. A worker should be able to move to another country to work or he can look for another job in his own town. Great stress has been laid on E.E.C. retraining schemes to help greater mobility between jobs in the same region rather than for greater mobility between regions.

The first move towards intra-community movement of workers came from a decision of the Council on 12 June 1961 to implement the first regulations. These came into force on 1 September 1961. The regulations provided that any vacancies on the national labour market could be filled within three weeks by the domestic administration from its own nationals but that after this period offers of employment would be transmitted to the other member-countries. Workers accepting this offer and moving to another Community country would be able to renew their labour permits there for the same occupation after one year of regular employment; for any other occupation for which they were qualified, after three years; and for any kind of paid work, after four years. Automatic granting of labour permits would apply in the case of occupations for which there was a labour shortage, while workers specifically applied for by an employer would be granted a permit without reference to the domestic labour market if supported by family reasons or the needs of the firm concerned. Since that first regulation came into force free movement has been virtually achieved, although in exceptional circumstances a fortnight's period of priority for local labour can be introduced if unemployment is unduly high in certain areas or skills. With a working population of over 75m. it will be seen from the table on the following page that, in fact, migration has been small.

Full mobility of labour for nationals of member-countries of the E.E.C. was achieved on 8 November 1968. Discrimination, because of nationality in jobs, housing and trade unions by a member-country against nationals of other member-countries became illegal.

The Treaty also provides for freedom of establishment of firms, branches, agencies and for individuals such as doctors, dentists, architects etc. and also the freedom to supply such services as building, banking, insurance, wholesale and retail distribution and the exercise of the liberal professions anywhere in the Community by the end of the transition period. A first directive was adopted by the Council of Ministers on 25 October 1961. The programme envisaged

*Intra-Community Movement of Workers since the entry into force of Regulations*

Figures relate to first work permits issued to workers of the member-state moving from one Community country to another

|      | E.E.C. total | Italian contribution to E.E.C. total |
|------|--------------|--------------------------------------|
| 1961 | 227,657      | 205,530                              |
| 1965 | 259,038      | 234,614                              |
| 1968 | 162,296      | 141,572                              |
| 1969 | 166,771      | 145,256                              |

the abolition of discrimination based on nationality hitherto restricting access to numerous activities, as follows:
By end-1963 for the textile, footwear, paper, basic chemicals, metalworking industries, wholesale trade, banking and dealings in property; by end-1965 for retail distribution, department stores and the food industry; by end-1967 for pharmacies (chemists), veterinary surgeons, insurance agents and transport; by end-1969 for education, film production and publicity material.

As for members of the medical profession, the suitability of equivalent qualifications has been established in principle, but the Treaty does not override all the different national laws relating to the practice of medicine. The unofficial, but very effective, Permanent Committee of the doctors of the Community is recognised as the spokesman for the medical profession in the Community and is engaged in the task of evolving a basis for implementing the principle and practice of the free movement of doctors.

The member-countries are not pledged to adopt identical legislation and regulations but must ensure that nationals of other member-countries enjoy equal rights with their own citizens.

The Commission has given as the chief reasons for the low mobility of labour:
(1) The standard of living has become more evenly balanced throughout the Community. Workers in the less prosperous areas

F

can find better-paid work in other parts of their own country. In Italy, the growing prosperity of the North is absorbing more of the Southerners seeking better work and Italians are no longer so interested in heavy, unskilled work available elsewhere in the Community.

There are, however, large numbers of Italian workers still in France and Germany. In 1968, there were 219,000 Italians in France and 287,000 in Germany. But the proportion of new Italian entries has fallen sharply from 27 per cent of the total, including non-E.E.C. migrant workers, in 1968 to 17 per cent in 1969, although it rose slightly in absolute terms from 130,000 to 136,000.

(2) Differences of language and culture still strongly discourage workers from taking jobs outside their own countries, and regional development policies are increasingly taking account of the wish of most workers to stay where they are.

(3) The fact that the economies of the Six are tending to develop more and more along parallel lines means that, where shortages of skilled labour occur, they tend to be in similar trades in all the member states.

(4) To meet the shortage of unskilled labour, Community countries have had to resort increasingly to the non-member states bordering the Mediterranean. These states supply labour under a network of bilateral agreements with the Six. The number of such agreements, which differ widely in character, is growing. Germany is intensifying its recruitment in most Mediterranean countries. France, because of her special relations with African states, has labour agreements with Mediterranean countries. In 1969, Belgium and the Netherlands signed new agreements with North African countries. The number of workers involved is very substantial. In 1968, there were 368,000 Spanish workers in France and Germany. France was also employing 170,000 Portuguese; Germany was playing host to 139,000 Turkish, 166,000 Greek and 100,000 Yugoslav workers. In 1969 the number of Yugoslavs in Germany rose to 226,000.

These immigrant workers from non-Community countries do not benefit from the Community regulations on free circulation and cannot move from one Community country into another without a permit from the latter—which means they must normally have a job to go to.

\*   \*   \*

Details of the aims of the European Social Fund are given in Chapters 3 (page 38) and 7 (page 69). The main aims of the Fund are to help finance vocational retraining, resettlement and other aids, in order to ensure the re-employment of workers who have to change their jobs.

CAPITAL

Without free movement of capital, it is unlikely that there would be real freedom of movement of labour or freedom of establishment of services. The first directive for the implementation of Article 67 of the Treaty on freedom of movement of capital was approved by the Council of Ministers in May 1960 and came into force in June 1960. It established:

(1) unconditional freedom of capital movements connected with the freeing of trade goods, of services, and of the movement of persons, and also with the free exercise of the right of establishment;

(2) unconditional and irreversible freedom for sale and purchase of stocks and shares quoted on the Community's stock exchanges;

(3) conditional freedom with regard to the issuing and placing of stocks and shares on capital markets, and for the purchase of un-quoted stocks and shares. Any member-country might, however, maintain or reimpose existing restrictions if their abolition was likely to hinder the achievement of its economic policy objectives.

A good example of this was the exchange control restrictions introduced by France following the devaluation of the franc in 1969. Action in this sphere has thus been restricted to studies of a technical nature by groups of experts on capital movements and securities markets. The Segré report on capital markets, presented to the Council in January, 1967, examined the problems arising from appreciable differences between member-states in their savings and investment mechanisms and in the organisation of their capital markets, and analysed the possible effects of an integrated Community capital market on certain national policies which are based principally on financial instruments. It contained five parts, dealing with (i) the creation of a European capital market; (ii) the instruments of economic policy in an integrated market; (iii) the extension of credit channels; (iv) the unification of stock markets and (v) the removal of disparities in access to financial markets. In 1969 the Commission submitted to the Council a memorandum entitled: 'The Case for Measures concerning Capital. Procedures to be adopted.' The suggestions made in this memorandum include certain measures for liberalising capital movements and for reducing discrimination, and measures for harmonising the organisation of the national capital markets and tax arrangements liable to influence capital movements. No action has yet been taken on this.

However, the Werner Report, on the creation of a full economic and monetary union, has recommended for implementation during the first stage (1971–3) the setting up of a liberalisation ceiling for issues of securities by the residents of other member-countries.

# CHAPTER 15

## *A Common Transport Policy*

The Treaty laid down the guide-lines of the Common Transport Policy and these are given on page 32. A memorandum on a Common Transport Policy on the lines of Article 79 (1) was submitted by the Commission to the Council of Ministers on 28 April 1961. After the Ministers of Transport of the Six had agreed on 28 November 1961, to consult each other about any future legislative or administrative changes in the transport policy of their own countries, the Council of Ministers asked the Commission in February 1962, to present detailed proposals for a common transport policy for roads, railways, and inland waterways by May of that year.

The Commission's programme was based on the principles of (1) equality of treatment; (2) financial independence; (3) freedom of action for transport enterprises; (4) free choice by the user of the means of transport; and (5) co-ordination of investment, the Commission's proposals included the following aspects:

*Access to the Market* The Commission's proposals for intra-Community traffic aimed at the rapid elimination of discrimination on grounds of nationality, easing of quotas on carriers, and the supervision of transport capacity. Regulations governing the admission to the market by member-states would be brought into line simultaneously. The Commission proposed that present bilateral quotas be gradually replaced by a Community quota open to carriers in the Six irrespective of nationality; this change would be spread over five years beginning in 1964 and be completed by 1969 by the introduction of a Community procedure for managing the quota. The programme also proposed a gradual procedure for admitting non-resident carriers to domestic road and inland waterways services.

*Transport Rate Policy* The Commission proposed for all types of transport a system of scales of charges subject to prior publication. Each transport undertaking would be free to determine its own tariffs with certain limits to be laid down by the public authorities concerned. From 1 July 1964, member-states would apply rate scales on the basis of the common principles though using their own procedure. From 1966 national systems would be harmonised so as to establish a common tariff system throughout the Community by 1969.

Various measures of harmonisation were proposed, including (*a*) the abolition of double taxation; (*b*) the harmonisation of the Rules governing duty-free entry of fuel in the tanks of motor vehicles; (*c*) the alignment of the basis of assessment of vehicle tax between member-states; (*d*) harmonisation of taxes on fuel; and (*e*) equal fiscal treatment of rail, road, and waterways transport.

The next landmark in transport policy was when the Council of Ministers agreed on 22 June 1965, a framework for a Community transport system which would regulate competition in all sectors by the progressive introduction of fixed-rate limits in two separate stages.

During the first stage, 1966 to 1969, only commercial transport between member-countries would be subject to E.E.C. regulations. Upper and lower tariff limits would be published for certain classes of road and rail traffic, though contracts could be made outside these rates under certain circumstances provided the details were published. This contrasts with the British system, where private hauliers may charge what the traffic will bear. Non-binding reference limits would be fixed for water transport, but contracts made outside these limits would also be published.

In the second stage, 1969 to 1972, the reference limit system would be extended to certain categories of national and international traffic of heavy goods (the Council had still to decide on a definition) and also on other forms of national transport. Following the decision of the Council of 22 June 1965 to produce the framework for such a policy, a virtual standstill had occurred in the discussions, and after an inconclusive meeting of the Transport Ministers on 20 October 1966, it was not until 13–14 December 1967, that they held another session. They then considered a memorandum of the E.E.C. Commission dated 10 February 1967, as well as an Italian memorandum of 21 September 1967, both concerned with the resumption of substantive talks, and agreed to take final decisions within six months, with their deputies meanwhile working out detailed draft regulations on certain basic aspects. The Council of Ministers, consisting on this occasion of the Transport Ministers of the Six, at its meeting of July 18–19 1968 adopted five regulations aimed at finally creating a common transport policy.

The five regulations adopted were:

*Rules of Competition*  This regulation, applying to rail, road, and inland waterways transport, banned with retrospective effect from 1 July 1968, all agreements which hindered, limited, or distorted competition within the Common Market. In particular it prohibited, with certain specific exceptions, (1) agreements directly or indirectly fixing prices and conditions of transport; (2) agreements limiting transport facilities, markets, technical developments, or investment; (3) market-sharing; (4) agreements which applied unequal conditions when charging the same rates; or (5) making acceptance of contracts dependent on the payment of additional charges.

*Intra-Community Licences*  While lorries from one E.E.C. country had hitherto been able to operate in other member-countries only under special licences issued under bilateral agreements, this regulation authorised the issue, until 31 December 1971, of 1,200 E.E.C. licences enabling their holders to operate goods traffic between the member-countries. The distribution of the licences would be: Belgium 161, France 286, Western Germany 286, Italy 194, Luxembourg 33, Netherlands 240.

*Fuel Rules*  From 1 February 1969, at the latest, goods vehicles registered in any E.E.C. country would be allowed to carry into another member-country 50 litres of fuel in their tanks duty free.

*Working Conditions in Intra-Community Road Transport*  This regulation laid down the minimum age for drivers; stipulated that drivers of vehicles of over 20 tons loaded weight who travelled over 280 miles (450 kilometres) between rest periods must be accompanied by another driver from the beginning of the journey or be replaced by another driver after 280 miles; and fixed the maximum hours of driving permitted for drivers of all goods and passenger vehicles as follows:

*From 1 October 1969*  50 hours per week or nine hours per day, with 10 hours permitted twice in any one week, and not more than $4\frac{1}{2}$ hours of continuous driving, followed by a half-hour rest.

*From 1 October 1971*  48 hours per week or 92 hours per fortnight or eight hours per day, with nine hours twice in any one week, and four hours of continuous driving, followed by a half-hour rest.

In addition minimum hours of rest were laid down as follows:

*Goods Transport*  Not less than 11 hours' rest in every 24 hours, though within any one week this might be reduced to two periods of nine hours or two periods of eight hours within any two 24-hour periods.

*Passenger Transport* Not less than 10 hours' rest in 24 hours, subject to extension to 11 hours when the week's total driving time includes two periods of the maximum of nine hours (or eight hours, see above) within any two 24-hour periods.

The above provisions would not prejudice agreements reached within the transport industry by collective bargaining or by Government action in any member-country introducing rules more favourable to transport workers.

The new regulation would apply to intra-Community road traffic from 1 October 1969, and to traffic within the member-countries from 1 October 1970. This interval had been agreed in order to enable the Six to have talks with the other European countries which signed the 1962 Geneva agreement on working conditions for road transport so that these countries would also agree to conform to their new regulations.

The regulation will apply equally to vehicles entering the Community from non-member countries, and is thus likely to have considerable impact on Switzerland and Austria, and to a lesser extent on other European countries, including Britain.

*Freight Charges for Intra-Community Road Transport* Under this regulation the appropriate authorities would publish fixed maximum and minimum charges, with the maximum permitted spread 23 per cent below the ceiling level. The basis of these rate-brackets would be a fixed price calculated on the average cost to a well-run firm for any particular traffic and route, and agreed between the member-countries directly concerned. Goods could be transported freely within these rate limits, though provision was made for private contracts to be undertaken outside the published brackets.

Private contracts, which must be immediately notified to the authorities, might be concluded for limited periods for carriage exceeding 500 metric tons per three months, in competitive conditions, or for special transport not provided for at the time of fixing the bracketed charges. If the transport market for some products was disturbed, however, all private contracts might be made subject, for a fixed period, to the prior approval of the authorities of the member-countries concerned.

To supervise the working of this regulation a special committee would be set up comprising representatives of the member-countries and the Commission. At the request of the Commission, the Committee would advise on the carrying out of the regulation, and it would also prepare six-monthly reports on market conditions.

The rate-bracket system for intra-Community road transport would continue in effect until 31 December 1971, subject to further extension for one year if the Council had not by that time agreed on the system to apply after that date.

At a meeting of Transport Ministers of the E.E.C. on 17–18 March 1969, three more regulations were adopted.

In order to bring about completion of the first stage of the Common Transport Policy, only one further regulation will have to be adopted dealing with the avoidance of double taxation on vehicles.

The three regulations adopted were: (1) *Working Conditions on Intra-Community Road Transport:* This regulation was agreed on 18–19 July 1968, but was held in suspense while international negotiations were carried on in Geneva for setting up a European Road Transport Agreement with other non-member European countries, on the ground that the regulations would apply, from 1 October 1970, to traffic between member-states and other European countries. (2) *Public Service Obligations:* This regulation laid down that public service obligations should only be maintained to the extent that they were necessary to provide adequate transport services. It also established how compensatory subsidies would be paid, including those arising from obligations to provide cheaper services for certain groups such as the armed services and larger families. The regulation became operative on 1 July 1969, and applied to the six national railway undertakings and other forms of inland transport, including inland navigation, except those engaged mainly in local or regional operations. (3) *Standardization of Railway Accounts:* This regulation, which was closely aligned to (2) above, established common rules for the standardization of railway accounts, to ensure that the pattern of subsidies paid to railways was identical in all member-countries and that all payments were fully disclosed in the national accounts. This method would also show to what extent railways were obliged to maintain uneconomic services or operations for social or other reasons.

# CHAPTER 16

# The European Coal and Steel Community and Euratom

E.C.S.C.

The European Coal and Steel Community (E.C.S.C.) set up in 1952, was the pioneer of European integration. It applied the Community method to the coal and steel industries as a first step towards integration of the economy as a whole. A decision to merge the executives of the E.C.S.C. and Euratom with the E.E.C. came into effect on 1 July 1967.

From the start the European Coal and Steel Community passed through a period of rapid growth. Steel output more than doubled from 42 million metric tons in 1952 to 85 million metric tons in 1966 and rose to 109 million metric tons in 1970. The action of the High Authority and the operation of the Community aided this development by bringing price stability, easing distribution of coal during the boom, providing new markets for iron-ore and steel through a more rational trade pattern, and stimulating competition. Since 1965, faced with the danger of excess supply the High Authority has intervened to restrain over-production of steel and to limit additions to capacity.

The coal industry, after expanding initially in conditions of acute shortage, found that a growing share of the energy market was being won by oil and other new sources of energy: in 1965 coal provided only 38 per cent of total energy consumption, compared with 53 per cent in 1960 and 73 per cent in 1950. In this situation the High Authority's task is to ensure the orderly retreat of coal at a pace which avoids social or economic disruption. Uneconomic pits are being closed and others regrouped and modernised. Average productivity in the Community rose from 1·4 tons per manshift underground in 1953 to 2·6 tons in 1966.

Since coal output first began to fall in 1957, the number of workers employed in the Community's coal industry dropped by over 400,000 to 650,000 in 1966. The E.C.S.C. Treaty's retraining and re-employment provisions have greatly eased the impact of this major change; an amendment to the E.C.S.C. Treaty in March 1960 extended and widened the High Authority's powers to apply such measures. The High Authority is also promoting industrial redevelopment in the areas until now mainly dependent on coalmining for their livelihood. A plan for cutting back Belgian coal capacity by one-third between 1960 and 1964 was carried out under High Authority supervision. In 1965 a High Authority decision authorised subsidies by member governments to ease the problems involved in mine closures and to speed up modernisation. In February 1967 the Six agreed on a system of subsidies for coking coal to enable Community production to compete with imported supplies.

The High Authority has direct powers to control restrictive trading practices. All company mergers in the coal and steel sector require the approval of the High Authority, which is given only if the resulting unit will not hold a dominant position in its sector of the market; any firm or group which already has a dominant market position is subject to strict High Authority control. Cartels and other trade agreements are illegal unless explicitly authorised.

The High Authority carries out an industrial policy for coal and steel by means of:

(1)   short and long-term Community-wide forecasts for supply and demand;

(2)   investment guidance and co-ordination, notably through loans to firms;

(3)   joint research programmes, aided by High Authority funds;

(4)   Community help for regional development.

Regular short-term forecasts supply detailed information on market developments in coal and steel, while medium and long-term forecasts, known as General Objectives, guide industry on modernisation, production and investment needs. Additional guidance on priorities is provided by the 'opinions' which the High Authority issues, in line with the General Objectives, on major investment projects, which firms are required to submit to it. It also aids certain key projects directly by re-lending the proceeds of loans which it raises on advantageous terms in the world's capital markets.

From 1954 to September 1966 the High Authority raised nearly $650 million in loans ($736 million if loan guarantees are included) and re-lent $850 million to part-finance new industrial projects worth in total more than twice this amount and representing well over 10 per cent of all investment in coal and steel in the Community during this period.

The High Authority also makes grants for pure and applied research projects related to coal and steel production, full details of which are supplied to all interested bodies in the Community. This aid, totalling $50 million for sixty-five projects by 1966, makes larger individual projects possible and cuts down duplication of effort.

Lastly, the High Authority provides loans to help regional development in areas affected by decline or changes in the coal, steel or iron-ore industries. It has lent $30 million to help build new factories creating employment for 9,000 workers and has earmarked a further $56 million for this purpose from 1966 onwards. The transition from coal or steel to new industrial activities is further softened by aid in retraining and re-employing workers.

The Community Executives believe that the coal problem can only be solved as part of a general Community policy for energy, including oil, gas, atomic power and hydro-electricity. With energy costs a basic factor in any industrial economy, a common energy policy is also vital to the completion of the common market.

Energy policy was not included as such in the Community treaties, since the E.C.S.C. the Common Market and Euratom each cover separate sectors of this field.

However, a special inter-Executive working group has been set up under the chairmanship of the High Authority, and this led to the signature in April 1964 of a Protocol of Agreement on Energy. This lays down the objectives of a common energy policy which must reconcile cheapness with an adequate guarantee for security of supply. At present, most Community-produced energy—for example, coal— is relatively expensive compared with imports, which in 1965 provided 46 per cent of Community power supplies. New Community sources of energy—natural gas and atomic power—should begin to provide significant amounts of cheaper energy in the mid-1970's, but imports will meanwhile continue to rise, and will eventually supply at least half the Community's requirements.

The first European labour card, enabling skilled coal and steel workers to move freely within the Community, was issued on 1 September 1957. On 7 December 1957 an agreement on Social Security for Migrant Workers was concluded, and was subsequently extended by the E.E.C. to all workers.

From 1955 to 1966 the High Authority approved re-adaptation projects involving 270,000 workers—including roughly 220,000 coal-miners—and expenditure of $81 million. The governments concerned contributed a like sum. Re-adaptation initially eased the consequences of increased competition in the common market, and now ensures that the brunt of structural and technical change in the coal and steel industries is not borne by the workers. It is playing a major part in the long-term reorganisation of the E.C.S.C. industries.

Re-adaptation provides for tiding-over allowances between jobs (maximum period two years; 90–100 per cent of previous earnings for first four months). The making-up of pay in the new job to 100 per cent of old wages (for up to two years). The payment of removal and transfer costs and the free training for a new job.

*Health, Safety, Social Surveys*

The High Authority has allocated $26 million as grants for research into industrial medicine and safety. Work on such problems as silicosis, pneumoconiosis, industrial noise, air pollution, and re-habilitation after accidents has been co-ordinated throughout the Community and stimulated where necessary. The High Authority has also carried out surveys of real wages, household budgets, employment, labour mobility, and housing conditions, which have provided the first Community-wide comparative data on which trade unions and employers can base their studies and claims.

After negotiations which began in Paris in June 1950, and had lasted for nine months, the draft of a treaty setting up a 'European Coal and Steel Community' (Communauté Européenne du Charbon et de l'Acier) under a supranational authority was initialled on 19 March, 1951, by representatives of France, West Germany, Italy, Belgium, the Netherlands, and Luxembourg, the Treaty itself being signed in Paris on 18 April 1951, by the Foreign Ministers of the six participating countries.

The six-nation conference for the pooling of the coal and steel resources of Western Europe under a supranational authority, based on the proposals outlined on 9 May 1950, by M. Robert Schuman, the French Foreign Minister, opened at the Quai d'Orsay on 20 June 1950, after the French Government's invitation to such a conference had been accepted by the Governments of West Germany, Italy, and the Benelux countries. The French delegation was led by M. Jean Monnet, Commissioner-General for Planning and Reconstruction, who, with M. Schuman himself, had played a major part in drawing up the 'Schuman Plan'; the West German delegation by Professor Walter Hallstein, Secretary-General for Foreign Affairs; the Italian delegation by Professor Paolo Taviani, a member of the Italian Parliament, who had been actively associated in the formulation of the Schuman plan; the Belgian delegation by M. Max Suetens, Ambassador in Paris; the Netherlands delegation by Dr. Dirk Spierenburg, of the Ministry of Economic Affairs; and the Luxembourg delegation by M. Albert Wehrer, Minister in Paris.

The conference was opened by M. Schuman, who stressed that 'no system such as that to which we look forward has ever been tried in practice', and that sovereign States had never before 'entrusted or even contemplated the delegation of a fraction of their sovereignty to an independent, supranational organisation' such as it was proposed to set up. He continued: 'We shall have to draw up a draft treaty which will define the main lines of this common authority, its powers, its machinery, the means of appealing against its decisions and of bringing its responsibilities into play. We shall have to consider—without, however, including them in the treaty—the technical details which will be embodied in agreements to be drawn up later, after the treaty itself has been ratified. Without losing sight of the special needs of our own countries, we must be aware that national interests nowadays consist precisely in finding, beyond national boundaries, the means of achieving a more rational economic structure, cheaper and greater production, and greater and more accessible markets.'

After emphasising that the French plan was not designed to conflict with or override other plans for the integration of the European economy, such as those formulated by Dr. Strikker in the O.E.E.C., M. Schuman drew attention to the fact that a special characteristic of the French proposals, over and above their economic implications, was their political value, arising from the French Government's desire 'to associate in a joint and permanent work of peace two nations which for centuries have clashed in bloody conflict'.

Expressing regret that the British Government had not seen its way to participate in the Paris conference, M. Schuman declared: 'We had earnestly wished that Britain might be present at our discussions. We cannot conceive of Europe without her. We know, and find comfort in the thought, that the British Government wishes our work well. Certain differences which prevented it from taking part, at least at the present stage, appeared in the course of explanations which were both frank and friendly. We continue to hope that the doubts and scruples, which a somewhat doctrinaire outlook was unable to overcome, will finally give way before more positive achievements. The French Government will act in accordance with the wishes of all the participating countries in keeping the British Government informed of the progress of negotiations, and will give it the possibility, if not of joining in our work—and this we continue to hope for—at least of bringing to our attention its own comments and observations, which might open the prospect of future co-operation.'

After initial exchanges of views between the delegations, the French Government issued on 27 June 1950, a series of draft proposals aimed at 'facilitating the formulation and the working out in common of a treaty to give effect to the French proposal of 9 May (i.e. M. Schuman's plan for the integration of coal and steel resources under a supranational authority). The conference was thereupon adjourned for a short period to enable these proposals to be studied by the various Governments, but re-assembled in Paris in 3 July 1950 when it was agreed to set up five expert 'working parties' to study the following specific problems raised by the French draft: (1) institutional questions such as the proposed supranational authority, democratic control of that body, and methods of arbitration in the event of disputes; (2) commercial policy; (3) definition of the terms 'coal' and 'steel' as envisaged under M. Schuman's proposals; (4) questions of production and prices; and (5) problems relating to wages and conditions of labour.

The five working parties completed their studies of specific aspects of the Schuman Plan on 10 August 1950 when the Quai d'Orsay announced that the preliminary phase of the negotiations had been completed and that the final phase of the conference would commence after a month's adjournment. The negotiations were resumed some three weeks later, and thereafter continued at intervals, with several adjournments, for another six months, during which period close contact was maintained with the national Governments with regard to the detailed provisions of the draft treaty.

On 19 March 1951 the draft of the treaty creating a 'European Coal and Steel Community' was signed at the Quai d'Orsay by the leaders of the French, West German, Italian, Belgian, Netherlands, and Luxembourg delegations. At the same time the text of the draft treaty was officially made public, together with an agreement covering the transitional period (fixed at five years) between the signing of the treaty and its application.

In a speech after the signing ceremony, M. Monnet laid special emphasis on three aspects of the treaty which, he declared, would transform the economy of Western Europe: (1) the supranational character of the European Coal and Steel Community; (2) the creation of a single market of 150,000,000 consumers and the pooling of the coal and steel resources of six nations; (3) 'the elimination of restrictive cartel practices and of excessive concentrations of economic power'. He also emphasised that, for the first time, six countries had come together 'not to seek a provisional compromise among national interests but to take a concerted view of their common interests', a development which represented 'a fundamental change in the nature of the relations among the countries of Europe, from the national form which has opposed and divided them to the supranational form which reconciles and unites them'. Speeches in support were made by the leaders of the other delegations, Professor Hallstein (West Germany) declaring that the treaty was an important step towards the achievement of a United Europe.

After the initialling of the treaty, the Governments of West Germany, Italy, Belgium, the Netherlands, and Luxembourg were invited by the French Government to send their Foreign Ministers to a further conference in Paris with the aim of reaching agreement on outstanding questions relating to the various organs of the European Coal and Steel Community which had not been settled in the draft treaty, e.g. the number of members of the High Authority, the Common Assembly, the Council of Ministers, the method in which those members would be chosen, and their voting powers. Accordingly, a conference of Foreign Ministers opened at the Quai d'Orsay on 12 April under the chairmanship of M. Robert Schuman (France), West Germany being represented by Dr. Konrad Adenauer (Federal Chancellor and Foreign Minister), Italy by Count Carlo Sforza, Belgium by Mr. Paul Van Zeeland, the Netherlands by Dr. Dirk Stikker, and Luxembourg by M. Joseph Bech. The conference was also attended by the Belgian Minister of Foreign Trade (M. Meurice), the Netherlands Minister for Economic Affairs (Professor van den Brink), and the leaders of the national delegation which had drawn up the treaty, including M. Monnet and Professor Hallstein.

The conference ended on 18 April when the six Foreign Ministers, together with M. Meurice and Professor van den Brink, signed a

Joint Delegation formally setting up the European Coal and Steel Community, the name under which the 'Schuman Plan' organisation will be officially known. The treaty, which was for 50 years, provided for the institution of a common market by the abolition of import and export duties, subsidies, and other restrictive practices on the movement of coal and steel between the participating countries, and the establishment of a High Authority, an Assembly, a Council, and a Court of Justice as the administrative institutions of the Community.

A summary of the main provisions of the Treaty constituting the European Coal and Steel Community is given below.

*Preamble*

'The President of the German Federal Republic, H.R.H. the Prince Royal of Belgium, the President of the French Republic, the President of the Italian Republic, H.R.H. the Grand Duchess of Luxembourg, and H.M. the Queen of the Netherlands;

'Considering that world peace may be safeguarded only by creative efforts equal to the dangers which menace it;

'Convinced that the contribution which an organised and vital Europe can bring to civilisation is indispensable to the maintenance of peaceful relations;

'Conscious of the fact that Europe can be built only by concrete actions which create a real solidarity and by the establishment of common bases for economic development;

'Desirous of assisting through the expansion of their basic production in raising the standard of living and in furthering the works of peace;

'Resolved to substitute for historic rivalries a fusion of their essential interests; to establish, by creating an economic community, the foundation of a broad and independent community among peoples long divided by bloody conflicts; and to lay the bases of institutions capable of giving direction to their future common destiny;

'Have decided to create a European Coal and Steel Community and . . . have designated . . . plenipotentiaries . . . and have agreed to the following provisions';

*The European Coal and Steel Community*

*Art. 1* 'By the present Treaty the High Contracting Parties institute among themselves a European Coal and Steel Community, based on a common market, common objectives, and common institutions. *Art. 2* 'The mission of the European Coal and Steel Community is to contribute to economic expansion, the development of employment and the improvement of the standard of living in the participating countries through the institution, in harmony with the general economy of the member-states, of a common market as defined in Art. 4.

'The Community must progressively establish conditions which will in themselves assure the most rational distribution of production at the highest possible level of productivity, while safeguarding the continuity of employment and avoiding the creating of fundamental and persistent disturbances in the economies of the member-states.'

*Art. 3* Within the framework of their respective powers and responsibilities, the institutions of the Community should: '(a) see that the common market is regularly supplied, taking account of the needs of third countries; (b) assure to all consumers in comparable positions within the common market equal access to the sources of production; (c) seek the establishment of the lowest prices which are possible without requiring any corresponding rise either in the prices charged by the same enterprises in other transactions or in the price-level as a whole in another period, while at the same time permitting necessary amortisation and providing normal possibilities of remuneration for capital invested; (d) see that conditions are maintained which will encourage enterprises to expand and improve their ability to produce and to promote a policy of rational development of natural resources, avoiding inconsiderate exhaustion of such resources; (e) promote the improvement of the living and working conditions of the labour force in each of the industries under its jurisdiction so as to make possible the equalisation of such conditions in an upward direction; (f) further the development of international trade and see that equitable limits are observed in prices charged on external markets; (g) promote the regular expansion and the modernisation of production, as well as the improvement of its quality, under conditions which preclude any protection against competing industries, except where justified by illegitimate action on the part of such industries or in their favour.'

*Art. 4* The following were recognised to be incompatible with the common market for coal and steel, and were therefore 'abolished and prohibited' within the Community: (a) import and export duties, or charges with an equivalent effect, and quantitative restrictions on the movement of coal and steel; (b) measures or practices discriminating among producers, buyers, or consumers, specifically as concerned prices, delivery terms and transportation rates, as well as measures or practices which hampered the buyer in the free choice of his supplier; (c) subsidies or state assistance, or special charges imposed by the state, in any form whatsoever; (d) restrictive practices tending towards the division of markets or the exploitation of the consumer.

*Art. 5* The Community would accomplish its mission with 'limited direct intervention', and to this end it would: 'enlighten and facilitate the action of the interested parties' by collecting information, organising consultations, and defining general objectives; place financial means at the disposal of enterprises for their investments and participate in the expenses of re-adaptation; assure the establishment, maintenance, and observance of normal conditions of competition, and take direct action with respect to production and the operation of the market only when circumstances made it absolutely necessary, publish the justifications for its action and take the necessary measures to ensure observance of the rules set forth in the Treaty. The institutions of the Community should carry out these activities with 'as little administrative machinery as possible' and in close cooperation with the interested parties.

*Art 6* Provided that the Community should have 'juridical personality' and that it should enjoy, in its international relationships, 'the juridical capacity necessary to the exercise of its functions and the attainment of its ends'.

### Economic and Social Provisions

*General Provisions (Arts. 46–48)* The High Authority might at any time consult the Governments, the various interested parties (enterprises, workers, consumers, and dealers) and their associations, as well as any experts, and should by these means:

(1) Carry on a permanent study of markets and price tendencies;

(2) Periodically draw up non-compulsory programme forecasts dealing with production, consumption, exports, and imports;

(3) Periodically work out general programmes with respect to modernisation, the long-term orientation of manufacturing, and the expansion of productive capacity;

(4) At the request of the interested Governments, participate in the study of the possibilities of re-employment, either in existing industries or through the creation of new activities, of workers set free

by the evolution of the market or by technical transformations; (5) Gather all information necessary to the appraisal of the possibilities of improving the living and working conditions of the labour force in the industries under its jurisdiction, and of the risks which menaced such living conditions.

The High Authority would not divulge information which by its nature was considered a professional secret, and in particular information pertaining to the commercial relations or the breakdown of the costs of production of enterprises. With this reservation, it should publish such data as might be useful to Governments or to any other interested parties. The High Authority might impose fines and daily penalty payments upon those enterprises which evaded their obligations resulting from decisions made in application of these provisions, or which knowingly furnished false information.

The right of enterprises to form associations was not affected by the Treaty, but membership of such associations must be voluntary; these associations could engage in any activity which was not contrary to the provisions of the Treaty or to the decisions or recommendations of the High Authority.

*Financial Provisions (Arts. 49–53)* The High Authority was empowered to procure the funds necessary to the accomplishment of its mission (a) by placing levies on the production of coal and steel (b) by borrowing, whilst it might also receive grants. The levies were intended to cover administrative expenses, the non-reimbursable assistance provided for re-adaptation (see below), and expenditures to encourage technical and economic research, but the funds obtained by borrowing might be used by the High Authority only to grant loans. The levies would be assessed annually on the various products according to their average value, but the rate of levy might not exceed 1 per cent unless previously authorised by a two-thirds majority of the Council.

*Investment and Financial Assistance (Arts. 54–56)* The High Authority might facilitate the carrying out of investment programmes by granting loans to enterprises or by giving its guarantee to loans which they might obtain elsewhere. With the concurrence of the Council acting by unanimous vote, the High Authority might assist by the same means in financing works and installations which contributed directly and principally to increase production, lower production costs, or facilitate marketing of products subject to its jurisdiction. In order to encourage co-ordinated development of investments,

however, the High Authority might require enterprises to submit individual programmes in advance.

If the High Authority found that the financing of a programme or
the operation of the installations which entailed would require subsidies, assistance, protection, or discrimination contrary to the Treaty,
it could prohibit the enterprise concerned from resorting to resources
other than its own funds to put such programme into effect.

The High Authority would encourage technical and economic research concerning the production and the development of consumption of coal and steel, as well as labour safety in these industries, and
to this end would establish appropriate contacts among existing
research organisations. After consultation with the Consultative
Committee, the High Authority might initiate and facilitate the
development of such research work either by encouraging joint
financing by the interested enterprises or by earmarking for that purpose any grants it might receive.

If the introduction of technical processes or new equipment within
the framework of the general programmes of the High Authority
should lead to an exceptional reduction in labour requirements in the
coal and steel industries, creating special difficulties in one or more
areas for the re-employment of the workers released, the High
Authority, on the request of the interested Governments, (a) would
consult the Consultative Committee; (b) might facilitate the financing of such programmes as it might approve for the creation, either in
the industries subject to its jurisdiction or, with the concurrence of the
Council, in any other industry, of 'new and economically sound'
activities capable of assuring productive employment to the workers
thus released; and (c) would grant non-reimbursable assistance to
contribute to: (i) the payment of grants to workers to tide them over
until they could obtain new employment, (ii) the granting of allowances to the workers for reinstallation expenses, (iii) the financing of
technical training for workers who were led to change their employment. The High Authority would grant non-reimbursable assistance,
however, only on the condition that the interested state paid a special
contribution at least equal to such assistance, unless a two-thirds
majority of the Council authorised an exception to this rule.

*Production (Arts. 57–59)* In the field of production the High
Authority would give preference to the indirect means of action at
its disposal (such as co-operation with Governments) to regularise or
influence general consumption, particularly that of the public

services, or intervention on prices and commercial policy as provided for in the Treaty.

In case of decline in demand and if the High Authority deemed that the Community was faced with a 'period of manifest crisis' and that the action provided for above was not sufficient to cope with the situation, it should, with the concurrence of the Council, establish a system of production quotas on an equitable basis. It might, in particular, regulate the rate of operation of enterprises by appropriate levies on tonnages exceeding a reference level defined by a general decision, the amounts thus obtained being earmarked for the support of those enterprises whose production rate had dropped below the level envisaged, especially with a view to ensuring for them as far as possible the maintenance of employment.

The system of quotas would be terminated automatically on a proposal made to the Council by the High Authority after consultation with the Consultative Committee, or by the Government of one of the member-states, except in the case of a contrary decision of the Council; such a decision must be taken by unanimous vote if the proposal originated with the High Authority, or by simple majority if it originated with a Government. The High Authority might impose upon enterprises violating the decisions taken by it in application of the present articles, fines not to exceed the sum equal to the value of the irregular production.

If, on the other hand, the High Authority found that the Community was faced with a serious shortage of certain or all of the products subject to its jurisdiction, it should establish consumption priorities and determine the allocation of the coal and steel resources of the Community among the industries subject to its jurisdiction, exports, and other consumption. On the basis of the consumption priorities thus determined, the High Authority should, after consulting the enterprises concerned, establish manufacturing programmes which the enterprises would be required to execute. If the quantities actually exported by a member-state were less than the scheduled quantities which were included in the basis for total allocations to the state in question, the High Authority would, to the extent necessary, redistribute among the member-states the additional availabilities for consumption thus created whenever a new allocation was made. It might in addition, with the concurrence of the Council, decide on the establishment in all member-states of restrictions on exports to third countries and might impose upon enterprises which violated the above decisions, fines not exceeding twice the value of the manufactures or deliveries prescribed and not executed or diverted from their proper use.

*Prices (Arts. 60–64)* Pricing practices contrary to the provisions of Arts. 2–4 were prohibited, particularly (a) unfair competitive practices (especially purely temporary or purely local reductions the purpose of which was to acquire a monopoly position within the common market), and (b) 'discriminatory practices involving the application by a seller within the single market of unequal conditions to comparable transactions especially according to the nationality of the buyer'. For the above purposes:

(a) The price scales and conditions of sales to be applied by enterprises within the single market would be made public to the extent and in the form prescribed by the High Authority after consultation with the Consultative Committee; if the High Authority considered that an enterprise had chosen an abnormal base point for its price quotations, in particular one which made it possible to evade the provisions listed in (b) below, it would make the appropriate recommendations to that enterprise;

(b) The prices charged by an enterprise within the common market, calculated on the base of the point chosen for the enterprise's price scale, must not as a result of the methods of quotation: (i) be higher than the price indicated by the price scale in question for a comparable transaction, or (ii) be less than this price by a margin greater than either the margin which would make it possible to align the offer in question on that price scale, set up on the basis of another point, which procured for the buyer the lowest price at the place of delivery, or a limit fixed by the High Authority for each category of products, taking into account the origin and destination of such products.

The High Authority might also fix for one or more products subject to its jurisdiction maximum and minimum prices within the common market, and maximum or minimum export prices. If the High Authority considered that such an action was appropriate 'in order to prevent the price of coal from being established at the level of the production costs of the most costly mine whose production was temporarily required to assure the accomplishment of the aims of Art. 3', it might authorise compensations (a) among enterprises of the same coal basin to which the same price scales were applicable; (b) after consulting the Council, among enterprises situated in different coal basins.

The High Authority might impose upon enterprises which violated these price provisions, or the decisions taken in application thereof, fines not exceeding twice the value of the irregular sales.

*Agreements and Concentrations (Arts. 65–66)* All agreements among enterprises, all decisions of associations of enterprises, and all concerted practices which would tend, directly or indirectly, to prevent, restrict, or impede the normal operation of competition within the common market were forbidden, especially those intended (a) to fix or influence prices; (b) to restrict or control production, technical development, or investments; (c) to allocate markets, products, customers, or sources of supply.

However, the High Authority would authorise enterprises to agree among themselves to specialise in the production of, or to engage in joint buying or selling of, specified products if it considered (a) that such specialisation, or such joint buying or selling, would contribute to a substantial improvement in the production or marketing of the products in question; (b) that the agreement in question was essential to achieve such effects, and did not impose any restrictions not necessary for that purpose; (c) that it was not susceptible of giving the interested enterprises the power to influence prices, or to control or limit the production or marketing of an appreciable part of the products in question within the Common Market, or of protecting them from effective competition by other enterprises within the Common Market.

Any transaction which would have in itself the direct or indirect effect of bringing about a concentration should first be submitted to the High Authority, which would only grant the authorisation if it found that the transaction in question would not give to the interested persons or enterprises the power (a) to influence prices, to control or restrain production or marketing, or to impair the maintenance of effective competition in a substantial part of the market for such products, or (b) to evade the rules of competition resulting from the application of the Treaty, particularly by establishing an artificially privileged position involving a material advantage in access to supplies or markets.

If a concentration should occur the High Authority would order the separation of the enterprises or assets wrongly concentrated, or the cessation of common control, as well as any other action which it deemed appropriate to re-establish the independent operation of the enterprises or assets in question and to restore normal conditions of competition. If the interested parties failed to fulfil their obligations the High Authority itself would take measures of execution and might impose fines.

*Impairment of the Conditions Competion (Art. 67)* Any action of a member-state which might have noticeable repercussions on the conditions of competition in the coal and steel industries would be brought by the interested Government to the attention of the High Authority. If such an action was liable to provoke a serious disequilibrium by increasing the differentials in costs of production otherwise than through variations in productivity, the High Authority, after consulting the Consultative Committee and the Council, might take the following measures:

(a)   If the action of the state concerned produced harmful effects for coal or steel enterprises coming under its jurisdiction, the High Authority might authorise that state to grant to such enterprises assistance, the amount conditions, and duration of which would be determined in agreement with the High Authority;

(b)   If the action of that state produced harmful effects for coal or steel enterprises subject to the jurisdiction of other member-states, the High Authority might address a recommendation to the state in question 'with a view to remedying such effects by such measures as that state may deem most compatible with its own economic equilibrium'.

*Wages and Movement of Labour (Arts. 68–69)* The methods of fixing wages and social benefits in force in the various member-states should not, as regards the coal and steel industries, be affected by the application of the Treaty, subject to the following provisions:

(a)   If the High Authority found that abnormally low prices practised by one or several enterprises were the result of wages fixed by those enterprises at an abnormally low level in comparison with the actual wage level in the same region, it should make the necessary recommendations to the interested enterprises after consulting the Consultative Committee;

(b)   If the High Authority found that a lowering of wages was leading to a drop in the standard of living of the labour force, and at the same time was being used as a means of permanent economic adjustment by enterprises or as a weapon of competition among enterprises, it should address to the enterprise or Government concerned a recommendation intended to assure the labour force of compensatory benefits to be paid for by the enterprise in question. This provision should not apply, however, to (i) overall measures taken by a member-state to re-establish its external equilibrium; (ii) wage decreases resulting from the application of the sliding scale legally or contractually established; (iii) wage decreases brought about by a decrease in the cost of living; (iv) wage decreases to correct abnormal increases previously granted under exceptional circumstances no longer in existence.

If an enterprise failed to conform to a recommendation made to it in the above connection, the High Authority might impose on it fines and daily penalty payments not exceeding twice the amount of the savings in labour costs unjustifiably effected.

The member-states further agreed to prohibit any discrimination in remuneration and working conditions between national workers and immigrant workers (without prejudice to special measures concerning frontier workers), and would work out among themselves any necessary arrangements so that social security measures did not stand in the way of the movement of labour.

*Transport (Art. 70)*   It was recognised that the establishment of the E.C.S.C. required the application of such transport rates for coal and steel as would 'make possible comparable price conditions to consumers in comparable positions'. Discriminations in transport rates, and conditions of any kind based on the country of origin or of destination of the products in question, were strictly forbidden for traffic among member-states whilst the application of special internal tariff measures in the interest of one or several coal- or steel-producing enterprises would be subject to the prior agreement of the High Authority.

*Commercial Policy (Arts. 71–75)*   Unless otherwise stipulated in the Treaty, the competence of the Governments of the member-states with respect to commercial policy would not be affected by the Treaty.

Minimum rates, below which the member-states were bound not to lower their customs duties on coal and steel with regard to third countries, and maximum rates, above which they were bound not to raise such duties, might be fixed by unanimous decisions of the Council upon the proposal of the High Authority; between the limits thus fixed, each Government could set its own tariffs according to its national procedure.

The administration of import and export licensing in relations with third Powers should be the responsibility of the Government on whose territory was located the point of origin for exports or the point of destination for imports, but the High Authority would be empowered to supervise the administration and control of such licensing where coal and steel were concerned.

The High Authority was also empowered to take all measures in conformity with the Treaty in the following circumstances: (a) if it was established that countries which were not members of the Community, or enterprises situated in such countries, were engaged in dumping operations or other practices condemned by the Havana Charter; (b) if a difference between the offers made by enterprises outside the jurisdiction of the Community and those made by enterprises within its jurisdiction was due exclusively to the fact that those of the former were based on competitive conditions contrary to the provisions of the Treaty; (c) if coal or steel was imported into the territory of one or several of the member-states of the Community 'in relatively increased quantities and under such conditions that these imports inflict, or threaten to inflict, serious damage on production, within the E.C.S.C., or similar or directly competitive products'.

The member-states bound themselves to keep the High Authority informed of proposed commercial agreements or arrangements relating to coal, steel, or the importation of other raw materials, and of specialised equipment necessary to the production of coal and steel.

The remaining clauses of the Treaty (Arts. 76–100) provided, *inter alia*, that the Community should enjoy on the territory of the member-states the privileges and immunities necessary to the exercise of its functions; that the seat of the institutions of the Community should be fixed by common agreement; and that the fiscal year of the Community should extend from 1 July to 30 June. The Treaty would apply to the European territories of the member-states, but each bound itself to extend to the other member-states the preferential measures which it enjoyed with respect to coal and steel in the non-European territories under its jurisdiction. It was expressly stated that the establishment of the Community in no way prejudiced the régime of ownership of the enterprises subject to the provisions of the Treaty. (Arts. 76–85.)

The member-states bound themselves to take all general and specific measure which would assure the execution of their obligations under the decisions and recommendations of the institutions of the Community, and to facilitate the accomplishment of the Community's purposes. They bound themselves to refrain from any measures compatible with the existence of the E.C.S.C., and agreed, to the extent of their competence, to take all appropriate measures to assure the international payments arising out of trade in coal and steel within the E.C.S.C., and to lend assistance to each other to facilitate such payments. (Art. 86.)

The signatories also agreed 'not to avail themselves of any treaties, conventions, or agreements existing among them to submit any difference arising out of the interpretation or application of the present Treaty to a method of settlement other than those provided for therein'. (Art. 87.)

If the High Authority considered that a state was delinquent with respect to any of the obligations imposed on it by the Treaty, it would take note of the delinquency in a decision accompanied by a justification. It would allow the state in question a period of time within which to execute its obligation, whilst the state would have the right to appeal to the Court's plenary jurisdiction within two months from the notification of the decision. If the state had not taken steps for the fulfilment of its obligation within the period fixed by the High Authority, or if its appeal was rejected, the High Authority could, with the concurrence of a two-thirds majority of the Council: (a) suspend the payment of sums which the High Authority might owe to the State in question; (b) adopt measures, or authorise other States to adopt measures, so as to correct the effects of the delinquency in question. If these measures should prove inoperative, the High Authority would lay the matter before the Council. (Art. 88.)

Any dispute among member-states concerning the application of the Treaty which could not be settled by a procedure provided for in the Treaty might be submitted to the Court at the request of one of the parties to the dispute. The Court would also have jurisdiction to settle any disputes between member-states relating to the purposes of the Treaty if such a dispute was submitted to it by virtue of an agreement to arbitrate. (Art. 89.)

If an enterprise did not make within the prescribed time limit a payment for which it was liable to the High Authority, the latter might suspend settlement of sums due by it to that enterprise up to the amount of the payment in question. All decisions of the High Authority imposing financial obligations on enterprises would be executory, and would be enforced on the territory of member-states through the legal procedures in effect in those States. Enforcement of such decisions could be suspended only by a decision of the Court. (Arts. 91–92.)

The High Authority would maintain whatever relationships appeared useful with the United Nations and with the Organisation for European Economic Co-operation, and would keep those organisations regularly informed of the Community's activities. The relations of the Community with the Council of Europe would be assured under the terms of an annexed Protocol. (Arts. 93–94.)

If, following the expiration of the transition period unforeseen difficulties which were brought out by experience in applying the Treaty, or a profound change in the economic or technical conditions which affected the common coal and steel market, made necessary an adaptation of the rules concerning the exercise by the High Authority of the powers conferred upon it, appropriate modifications might be made provided that they did not modify the provisions of Arts. 2, 3 and 4 or the relationship among the powers of the High Authority and of the other institutions of the Community. These modifications would be proposed jointly by the High Authority and the Council, acting by a five-sixths majority; would then be submitted to the opinion of the Court; and after examination by the Court would be transmitted to the Assembly, which could approve them by a majority of three-quarters of the members present and voting, compromising two-thirds of the total membership. (Art. 95.)

Following the expiration of the transition period, amendments might be proposed by member-states or by the High Authority; the Council, on a two-thirds majority vote, could then approve the calling of a conference of Government representatives of the member-states to consider such amendments. (Art. 96.)

The Treaty would run for a period of 50 years from the date of its entry into force (Art. 97), and other European States might accede to it by a unanimous vote of the Council. (Art. 98.)

The Treaty would be ratified by all the member-states (instruments of ratification being deposited with the French Government), and would enter into force on the date of deposit of the last instrument of ratification. If all the instruments of ratification had not been deposited six months after the signing of the Treaty, the Governments of the States which had ratified would consult among themselves on the measures to be taken. (Art. 99.)

EURATOM

The European Atomic Energy Community (Euratom) was set up in 1958 to help develop a civil nuclear industry in Europe and thereby help to raise living standards, which are closely linked to the level of energy consumption. In 1967 its executive was merged with E.E.C. and E.C.S.C. Since 1967 very little progress has been made within this community and it is considered by many to be the least successful.

Electricity consumption in western Europe, as in all industrialised countries, is rising rapidly. In the Community it is doubling every decade, and by 1980 at least four times as much electricity will be needed as in 1960. The role of atomic energy in producing electricity will also rise rapidly. In 1965 only 1 per cent of all electricity generated was of nuclear origin; the proportion was 3 per cent in 1968 and in the range of 20–25 per cent by 1980. Nuclear power stations which came into operation in 1968–70 are competitive with conventional stations in many areas of the Community.

Euratom's role is to ensure that the Community undertakes the research necessary for the development of nuclear energy not only for power production, but also through the use of radioisotopes and radioactive sources, for agricultural, industrial and medical purposes.

Euratom supplements and co-ordinates research undertaken in the Community, pools and disseminates scientific information, and promotes the training of scientists and technicians. For its first five-year research programme (1958–62) the Commission had at its disposal $215m.; for the second five-year programme (1963–67) this sum was doubled to $432m. Euratom research takes place:

(a)   in its own research centres:

*Ispra*, north of Milan, Italy, where work is at present concentrated on the fields of experiment opened up by the ORGEL heavy-water reactor;

*Geel*, Belgium: the Central Nuclear Measurements Bureau;

*Karlsruhe*, Germany: the European Transuranium Institute;

*Petten*, Holland: a general-purpose establishment.

(b)   through 'association contracts' under which Euratom and a partner organisation in a member-country jointly finance certain large-scale research projects, Euratom assigning scientific staff to joint teams. For instance, all fast-reactor and thermonuclear-fusion research in the Community is tied into the Euratom network of association contracts.

(c)   by contracting specific assignments to national centres or firms. Altogether over 700 such contracts have been executed or are under way.

(d)   by joining international projects such as the European Nuclear Energy Agency (E.N.E.A.) Dragon project at Winfrith, England.

Euratom has organised a large Information and Documentation Centre and has worked out a Community policy on the ownership of patents resulting from Euratom research.

Euratom also encourages the development of the Community's nuclear industry. It has brought into being, since 1 January 1959, a common market for all nuclear materials and equipment, and a low or suspended common external tariff on imports of nuclear materials from non-member countries.

Euratom has:

(a)   put into force a plan for the free movement of qualified atomic workers;

(b)   drawn up with other European countries an insurance convention providing joint Community coverage—supplementary to that of O.E.C.D.—for large-scale atomic risks;

(c)   earmarked $32m. to help build power plants of special importance to the Community. The installations aided in return pass on to the Euratom Commission their constructional and operational experience, which will then be made available to all requiring it;

(d)   granted 'joint enterprise' status to three power-reactor projects; joint enterprises, which must be projects of outstanding importance to the Community, enjoy special fiscal and other privileges.

(e)   set up a radioisotope information bureau to provide information on the rapidly increasing uses of isotopes in industry.

To safeguard both nuclear workers and the general population, Euratom has laid down Basic Standards for health protection which have been incorporated into the laws of the Community countries. These Basic Standards, which are among the most up-to-date and comprehensive in the world, are subject to continuous revision in the light of scientific advance. In addition, the Commission maintains a constant check on the level of radioactivity in the atmosphere, water and soil, on the basis of data regularly supplied by the six countries' control posts.

Euratom is pledged to ensure that ores, raw materials and fissile matter are not diverted from their declared use. Enterprises submit to the Commission details of the equipment of their installations and regular returns on their stocks, transfers and transactions of materials. The Commission operates an international on-the-spot inspection system to check on the returns. Any enterprise breaking these regulations may be subjected to sanctions, but no significant contraventions have been detected up to now.

The Treaty of the European Atomic Energy Community (Euratom) was signed and came into force on the same day as the Treaty creating the E.E.C.

The aims of the Community were defined in the preamble as the raising of living standards in the member-countries and the promotion of trade with non-Community countries. The tasks of Euratom were defined in Article 1 of the Treaty as the creation within a short period of the technical and industrial conditions necessary to utilise nuclear discoveries, and especially to produce nuclear energy on a large scale. This result would be achieved by joint measures of the member-countries and through the activities of the institutions of the Community.

*Provisions for Nuclear Development*

These provisions of the Treaty (Articles 4–106) were divided into sections dealing respectively with the development of nuclear research, dissemination of nuclear information, protection of health, investments, Community undertakings, supplies of nuclear materials, security measures, ownership of fissile material, and external relations. Details were as follows:

*Development of Research* The Commission would promote and facilitate research in the member-countries by the following means:

(1) It would set up a Community Nuclear Research Centre to ensure the execution of research programmes. This Centre would also be responsible, *inter alia*, for standardising nuclear terminology and measurements, and a Central Nuclear Measurements Bureau would be established in this connexion. Schools for training specialists would be set up in conjunction with the Centre, and an institution of university rank would be created at a later stage.

(2) To supplement nuclear research by member-countries, the Commission would work out research and training programmes, not exceeding five years, to be carried out by the Community Nuclear Research Centre. It might, however, conclude research contracts for part of these programmes with undertakings or nationals of member-countries, and also with international organisations or with nationals and undertakings of non-Community States. These pro-

grammes would require the unanimous approval of the Council of Ministers.

(3) The Commission would endeavour to co-ordinate the research conducted in the individual member-states. To this end, it would invite member-states, undertakings, and individuals to inform it of their research programmes in a specified field, and would express an opinion on these programmes. It would also attempt to prevent wasteful duplication and to direct research into less well-explored channels; would regularly consult public and private research bodies; would publish (with the agreement of the interested parties) the research programmes in operation; and might convene representatives of public and private research centres for mutual consultation and exchanges of information.

(4) The Commission might extend financial and/or technical assistance for research work as follows: (a) by a direct financial contribution repayable or otherwise; (b) by the organisation of joint financing by those concerned; (c) by supplying raw or fissile materials, either against payment or free of charge; or (d) by making available installations, equipment or experts, either against payment or free of charge.

*Dissemination of Information*

(1) The Commission would be obliged to pass on to interested persons and undertakings in the member-countries all the information acquired by the Community, and to issue to them at their request non-exclusive licences, provided they were in a position to exploit them effectively. A special procedure would apply to information which had to be kept secret for defence reasons (see below).

(2) The Commission would also seek (by way of agreement) to obtain information from the member-countries on all patents, patent applications, or working models covering inventions which would be useful to the Community. It would do its utmost to promote the issue of licences for such patents, etc.

(3) A compulsory notification procedure would apply to certain inventions. Under this procedure, member-countries would be required to notify the Commission, within 18 months of the lodging of such applications, of the details of any applications for patents for 'specifically nuclear objects'. In the case of applications covering objects which, while not specifically nuclear, were considered after

G

preliminary examination to be directly connected with the development of nuclear energy, member-countries would be obliged to notify the Commission within 18 months, and to communicate full details within another two months if requested by the Commission. A special procedure would again apply to secret defence inventions.

(4)  For inventions covered by the foregoing paragraph, certain compulsory powers would be available to the Commission, which could demand the issue of a licence if it considered this desirable even though no amicable agreement had been reached between the holder of the patent and the applicant for a licence. In all cases where such a licence was issued, the amount of compensation to be paid would be settled between the owner of the patent and the holder of the licence.

(5)  An arbitration Committee would be set up to deal with disputes between either (a) the Commission and the owner of a patent; or (b) the owner of a patent and a licensee on the subject of compensation. The Committee's members would be appointed by the Council of Ministers on the proposal of the Court of Justice. The final decisions of the Committee would have the force of *res judicata* as between the parties involved; but, after a lapse of one year, a request might be made for the revision of a decision if fresh circumstances had arisen to justify such a step.

(6)  Special confidential procedures would be adopted in the case of information which the Community had acquired from its research programme, and the disclosure of which might be considered detrimental to the defence interests of one or more member-countries. The Council of Ministers would draw up the necessary security regulations defining the various categories of secrecy and the security measures to be adopted.

(7)  The Commission would evolve a system whereby member-states, undertakings or individuals could exchange progress or final reports about their research. This system would have to guarantee the confidential nature of such exchanges, but the Commission would be entitled to transmit such reports to the Community Nuclear Research Centre for information, on the understanding that the Centre would have no right of utilisation save with the consent of the originators.

*Public Health*  The Community would establish a code of basic standards governing personal safety against dangers resulting from ionising radiation. This code would be drafted by the Commission, and submitted to the Council of Ministers for approval, after the Commission had heard the views of a group of persons selected by the Scientific and Technical Committee from amongst scientific experts in the field of public health. In addition, an information and study centre for personal safety problems would be set up within the Community Nuclear Research Centre.

*Investments* To stimulate initiative by public and private undertakings in the nuclear energy field, and to promote a planned development of their investments, the Commission would publish programmes indicating the Community's production aims and the capital investments thereby implied, after hearing the views of the Social and Economic Committee.

Public and private undertakings in member-countries which were contemplating investments in the nuclear energy field would be required to inform the Commission at least three months before work began or the first contracts were concluded. Such investment projects would be published, subject to the agreement of the parties concerned and their Governments.

*Community Undertakings* Undertakings of outstanding importance for the development of nuclear industry in the Community might be declared Community undertakings by a decision of the Council of Ministers, taken on a proposal by the Commission. This proposal would cover the statutes and site of the undertaking. The necessary finance, and the participation of the Community as well as of non-Community countries, international institutions, or foreign nationals, in the financing or management of the undertaking.

A Community undertaking would enjoy a special status; would be a legal entity of its own with the right to own property, enter into agreements, and assume rights and obligations; but, unless otherwise stipulated, would be subject to general industrial and commercial laws and regulations.

The Council could grant Community undertakings all or some of a certain number of privileges—viz., special facilities for the purchase or expropriation of property; exemption from dues and taxes; exemption from transfer, re-transfer, and registration dues and charges; exemption from Customs duties and from economic or fiscal restrictions on scientific and technical material, or substances treated by the undertaking; and the right to hold funds and foreign currency of any kind, with freedom of transfer.

Council decisions on the creation of Community enterprises would in general be taken by a qualified majority, but the following decisions would require unanimity: (i) Financial participation by the Community; (ii) the granting of the above-mentioned privileges; (iii) participation of non-Community States or their nationals in the financing or management of the enterprise.

Amendments to the statutes of such enterprises would have to be approved by the Council of Ministers. Disputes affecting them would be settled by the competent national courts, except for those matters reserved to the Court of Justice of the Community.

*Supplies*  A joint policy would be pursued with regard to the supply of ores, raw materials, and special fissile matter on the basis of the principle of equal access to resources. For this purpose the Commission would set up a Commercial Agency which would be a corporate body, vested with financial independence and able to conduct its affairs according to business rules, but controlled by the Commission. The Agency (the majority of whose capital would have to be owned by the Community and the member-countries) would possess (i) an option to purchase any of the materials in question produced in member-states; and (ii) the exclusive right to conclude contracts for the purchase or sale of such materials outside the Community.

*Resources within the Community*  All producers of ores, materials, and special fissile matter would be under an obligation to offer their products to the Agency immediately they became available, and the Agency would normally exercise its option by means of contracts with the producers. The Agency could exercise this option at any stage of production except in the following cases; (i) a producer engaged in the mining of ores as well as in the production of nuclear material need offer his product to the Agency only once, the same applying to a group of undertakings co-operating with each other in these processes; (ii) Community undertakings would supply ores, raw materials, and special fissile matter produced by them according to their statutory or contractual obligations; (iii) in the case of special fissile matter the Agency, while exercising its option, might leave the material with the producer, either to be used by the latter, or to be placed in stock, or to be placed at the disposal of undertakings associated with the producer for the execution of programmes of which the Commission had been notified.

When the Agency did not exercise its option the producer might continue to use or process the material himself, or he might be authorised by the Commission to dispose of the material outside the

Community at a price not less than that of his previous offer to the Agency. In the case of special fissile material, however, only the Agency could export this to other countries, with the Commission's consent.

*Resources outside the Community*   While the Agency would normally have the exclusive right to conclude contracts for supplies from non-Community countries, consumers would be entitled to do so if the Commission found at any time that the Agency's prices for such supplies were excessively high, or that the Agency could not deliver all or some of the required supplies within a reasonable time; the Commission's ruling would be taken on an application from the consumers concerned. Any contracts concluded by consumers would have to be notified to the Commission, which might object to them within one month if they violated the aims of the Community.

*Transactions with Agency—Prices*   To enable the Agency to satisfy all demands, producers and users would notify it at regular intervals of their available output and requirements. The Agency would endeavour to satisfy all applications for ores, materials, or special fissile matter, but if unable to do so fully would distribute the available supplies on a proportional basis.

Prices would be regulated by the interplay of supply and demand, member-countries being forbidden to infringe this rule by national legislation. Price adjustments designed solely to give certain consumers a monopoly would likewise be prohibited. On a proposal of the Commission the Council of Ministers could fix prices by unanimous vote. The Commission would also be entitled to put forward proposals to consumers for the standardisation of prices.

*Other Provisions* The Commission would be entitled to make recommendations regarding prospecting and the exploitation of mines, and might participate financially in such activities. Member-states would be required to send the Commission annual reports on prospecting, reserves and mining investments.

After seven years from the entry into force of the Treaty, the Council of Ministers would either confirm or replace all provisions relating to supplies.

*Security*   The Commission would be required to ensure (i) that ores, raw materials and special fissile matter were not diverted from their intended use as declared by their consumers; and (ii) that arrangements for their supply, and any special control measures accepted by the Community in an agreement with a non-Community State or international organisation, were observed.

To this end, the Commission would:

(a)  Request declarations from all the undertakings concerned describing the basic technical characteristics of their equipment;

(b)  Request statements of all transactions in order to facilitate accounting of ores, raw materials and special fissile matter;

(c)  Insist, if necessary, on all surplus special fissile matter temporarily not in use being placed in deposit;

(d)  Arrange for its inspectors to carry out checks and, where necessary impose sanctions ranging from a warning to the complete withdrawal of raw materials or special fissile matter.

*Ownership of Special Fissile Matter*  All special fissile matter would be the property of the Community. Member-states, undertakings or individuals, however, would be entitled to the widest possible utilisation and consumption of the special fissile matter which had legitimately come into their possession.

On behalf of the Community, the Agency would keep a special account relating to fissile matter transactions and entitled 'Financial Account for Special Fissile Matter'. This account would not show any changes in the value of the fissile matter, which would be entirely at the risk of those having the matter in their possession, leaving neither profit nor loss to the Agency.

*Common Market in Nuclear Materials*  A common market in nuclear materials would be set up, involving the following obligations on member-countries;

(a)  to introduce, one year after the coming into force of the Treaty, a common Customs tariff for nuclear minerals and products imported from non-Community Countries;

(b)  to repeal between each other, after the same one-year period, all import and export duties and taxes on such minerals, materials and products (the non-European territories of member-states being entitled, however, to continue to levy duties and taxes of a purely fiscal character);

(c)  to apply the procedure laid down in the Common Market Treaty for the gradual abolition of internal tariffs and quantitative import restrictions between member-countries, and for the introduction of a uniform Customs tariff, to all other products which might be used in the nuclear industry;

(d)  to admit nationals of the other member-countries, without discrimination, to all posts and occupations requiring qualifications in the nuclear sphere, as well as to participation in the construction of nuclear undertakings;

(e)  to set up an insurance scheme covering risks arising from the use of atomic energy;

(f)  to facilitate the transfer between member-countries of capital needed for nuclear projects, and to permit the transfer to other member-countries of payments in connection with nuclear transactions and employment in nuclear industries or research.

*External Relations*  The Commission would be responsible for any liaison needed with the various international organisations and, subject to the Council's approval, might conclude agreements with these bodies or with non-Community countries. Member-states would be required to notify the Commission of any clauses in agreements or arrangements concluded, or to be concluded, with non-Community States which fell within the scope of the Treaty. The Commission would consider whether such clauses were compatible with the Treaty and would be entitled, if necessary, to bring any such matter before the Court of Justice.

*Financial and General Provisions*

The remaining principal provisions of the Treaty covered the following subjects *inter alia*:

*Finance*  Estimates of all the Community's revenue and expenditure (apart from those of the Commercial Agency and the joint undertakings) would be drawn up for each financial year and entered either in the operational budget or the research and investment budget. The revenue and expenditure of the Agency, which would operate on commercial lines, would be estimated separately.

The receipts of the operational budget would consist mainly of the financial contributions of the member-countries, in the following proportions: France, Italy and West Germany, each 28 per cent; Belgium and the Netherlands, each 7·9 per cent; Luxembourg, 0·2 per cent. The receipts of the research and investment budget would consist of similar contributions, but with a slightly different proportionate scale, viz. France and West Germany, each 30 per cent; Italy, 23 per cent; Belgium 9·9 per cent; the Netherlands, 6·9 per cent; Luxembourg 0·2 per cent.

The above contributions might be replaced, in whole or part, by the proceeds of taxes levied by the Community in the member-countries; the introduction of such taxes would be decided

by the Council of Ministers on the proposal of the Commission.
The Community would also be entitled to raise loans to finance
research or investment.

The preliminary draft budgets of the various Community institutions under the aegis of the Commission would have to be submitted
to the Council of Ministers not later than 30 September of each year
(the financial year being 1 January–31 December). The Council
would be entitled to propose amendments but would be required, in
its turn, to submit the budgets to the Assembly by 21 October at the
latest. If the Assembly either signified its approval or expressed no
opinion within a month, the draft budgets would be deemed to be
finally adopted. If the Assembly proposed amendments, the final
decision would lie with the Council of Ministers.

The Council's decision would be taken by a qualified majority. For
the adoption of the operational budget this would be the normal
qualified majority—i.e. at least 12 out of 17 votes. For the adoption
of the research and investment budget, however, the votes of the
Council members would be weighted as follows:

France 30, West Germany 30, Italy 23, Belgium 9, the Netherlands
7, and Luxembourg 1. A qualified majority in this case would require
at least 67 votes.

*Overseas Territories*   Unless otherwise provided, the Treaty would
apply to non-European territories under the jurisdiction of member-
states.

*Amendment of the Treaty*   The Commission or any member-state
would be entitled to submit proposals for amending the Treaty to the
Council of Ministers, which could then decide to convene a conference of the member-states to consider such proposals.

*Admission of New Members*   Any European State could apply to
become a member of the Community, and could be admitted by
unanimous vote of the Council of Ministers. In the case of a successful application, the conditions of admission and the resultant changes
in the Treaty would be set out in an agreement between the member-
states and the applicant State.

A fundamental problem facing Euratom is whether it should
continue to work with the member-states' research programmes in
addition to maintaining research in its own research laboratories.
France and Italy would prefer to see 'national' laboratories run and
financed by the individual countries but West Germany and the
Netherlands oppose this. This fundamental disagreement has delayed

budgetary procedure and also Euratom's second five-year plan. Movement began again after 'The Hague Summit' (see page 13) and a budget was agreed. By the end of 1972, terms of reference to carry Euratom through to the end of the decade will have to be constructed.

# CHAPTER 17

## Regional Policy in an Enlarged Community

The disparity in industrial activity and employment between regions is common to almost all the west European countries.

The economies of these countries grew from the industrial revolution onwards under free and private enterprise which established industries as and when and where it was profitable to do so without making provision for future changes in the pattern of world trade even if such changes could have been foreseen.

The earlier the industrial revolution took place in the different countries the more acute the problem is.

The Regional Policy of the European Economic Community is still in its formative stages, in contrast with the Community's Common Agricultural Policy, which is clearly defined and firmly established.

The Communities have worked on the broad principles of Regional Policy for a long time. The European Coal and Steel Community's retraining of more than 400,000 ex-miners and steel workers and its loans to help the establishment of new industries in coal and steel areas faced with decline as well as the operation of the Guidance Section of the European Agricultural Fund are in line with the principle of Regional Policy.

The Treaty of Rome prescribes the arrangements for ensuring the harmonious development of the member States by strengthening their economies and reducing the differences between the various regions. The Council, by virtue of Article 235 of the Treaty, has powers to implement these aims and has decided to develop plans for doing so as a matter of urgency. The following regions of the Community are considered to have special priority:

(1)  Regions lagging behind in development, mainly because of the predominance of agricultural activities.

(2)  Frontier regions where the need to co-ordinate action of member states is felt strongly.

(3)  Regions where there is structural unemployment.

(4)  Regions which are declining because of the trend of predominant economic activity.

The powers granted to the Commission to implement the plan are widespread and include a Regional Development Rebate Fund, managed by the Commission and replenished by budget contributions, from which aid may be granted in the form of interest rate rebates or guarantees for loans made by the European Investment Bank or other financial institutions.

The methods which the different member-countries have evolved to encourage developments in areas of economic changes are summarised below. All have the same objectives, though, for national geographical social and demographic reasons, the instruments used for attaining the objectives differ in each country.

## REGIONAL POLICY IN GERMANY

Responsibility for regional policy lies primarily with the Lander, with the Bund (Federal Government) intervening secondarily where the Lander are unable to discharge their functions. Furthermore, the Bund furnishes a considerable proportion of the funds for promoting the establishment of industry.

The instruments of regional policy include:
(1)   Investment grants of up to 25 per cent of the cost of establishing new enterprises.
(2)   Loans to industrial enterprises covering up to 50 per cent of the total investment, at low interest rates.
(3)   3 per cent interest rate rebates during the first three years for loans granted for the rationalisation of industrial enterprises.
(4)   Grants of up to 60 per cent of the cost of developing industrial land.
(5)   Rapid write-off for movables—50 per cent in the first year.
(6)   Freight compensation in the area bordering the Eastern zone.
(7)   Tax relief for investment allowance of 10 per cent of capital expenditure.

## REGIONAL POLICY IN FRANCE

The objectives of French policy crystallise around three points:
(1)   Decentralisation of activities from Paris and Lyons areas.
(2)   Development areas where new enterprises are needed to re-employ workers from industries which are declining or disappearing, notably the coalfields and some iron and steel areas.
(3)   The establishment of industrial activities in the west and south-west which are heavily dependent on agriculture.

The instruments of French regional policy are largely methods of constraint, for example any industrial structure of more than 1,000 square metres in Paris and Lyons requires authorisation. Government departments and other establishments in Paris are strongly encouraged, if not constrained, to move elsewhere.

On the financial side:

(1)   10 to 15 year loans at 6 per cent interest are granted to encourage decentralisation.

(2) Industrial development grants are made for industrial adaptation in declining regions, varying from 15 per cent to 25 per cent based upon the number of new jobs to be created.

(3)   Decentralisation and closure grants to enterprises which leave Paris together with training grants, reduced prices for new industrial sites and, where applicable, for natural gas from Lacq or electricity power in Brittany.

(4)   Reduction in conveyancing tax and business tax.

The aim of the French regional policy is to effect the release of a million workers in agriculture and the re-employment of 300,000 workers in the mines, in coal and steel and in textiles, mainly in the north and east.

REGIONAL POLICY IN ITALY

The most serious problem in Italy is still the emigration from the south to the north, depriving the south of the manpower needed for industrial growth, which characterises the Mezzagiorno problem.

International industrial finance, promoted by the Instituto Mobiliare Italiano, is being used and a loan of 50 million Eurodollars is being drawn upon to set up industries in the Mezzogiorno to make plastics, chemicals and chemical fibres, petrochemicals and similar products.

Government instruments for regional policy include:

(1)   Capital grants of up to 20 per cent for buildings and 30 per cent for machinery.

(2)   3 per cent interest rate rebates.

(3)   Preferential loans at low interest rates.

These inducements can cover in all up to 85 per cent of total investment. In addition, profits and 50 per cent of investment outlay are exempted from Corporation and Income Tax, in some cases up to 10 years.

Other measures include 50 per cent reduction in the duty on energy,

50 per cent on railway freight charges on goods to be used for invest-ment purposes in the south and payment by the state of 20 per cent of the Social Service charges.

## REGIONAL POLICY IN BELGIUM

There are specific laws and decrees which both set out the problem of establishing measures to promote new enterprises, the designa-tion of areas to which they apply and the financial appropriations needed to carry them out.

The instruments include:

(1)  Interest rate rebates from 2 per cent to interest free for the first two years.

(2)  State underwriting of repayment of loans.

(3)  Capital grants of up to 20 per cent of investment in buildings and $7\frac{1}{2}$ per cent of investment in equipment, which can be increased to 30 per cent and 10 per cent respectively in certain cases.

(4)  (a)  Tax reliefs amounting to tax exemption for capital subsidies provided by the State.

    (b)  Ten year exemption for property tax on buildings and land, constructed with state assistance.

    (c)  Deduction of subsidies when calculating amortisation.

    (d)  Authorisation to write off buildings, material and equip-ment at twice the normal depreciation rate for the first three years.

Belgian regional policy applies to a geographical area which covers nearly 40 per cent of the country. It is said that it has done much to improve conditions in the northern area, but that the south-ern area has deteriorated markedly in the last ten years; and, on the whole, regional policy has led to new enterprises being set up in areas faced with the less serious problems because the law does not apportion the amount of aid according to the acuteness of regional necessities.

## REGIONAL POLICY IN THE NETHERLANDS

One of the principal reasons for regional imbalance in the Nether-lands is concentration in the Amsterdam, Rotterdam, The Hague and Utrecht conurbations, 10 per cent of the total area with 37 per cent of the population.

As in other Community countries, coal mining and textiles are declining industries.

Dutch regional policy currently applies to four 'regional units', covering 46 per cent of the area and 21 per cent of the population.

The instruments include:

(1) Infrastructure improvements, for example, canals, roads, the development of industrial areas and the modernising of public services in all of which the State can contribute up to 95 per cent of the cost.

(2) Financial aids, which vary according to the geographical location, for example:

    (a) Grants of up to Fls. 60 (approximately £7·00) maximum per square metre for buildings.

    (b) 25 per cent of capital expenditure for establishing new enterprises.

    (c) 50 per cent reduction in the purchase price of land for new factories.

    (d) 3 per cent interest rate rebates for fifteen years in certain areas.

    (e) State underwriting of loans from National Investment Bank.

    (f) The state can acquire direct ot indirect holdings in the capital of enterprises set up in the north.

60,000 new industrial jobs were created in the Netherlands from 1957 to 1967 and 56 per cent of these were created by concerns which had received the regional development grant.

REGIONAL POLICY IN BRITAIN

Responsibility for attracting industrial development in the 'Development Areas' lies primarily with the Department of Trade and Industry.

The instruments of regional policy consist of a number of incentives of which the following are some:

(1) The English, Scottish and Welsh Industrial Estates Corporation may offer D.T.I. factories for rent or sale. These factories may be custom-built or ready to occupy.

(2) Grants of 35 per cent to 45 per cent of the cost of building a factory or buying a building not previously occupied.

(3) Loans for buildings, plant and working capital depending on the number of new jobs to be created.

(4) Grants towards the cost of removal from some part of Britain outside a Development Area.

(5) Tax Allowances: Machinery and Plant: 100 per cent allowance on capital expenditure for new machinery for the period in which the expenditure is incurred.

Buildings: 44 per cent of the cost, less any grant, can be written off against the first year, then 4 per cent per year.

(6) A Regional Employment Premium is paid of £1·50 for whole time men and £0·75 for whole time women (up to September 1974) in addition to the refund of Selective Employment Tax.

(7) Financial help of up to £10 per week for men is given to an employer who provides training for new, reasonably permanent jobs in a Development Area, and additional finance for building and machinery for that purpose.

In certain designated Special Development Areas—parts of Scotland, the north-east, the north-west and Wales—additional incentives are available in the form of rent-free periods and operational grants of up to 30 per cent of eligible wage and salary costs during the first three years of operation.

It must, however, be noted that Regional Policy in Britain still hinges largely on the Industrial Development Certificate concept which, in itself, promotes conflict between different Ministries and between Ministries and Local Government and would stand to gain immeasurably from harmonisation of Regional Policy in the enlarged Community.

It has been said that in applying Community resources to Britain's regional policy she would have to contribute as much to the Community pool as she would be able to draw out. This may be true, though it is hard to accept that Britain's regional requirements are lower in priority than those of France's agricultural needs, which, as far as subsidies from the common agricultural fund are concerned, will not continue at the present level for ever and that, at some time, the redeployment of Community resources from agricultural to industrial aid may not only be desirable, it may be essential.

THE COMMUNITY'S PLANS

In addition to plans which may be regarded as the beginning of a Regional Policy designed to supplement national efforts in special cases, the Commission has worked out, (and in due course the Community will apply) a Common Policy on what they call the 'Central Regions'.

The object of this plan is to reduce the escalation of subsidies for attracting new industry, especially from outside the Community, which bid up their state aids to attract investment in areas of the Community which are already prosperous and industrially developed.

Regions qualifying for state aid must genuinely need it for special social and economic reasons and aids must be accurately calculated.

Furthermore, a common method of measuring existing regional aids has been agreed, based broadly upon the percentage of the aid relative to the total amount of the investment in question.

M. Albert Borschette, member of the European Commission with special responsibility for regional policy, speaking in Bristol in September 1971 said 'We hope that Britain, Norway, Denmark and Ireland from the moment they become part of the enlarged Community will join us in working out a common regional policy to supplement their national policies'.

# CHAPTER 18

## *Agreements of Association and Trade*

AGREEMENT ON ASSOCIATE MEMBERSHIP OF GREECE
An agreement was initialled in Brussels on 30 March 1961 whereby
Greece became associated with the European Economic Community
in a customs union, with provision for her to become a full member
of the E.E.C. when her economic progress permitted. The agreement
became effective on 1 November 1962. It was planned that Greece
should become a full member of the E.E.C. by 1984 but since 1967
all progress towards this goal has been halted by the Six. This
action has also resulted in a standstill in harmonisation of agricultural
policies and in the restructuring of industry which was dependent on
loans from European Investment Bank.

The Greek request for association had been accepted in principle
by the member-countries of the E.E.C. on 25 July 1959, but negotiations on details extended over the next two years, in the course of
which Greek ministers and officials had numerous meetings with
officials of the E.E.C. and with ministers and officials of individual
countries of the Community.

The chief topics covered in these negotiations were as follows:
(1)  The date at which tariff reductions by Greece *vis-à-vis* the
Six should commence and the speed at which they should be effected,
having regard to the state of developments of the Greek economy.
(2)  The expansion of markets for Greek agricultural products
(especially tobacco and citrus fruits) in the member-countries of the
E.E.C. Italy expressed particular concern at the possible effects
which Greek exports might have on her own exports of citrus fruits,
but a  compromise was finally reached whereby a ceiling was fixed
on the quantity of fruits which might be exported by Greece under
conditions of equal treatment with exports by E.E.C. member-
countries. A compromise was also eventually reached with Italy on
the level of Italian imports of Greek tobacco.
(3)  Greece's trade relations with third countries, in which connection Greece demanded the right to accord favourable treatment to
products imported from third countries in order to promote the
export to those countries of her own agricultural products, so long

as the E.E.C. could not guarantee that Greece's output of these products would be fully absorbed in the markets of the E.E.C. member-countries.

(4)   The nature of an 'escape' clause.

(5)   The granting of loans to Greece by the E.E.C. Originally the E.E.C. had proposed to make new loans dependent on the settlement of Greece's pre-war debt totalling the equivalent of £75,000,000 (with an additional £75,000,000 representing accumulated unpaid interest since 1941); of this sum, nearly 80 per cent was in sterling, 17 per cent in dollars, and the remainder in French francs.

Greece put forward the argument that only a very small portion of the debt was owed in E.E.C. member-countries, that Germany and Italy had been responsible for war devastation in Greece, and that post-war reparations had been insufficient to enable Greece to develop her economy to the point at which she could resume repayment of the debt. A statement issued by the Greek Ministry of Finance on 24 August 1960, declared that Greece had 'repeatedly expressed her eagerness for a settlement of the pre-war public debt based on the capabilities and needs of the Greek people . . . in spite of the terrible trial of her economy during the war and post-war periods and the need to concentrate all her resources and capabilities on her economic cevelopment'; discussions had, however, revealed a conflict on basic points which made agreement impossible.

Eventually, however, agreement on the unconditional granting of loans was reached and embodied in a special protocol.

The main provisions of the final agreement are summarised below:

*Greek Association with the E.E.C.* Under Article 238 of the Treaty of Rome Greece would not become a full member of the European Economic Community but associated herself with it on the basis of a customs union, with the prospect of her incorporation into the Community when the progress of her economy allowed her to assume fully the obligations deriving from the Rome treaty.

The object of the Association was defined as the 'continuous and balanced strengthening of trade and economic relations between the contracting parties, having particular regard to the need to secure an accelerated development of the Greek economy'.

INTERNAL TARIFFS BETWEEN GREECE AND E.E.C.

*Member-countries* A customs union would become fully effective after a transitional period during which Greece would receive special consideration. In principle she would reduce her tariffs over twelve years from the date of the Agreement coming into force, at the rate of 10 per cent immediately, 10 per cent at the end of each 18-month period for the first nine years, and a further 10 per cent at the end of each of the remaining three years.

In order to assist in the development of Greek industry, however, there would be special concessions in the case of most industrial goods purchased in Greece, the transitional period for these lasting 22 years. Thus, during the first 10 years tariffs would be reduced by a total of 20 per cent, i.e. a 5 per cent reduction on the date of the Agreement coming into effect, and three reductions of 5 per cent each at intervals of 2½ years; from the end of the tenth year until the end of the twenty-second, the remaining 80 per cent of the original tariffs would be reduced at the rate laid down for normal tariff elimination, i.e. one-tenth (or 8 per cent of the original tariff) at the end of the tenth year, one-tenth at the end of each 18-month period for the next nine years, and one-tenth at the end of each of the last three years. It was estimated that the 22-year transitional period would apply to approximately one-third of Greece's imports from the Community.

Tariff reductions which had already taken place among the six member-countries of the E.E.C., as well as any further reductions, would, upon the Agreement coming into effect, immediately and automatically apply to Greek products. Thus the tariff would immediately be reduced by 30–40 per cent for Greek industrial products and by 20–30 per cent for Greek agricultural products, all tariffs *vis-à-vis* Greece being completely eliminated by 1969 at the latest.

In order to protect newly established industries, Greece would be permitted during the 12-year transition period to impose new tariffs or to increase existing ones by a maximum of 25 per cent *ad valorem*, provided that imports from the E.E.C. of the products affected did not exceed 10 per cent of the total imports from the member-countries of the Community in 1958. These tariffs might be maintained for nine years and would then be progressively reduced, being eliminated in any case by the end of the 22-year transitional period.

*External Tariffs* Greece accepted the tariffs of the E.E.C.'s common external tariff scale, so that at the end of the 13- or 22-year transitional period (whichever applied to the articles in question) goods imported from third countries would be subject both in Greece and in the E.E.C. member-countries to a common external tariff.

In the case of tobacco, raisins, olives, colophony and turpentine (the five products in which Greece has a 'special and increased interest') the following special provisions in favour of Greece would apply during the first 12 years: (i) the *ad valorem* tariff of the common external tariff scale on 1 Oct. 1960 might not be modified by more than 20 per cent without the prior consent of Greece, e.g. the E.E.C. *ad valorem* tariff *vis-à-vis* third countries of 30 per cent on tobacco might not be reduced below 24 per cent; (ii) the prior approval of Greece would also be sought before any special tariff quotas were granted by the E.E.C. member-countries for more than 22,000 tons out of the total of 130,000 tons of tobacco imported annually from third countries, and for more than 15 per cent of the annual E.E.C. imports from third countries of raisins, olives, colophony and turpentine.

For up to 10 per cent of her imports from third countries, Greece would be permitted to grant special tariff quotas without the prior approval of the E.E.C. provided the special tariffs would equal those currently applied for corresponding imports from E.E.C. member-countries.

*Quantitative Restrictions*  These would be progressively eliminated between Greece and the E.E.C. In particular, the equivalent of 60 per cent of Greek private imports from E.E.C. countries in 1958 would be permanently liberalised within one year, rising to 75 per cent at the end of the fifth year and to 80 per cent at the end of the tenth year. Global quotas for E.E.C. member-countries equal to Greece's imports from those countries in the first year after the Agreement came into effect would be increased from the third to the tenth year by 10 per cent per annum on a cumulative basis; after the tenth year the rate of increase would be raised to 20 per cent for each 18-month period, all quantitative restrictions being eliminated by the end of the 22-year period. The expansion of import quotas and import liberalisation already effected or to be carried out in the future between member-countries of the E.E.C. would be extended to Greece.

*Special Agricultural Provisions*  The Agreement aimed at harmonising the agricultural policies of the signatory countries, so that Greek agricultural products would receive equal treatment with similar products of the Six. If for any reason Greece found that such a harmonisation for a particular product ran contrary to her interests, she might decline to implement it, in which case she would be entitled to enjoy at least a most-favoured-nation status as regards her relations with the Community for that particular commodity.

All Greece's key farm products (tobacco, raisins, olives, etc., and all fruit and vegetables) would immediately enjoy equal treatment with similar products of the six member-countries of the Community. For Greek wines quotas had been fixed covering the normal maximum annual exports in recent years, within which they would enjoy equal treatment; these quotas would be increased whenever the quotas prevailing among the Six underwent an increase.

At the special insistence of Italy, a protocol was added providing that if the export trade of any E.E.C. member-country was adversely affected by Greek exports of citrus fruits, grapes and peaches, the E.E.C. Council of Ministers might decide that Greek exports of these products which were in excess of the amount stipulated in the protocol would not enjoy the status provided by the Agreement. The limits were set at 22,000 tons for citrus fruits, rising to 45,000 tons by the end of the fifth year; 15,000 tons for fresh grapes, rising to 31,000 tons; and 40,000 tons for peaches, rising to 83,000 tons, After the fifth year the limits would be agreed by both sides until Greek agricultural policy was completely harmonised with that of the Six. In the case of citrus fruits, the limits might be subject to revision if Greece experienced particular difficulties with her exports to third countries with which she was linked by bilateral clearing agreements.

A more rapid tariff reduction by the Six would be applied to Greek exports of raisins and tobacco, viz. the tariffs in force on 1 January 1957 would be halved immediately the Agreement came into force, and would be completely eliminated in the case of raisins within six years and in the case of tobacco by the end of 1967.

The French Monopole du Tabac would stabilise its purchases of Greek tobacco at the average level of the years 1957–59, and would increase them in the same proportion as those countries which imported tobacco freely; the Italian Tobacco Monopoly would procure from Greece at least 60 per cent of its purchases of tobacco for internal consumption (i.e. excluding tobacco destined for re-export), with a guaranteed annual minimum value of $2,800,000.

The tariff and quota status for imports of other farm products by either side would become permanent at the level in force when the Agreement came into effect. In the case of meat and dairy products, however, Greece would grant limited tariff reductions, amounting in general to 20 per cent within the first 10 years but to 40 per cent for ham, 35 per cent for cheeses, and 30 per cent for butter.

*Other Provisions*  The Agreement also provided for the establishment of a common economic policy on the model of the Treaty of Rome, taking into account the needs and resources of Greece. The movement of workers, services, and capital would be liberalised; a common policy would be established for vocational training and the exchange of young workers; and tax legislation, currency policy, transport systems, and the rules of competition would be harmonised. The Council of the Association (see below) would determine the exact conditions for the implementation of these provisions.

*Institutions*  The application of the Agreement would be supervised by a newly created Council of the Association, composed of members of the Council of Ministers and of the Commission of the E.E.C. and of the Greek Government. Each side would have one vote and the Council would take its decisions on the basis of unanimity; if it found itself unable to solve the differences submitted to it, it might refer them to the European Court of Justice or to arbitration. In the latter case, the E.E.C. and Greece would each appoint one arbitrator, and these two arbitrators would then co-opt a third as Umpire. The President of the European Court of Justice would act as Umpire for the first five years, and thereafter the Umpire would, in case of dispute, be appointed by the President of the International Court of Justice.

*Escape Clause*  In the case of serious difficulties being encountered by any member of the Association, the E.E.C. member-countries would have the right of recourse to Article 226 of the Treaty of Rome, while Greece would enjoy equal status as regards the application of this Article. This right, however, would remain in force only during the transitional period of the Treaty of Rome and, in the case of the E.E.C. countries, might only be applied after prior consultation with Greece. Moreover, in such a case it would not be possible for all the E.E.C. member-countries to take joint protective measures against Greece, and the member-country in difficulties could not direct its protective measures against Greece alone, but would have to apply them against all the other E.E.C. member-countries. Up to 1969, Greece would be entitled to resort to protective measures in the event of difficulties in any sector of her economy, and might resort to such measures unilaterally after prior consultations with the E.E.C.

*Loans to Greece*  A special protocol provided for loans to Greece of up to $125,000,000 to be used during the first five years of the Agreement. These loans would be for 25 years, and might be spent either in drachmas or foreign currencies. The Six would subsidise by up to 3 per cent per annum the rate of interest on loans representing two-thirds of the total financial support (i.e. on a maximum of approximately $83,000,000). They also agreed to consider within the first five years the provision of additional financial support, specifically through the recognition of Greece's need to apply for loans to the European Investment Bank.

The principal developments under the Association Agreement have been that in accordance with the provisions of the Association Agreement the E.E.C. extended to Greek products the internal tariff reductions introduced within the Six on 1 January 1966 but a more favourable treatment was granted for the Greek key export products —raisins and tobacco. Greece reduced her customs duties in November 1965 for imports from the E.E.C. by 30 per cent for most products and by 10 to 20 per cent for products subject to slower rates of dismantlement. For imports from non-E.E.C. countries Greece has started to align her tariffs on the Community's common external tariff on 1 November 1965.

At a meeting of the Council of Association held in Brussels in June 1964 it was agreed that a plan to bring the Greek and the E.E.C. agricultural policies into harmony would be in two stages:

(a) The first stage would allow Greece the levies and other mechanisms of the common agricultural policy, without, however implementing the Common Market price structure; at the same time Greek agricultural produce would receive qualified preference on the E.E.C. markets.

(b) In the second stage Greece would progressively align her agricultural prices and protection levels on those prevailing in the E.E.C. would open her markets to Community farm exports while U.S. agricultural assistance would have to be discontinued. The Ministers were unable to agree a time-table for this plan, the Greek government asked for a longer period for the first stage when 31 December 1967 was suggested as an ending date. These difficulties made it impossible to reach a decision on harmonisation within the time-limit laid down in Article 35 of the Association Agreement, i.e. 12 November 1964 and therefore the period has been extended several times.

AGREEMENT ON ASSOCIATE MEMBERSHIP OF TURKEY

An agreement and two supplementary protocols whereby Turkey became associated with the European Economic Community in a

Customs union, with provision for her to become a full member of the E.E.C. when her economic progress permitted, were initialled in Brussels on 25 June 1963 and signed in Ankara on 12 September 1963. After ratification documents had been exchanged on 28 October 1964 the association agreement came into force on 1 December 1964.

The Turkish Government first applied for the association of Turkey with the E.E.C. on 31 October 1959. The Community for its part was interested in associating a country situated on the confines of Europe, but the content of association agreement had to take into consideration Turkey's need to speed up industrialisation, modernise agriculture, and improve infrastructures before planning any mutual reduction of Customs duties leading to a Customs union. The final agreement laid down that its objectives should be attained by stages, its main provisions are:

*The First or Preparatory Stage*

During an initial period of five years Turkey would continue her efforts to strengthen her economic and commercial position. The E.E.C. would assist these efforts in two main ways:

(1) By granting tariff quotas to ensure that Turkey could sell in the Common Market specified amounts of four agricultural products which made up 37 per cent of her total export trade. Annual tariff quotas would accordingly be opened by member-states for 12,500 tons of tobacco, 30,000 tons of dried grapes, 13,000 tons of dried figs, and 17,000 tons of hazel-nuts. After a period of two years from the entry into force of the agreement, the Council of Association would be able to increase the tariff quotas and, after three years, to take measures to promote the marketing of other products in the Community. In the first year of the Association (1965) the quota for tobacco was taken up by Turkish exporters to 76 per cent: raisins by 83·5 per cent; dried figs by 98·5 and hazel-nuts by 100 per cent. Increased quotas were arranged for 1966 and 1967.

(2) By granting loans to Turkey through the European Investment Bank. Under a Finance Protocol these loans would total $175,000,000 and would be applied to capital projects serving to increase the productivity of the Turkish economy, contributing to the attainment of the agreement's objectives, and fitting into the framework of the Turkish development plan. Loans would be made by the E.I.B. directly to the responsible Turkish organisations, but loans for

normal profit-making projects would be made to the Turkish State, which would re-lend the money to the appropriate body or enterprise. The E.I.B. and the Turkish Government signed a general convention on these loans on 8 December 1964.

## The Second or Transitional Stage

During this stage, which might last up to a maximum of 12 years, a Customs union between Turkey and the E.E.C. would gradually be established on the basis of mutually balanced obligations. Details of this stage have not yet been planned because they will depend on the situation existing when the move is made from the preparatory stage. The framework of the trade and economic arrangements was, however, laid down as follows:

(i) The Principles of the Customs union and its timing would be on the basis of Article XXIV of GATT. It would cover all trade and would entail the adoption by Turkey of the common Customs tariff. With a few exceptions it was planned to have the union fully established in 12 years. A special system would be introduced for agricultural products in order to take into consideration the Community's agricultural policy. Detailed arrangements would be made by the Council of Association and laid down in a protocol.

(ii) During this preparatory stage Turkey would bring her economic policy into line with that of the Community, particularly as regards: free movement of persons; (2) transport policy; and (3) rules of competition.

## The Third or Definitive Stage

The third stage would be based on a full Customs union between Turkey and the E.E.C. including a common external tariff and with growing co-ordination and integration in all fields of economic policy. The agreement envisaged that when a full Customs union had been achieved Turkey would be eligible to apply for full membership of the European Economic Community.

*Institutions* The application of the Agreement would be supervised by a newly created Council of the Association composed of members of the six Governments and the Council of Ministers and Commission of the E.E.C., and of the Turkish Government. Each of the two parties would have equal voting rights and the chairmanship would alternate between Turkey and the E.E.C. every six months. During the preparatory stage the Council of Association would be the forum for periodical discussions on how the association was working, and would be competent to resolve any dispute or difficulty concerning the association or to refer such disputes or difficulties to an existing juridical authority.

### Protocol on Transition from First to Second Stage

A 'Provisional Protocol' attached to the agreement stipulated that the Council of Association should examine after four years the question of whether the transition to the second stage could be implemented having regard to Turkey's economic progress, and whether agreement could be achieved on the conditions, details, and time-schedules for the implementation of the second stage, Such an agreement would have to be laid down in a supplementary protocol requiring unanimous acceptance and ratification by all the countries concerned before the transition to the second stage could come into effect. If no such protocol was signed after the first four years, the preparatory stage would be extended by up to another six to a maximum of ten years, and the Council of Association would then have to decide about the arrangements to take effect after the tenth year.

On 23 November 1970 Turkey and the Six signed a protocol in Brussels governing Turkey's relations with the E.E.C. in the second phase of its association.

AGREEMENT ON MEMBERSHIP OF THE ASSOCIATION OF AFRICAN STATES

The Convention of Association between the E.E.C. and the associated African States and Madagascar was signed on 20 July 1963, at Yaoundé (Cameroon), after protracted negotiations on certain of its terms, especially the total amount of financial aid to the associated countries had been successfully concluded, the figure finally agreed being $730,000,000. In view of the delay, the European Parliament had proposed on 25 March 1963, that certain adjustments in the transitional provisions would be required, including financial authority for the Commission to continue technical assistance after 1 July 1963, and the duty-free admission of certain tropical products by member-countries.

After ratification the Convention came into force on 1 June 1964, together with a parallel decision of the E.E.C. on the association arrangements between the Community and overseas dependent territories and French overseas departments.

The principal provisions of the Association Convention were as follows:

*Trade*

(a)  Exports from the associated states to the E.E.C. member-states would benefit from the same gradual elimination of duties and expansion of quotas as the member-states were to apply amongst themselves.

(b)  Pineapples, coconuts, coffee, tea, cocoa, pepper, vanilla, cloves, and nutmeg would enter member-states duty free. The common external tariff would operate for these products at reduced rates.

(c) When fixing common agricultural policy the E.E.C. would protect the interests of associated states with respect to those products which were similar to, or competed with, European products, particularly oilseed and sugar.

(d)  Not later than six months after the effective date of the Convention, the associated states would extend the same tariff treatment to products originating in all member-states and would gradually abolish quantitive restrictions. They might nevertheless retain or introduce Customs duties on products imported from member-states when such duties corresponded to the requirements of their development and industrialisation or were intended to contribute to their budgets; in the event of these measures proving inadequate because of balance-of-payments difficulties, the associated states might also retain or introduce quantitative restrictions.

(e)  The E.E.C. would help finance schemes which would enable certain products of the associated states to be marketed throughout the Community at competitive prices.

*Financial and Technical Co-operation*  The object of the Convention —to foster the economic and social development of the associated states—would, as in the earlier convention, be achieved mainly by means of the European Development Fund (E.D.F.). The Fund would, however, be assisted by the European Investment Bank (E.I.B.), which had hitherto only operated for the benefit of the E.E.C. member-states themselves.

There were four main features in the new association system:

(a)  An increase in the amount of aid. In the initial period, aid from the European Development Fund to African and other dependent territories amounted to $581,000,000 but under the new association system the total would be $800,000,000. Of this sum $730,000,000 would be allotted to the eighteen associated states and $70,000,000 to the dependent territories and the four French overseas departments. The new total represented a 38 per cent increase in aid.

(b)   Whereas previously the E.E.C. had only been able to grant aid outright, under the new convention a much wider range of financial methods was provided. Thus, the $730,000,000 to be allocated to the associated states would be distributed as follows: (i) Non-reimbursable grants by E.D.F.—$620,000,000; (ii) E.D.F. loans on special terms such as very long periods of repayment, periods of grace, and low rates of interest—$46,000,000; (iii) E.I.B. loans on ordinary terms—$64,000,000; (iv) Interest rebates subtracted from the total amount of non-reimbursable grants, thus enabling the E.D.F. to cut to 3 per cent the interest on E.I.B. loans; (v) Short-term advances to stabilise commodity prices up to a ceiling of $50,000,000 from the cash holdings of the Fund.

(c)   Hitherto the E.E.C. could only finance capital investment and, on occasions, certain technical assistance schemes. Under the new Convention the scope of its aid was widened as follows: (i) Traditional type of capital investment: $500,000,000; (ii) Aids to production, including additional bonuses so that products could gradually be marketed at competitive prices, structural aids to production, and aids to diversification to remedy weaknesses in single-crop economies; (iii) Stabilisation measures to mitigate fluctuations in prices for agricultural products; (iv) Technical assistance.

(d)   In the first period of association the E.E.C. was not formally entitled to intervene in the field of technical co-operation, but experience had shown that it was imperative for the E.E.C. Commission to be empowered to finance, through the E.D.F. schemes for technical co-operation connected with investments.

*Right of Establishment, Services, Payments and Capital*
The provisions on establishment were based on the principle of non-discrimination in the associated states against national and companies from the member-states, subject to reciprocity with respect to nationals and companies from the associated states in the member-states. At the same time the signatories undertook to free payments and capital movements connected with the facilities for establishment.
*The Institutions*   Both the E.E.C. and the associated African states

and Madagascar would be equally represented on the institutions of the Association, viz. (a) The Council of Association assisted by the Associated Committee; (b) The Parliamentary Conference of the Association; (c) The Court of Arbitration of the Association.

The Council of Association would consist of the members of the E.E.C. Council of Ministers, members of the E.E.C. Commission, and one member of the Government of each associated state. The Council would meet at least once a year and the chairmanship would be held in turn by a member of the E.E.C. Council and a member of the Government of an associated state.

The Association Committee would comprise one representative from each member-state, one of the Commission, and one from each associated state, the chairmanship procedure being the same as for the Council. The committee, whose aims and terms of reference would be determined by the Council, would have to ensure the continuity necessary for the smooth functioning of the Association.

The Parliamentary Conference of the Association would consist of members of the European Parliament and members of the Parliaments of the associated states.

The Court of Arbitration of the Association would deal with disputes in Association matters which could not be settled in the Council of Association. It would have five members appointed by the Council, viz., a president, two judges appointed after nomination by the E.E.C. Council, and two after nomination by the associated states. Majority rulings would be binding on the litigants to the disputes.

*General Provisions*  The Convention would be valid for five years, but might be terminated at six months' notice by the Community in respect of any associated state or by any associated state in the respect of the Community.

The Associated African States, eighteen in number, are Burundi, Cameroon, Central African Republic, Chad, Congo (Brazzaville), Dahomey, Gabon, Ivory Coast, Madagascar, Mali, Mauritania, Niger, Rwanda, Senegal, Somalia, Togo, Upper Volta and Zaire.

A second convention was signed on 29 July 1969 and came into force on 1 January 1971. This convention is due to expire in 1975 and stresses the need to develop industrialisation in the associated countries. The European Development Fund will provide aid to this end totalling $918,000,000 compared with $800,000,000 under the first convention.

AGREEMENT OF ASSOCIATION OF KENYA, UGANDA, AND
TANZANIA

A four-year association agreement, the 'Arusha Convention', was
signed on 24 September 1969. An earlier agreement signed on 26 July
1968 had not been ratified by all the E.E.C. members before the
expiry date. The provisions are similar to those in the Yaoundé
agreements except that there is no arrangement for development
and the preferential agreement for E.E.C. goods is more limited,
and expires at the same time in 1975.

AGREEMENT OF ASSOCIATION OF MALTA

An Association agreement with Malta was signed on 5 December
1970 with the E.E.C. and came into force on 1 April 1971. It provides
for a customs union to be established within ten years. This to be
achieved in two phases of five years each. In the first phase Malta will
reduce customs duties on most goods by 35 per cent. In return, the
E.E.C. will reduce its duties on imports from Malta by 70 per cent,
although some textile, agricultural and petroleum products are
excluded or are subject to special quota conditions. In the second
phase the aim will be to abolish tariffs.

'PARTIAL' AGREEMENT OF ASSOCIATION OF MOROCCO AND
TUNISIA

An agreement, known as the Mahgreb Agreement, was signed in
Rabat on 31 March 1969 and in Tunis on 28 March 1969. This
allows the two countries to sell their manufactured goods to the
E.E.C. without duty or other restriction. Exceptions are coal, steel
and cork. Agricultural products, such as citrus fruits, are allowed up
to 80 per cent preference into the E.E.C. markets. The agreement is
to be reviewed in 1972 with the aim of full associate membership for
the two countries.

AGREEMENT OF ASSOCIATE MEMBERSHIP OF NIGERIA, LATER
ABANDONED

An agreement which would have made Nigeria an associated member
of the European Economic Community was signed in Lagos on
16 July 1966, by Brigadier B. O. A. Ogundipe (then Chief of Staff)
on behalf of Nigeria and Dr. Joseph Luns (then Netherlands Foreign

Minister) on behalf of the E.E.C. When the Association Convention with the French-speaking African states was concluded at Yaoundé on 20 July 1963, the member-states of the E.E.C. declared their readiness to negotiate in a sympathetic spirit with any other country who so requested and whose economic structure and production was comparable with those of the Associated States.

This agreement was never ratified partly because of the Nigerian civil war, but is interesting in that other Commonwealth countries will apply for associate membership when Britain signs the Treaty.

The draft agreement was divided into three main sections:

All Nigerian exports, with the exception of four commodities, would enter the E.E.C. free of duty when the agreement came into force.

The four exceptions would be groundnut oil, palm oil, cocoa beans, and plywood; all of which would be subject to a tariff quota based on the average of Nigeria's exports of these products to the Common Market in the years 1962, 1963 and 1964. The quota would increase by 3 per cent per annum, or by 6 per cent, with free entry of plywood, if Nigeria increased from 2 per cent to 5 per cent its tariff preference on certain imports from the Community. The twenty-six products involved included macaroni, spaghetti, vermouth, some agricultural machinery, radios, radiograms and household goods. These products accounted in 1963 for £3,500,000 worth of exports from the E.E.C. to Nigeria, compared with only £108,000 worth of exports by Britain.

Nigeria would be allowed to keep various restrictions on her imports from the Community because of her industrial and development needs. This provision would allow her, in particular, to impose quantitative restriction on imports from the E.E.C. if her financial stability or the economic health of any sector of her economy were to be impaired.

In the event of Nigeria applying export taxes she would not discriminate between member-countries of the E.E.C. Nigeria retained the right to establish customs unions or free trade areas with other countries.

The agreement provided that nationals and companies of every member-country would be treated on an equal footing. Reciprocity could not be granted to Nigeria until such time as the E.E.C. had a common policy on the right of establishment.

The E.E.C. and Nigeria would authorise payments and transfers for goods and services.

Nigeria would endeavour not to impose new exchange control restrictions, and the E.E.C. in turn would not put new restrictions on the flow of private capital to Nigeria.

An Association Council would be established consisting of an E.E.C. and a Nigerian representative, each representative having one vote. The Council would meet at least once a year at ministerial level and more frequently at ambassadorial level.

Its Secretariat would be headed by a Nigerian and a Community representative.

An *ad hoc* arbitration tribunal, composed of one member nominated by Nigeria, one nominated by the Community, and one nominated by the Association Council after consultation with Nigeria and the Six, would settle any disputes which might arise.

Following the publication of the draft agreement, both the United States and the British Governments officially objected to its terms, but Nigeria did not accept their point of view.

The British attitude, which coincided with the U.S. viewpoint, took the form of representations that the proposed agreement, introducing preferences for E.E.C. and Nigeria in each other's markets, would not establish a free trade area and would not therefore conform to GATT rules. (To be accepted by GATT an agreement not covering a free trade area would require specific waivers granted by Britain, the U.S.A. and other members affected in order to make it permissible.)

Nigeria, on the other hand, claimed that she had a strong case for defending her traditional trading interests, which had been seriously undermined by the creation of the Common Market, because her large sales to the E.E.C., and particularly to West Germany and the Netherlands, had been jeopardised by the E.E.C. preferences granted to the present African Associates. Nigeria also argued that the new preferences would harm Britain very little, and in any case would be far less damaging than a full free trade area.

The agreement as finally signed on 16 July 1966, conformed to the draft approved a year earlier and was valid until 31 May 1969, i.e. the same date on which the first Yaoundé Convention terminated.

A Nigerian proposal to implement the agreement before ratification by the Community and its six member-countries was rejected by the E.E.C.

TRADE AGREEMENTS

Trade agreements have been signed with Iran, Israel, Spain and Yugoslavia and discussions are in progress with Algeria, Argentina, Egypt, Lebanon, and Uruguay. Lebanon had signed a three-year trade and technical co-operation agreement with the E.E.C. in 1965.

# Some suggestions for further reading

*Chapter 1:* POST-WAR EUROPE
Henderson, W. O., *The Genesis of the Common Market* (London, 1962).
*General Report on the Activities of the Community* (Annual from 1958).

*Chapter 2:* THE TERMS OF BRITAIN'S ENTRY INTO THE E.E.C.
Pisani, E., and others, *Problems of British Entry into the E.E.C.* (London, 1969).
*The United Kingdom and the European Communities.* (Cmnd. 4715, H.M.S.O., 1971).

*Chapter 3:* THE TREATIES OF ROME AND BRUSSELS
Calmann, J., *The Rome Treaty—the Common Market Explained* (London, 1967).

*Chapter 4:* THE INSTITUTIONS OF THE EUROPEAN COMMUNITIES
Mayne, R., *The Institutions of the European Community* (London, 1968).
Oudenhove, G. van, *The Political Parties in the European Parliament* (Leyden, 1965).

*Chapter 5:* THE TARIFF STRUCTURE OF THE COMMON MARKET
Walsh, A. E. and Paxton, J., *Trade in the Common Market Countries* (London, 1968). *Trade and Industrial Resources of the Common Market and EFTA Countries* (London, 1971).

*Chapter 6:* COMMUNITY LAW IN THE MEMBER-STATES
Bebr, G. *Judicial Control of the European Communities* (London, 1962).
Scheingold, S. A., *The Rule of Law in European Integration: The Path of the Schuman Plan* (Yale Univ. Press, 1965).

*Chapter 8:* AGRICULTURE AND FISHERIES
Butterwick, M. and Neville-Rolfe, E., *Agricultural Marketing in the E.E.C.* (London, 1971).

*The Common Agricultural Policy of the European Community* (Cmnd. 3274, H.M.S.O, 1967).
*Farmers and Growers Guide to the E.E.C.* (London, 1971).

*Chapter 9:* SALES AND TURNOVER TAXATION
Dale, A., *Tax Harmonization in Europe* (London, 1963).
*Report of the Committee on Turnover Taxation* (H.M.S.O., 1971).
*Value-added Tax.* Report of the National Economic Development Office (H.M.S.O., 1971).

*Chapter 10:* THE RULES OF COMPETITION
Swann, D., and McLachlan, D. L., *Competition Policy of the European Community* (London, 1967).

*Chapter 11:* INDUSTRIAL PROPERTY: PATENTS AND TRADE MARKS
*Second Preliminary Draft of a Convention Establishing a European System for the Grant of Patents.* 2 vols (Brussels, 1971).

*Chapter 12:* INDUSTRIAL STANDARDS
*Standards and European Trade.* Report of a conference presented by C.B.I. and B.S.I. in February 1971 (London, 1971).

*Chapter 15:* A COMMON TRANSPORT POLICY
Despicht, N., *The Transport Policy of the European Community* (London, 1969).

*Chapter 18:* AGREEMENTS OF ASSOCIATION AND TRADE
Okigbo, P.N.C., *Africa and the Common Market* (London, 1967).
Zartman, I. W., *The Politics of Trade Negotiations between Africa and the E.E.C.* (London, 1971).

*Chapter 17:* REGIONAL POLICY
Barzanti, S., *The Underdeveloped Areas within the Common Market* (Princeton Univ. Press, 1965).

# APPENDIX I

*Who sells most to Britain and the*
*Common Market Countries?*

The following tables show, for 27 commodity groups, where Britain and each country in the Common Market buy their supplies of those commodities. In the table, each country's total imports under the commodity group are given, together with the share of the exporting countries which account for the bulk of the supplies.

An important feature of these tables is the Export : Import Ratio shown against each commodity group. This figure provides a measurement of the strength of the domestic industry in terms of its ability to export or its dependence on imports.

The Export : Import Ratio is expressed as an Index (Exports = 100).

The figures are for the year 1969 and have been approximated in $ million in value and to the nearest integer in percentages.

Where '—' is shown in the tables, the relevant figure is nil or negligible.

Source: O.E.C.D. Trade by Commodities, 1969.

| Product | Importing Country | Total World Imports | PRINCIPAL SUPPLIERS SHARE OF IMPORTS | | | | Export:Import Ratio |
|---|---|---|---|---|---|---|---|
| | | | U.K. | E.E.C. | U.S. | Other | |
| | | $ Million | % | % | % | % | |
| | Bel./Lux. | 83 | — | 83 | — | 17 | 100: 82 |
| | Netherlands | 92 | 1 | 96 | — | 3 | 100: 23 |
| | Germany | 291 | — | 88 | — | 12 | 100: 230 |
| Dairy | France | 55 | — | 70 | — | 30 | 100: 15 |
| Produce and | Italy | 249 | — | 82 | — | 18 | 100: 600 |
| Eggs | U.K. | 441 | — | 8 | — | 92 | 100:1350 |
| | Norway | 1·7 | — | 9 | — | 91 | 100: 15 |
| | Denmark | 5 | 3 | 26 | — | 71 | 100: 3 |
| | Ireland | 0·8 | — | 11 | — | 89 | 100: 1 |
| | Bel./Lux. | 290 | — | 60 | 20 | 20 | 100: 249 |
| | Netherlands | 327 | — | 52 | 31 | 17 | 100: 194 |
| | Germany | 570 | — | 65 | 17 | 18 | 100: 445 |
| Cereals and | France | 145 | 1 | 29 | 44 | 26 | 100: 15 |
| Cereal | Italy | 471 | — | 15 | 25 | 60 | 100: 611 |
| Preparation | U.K. | 604 | — | 23 | 20 | 57 | 100: 978 |
| | | 22 | | 10 | 8 | 69 | 100:1758 |

|  | Country | | | | | | |
|---|---|---|---|---|---|---|---|
| Sugar and Sugar Preparations | Germany | 77 | 3 | 72 | 1 | 24 | 100: 264 |
| | France | 68 | 1 | 15 | — | 84 | 100: 58 |
| | Italy | 51 | 1 | 79 | — | 20 | 100: 480 |
| | U.K. | 270 | — | 2 | — | 98 | 100: 402 |
| | Norway | 19 | 27 | 7 | — | 66 | 100:3068 |
| | Denmark | 7 | 25 | 35 | 1 | 39 | 100: 55 |
| | Ireland | 6 | 43 | — | — | 57 | 100: 115 |
| Feeding Stuffs for Animals including Unmilled Cereals | Bel./Lux. | 116 | — | 36 | 12 | 52 | 100: 339 |
| | Netherlands | 216 | 1 | 20 | 31 | 48 | 100: 223 |
| | Germany | 339 | — | 12 | 26 | 62 | 100: 515 |
| | France | 159 | — | 19 | 42 | 39 | 100: 169 |
| | Italy | 115 | — | 51 | 20 | 29 | 100: 900 |
| | U.K. | 195 | — | 62 | 1 | 37 | 100: 875 |
| | Norway | 13 | 4 | 11 | — | 85 | 100: 22 |
| | Denmark | 70 | 1 | 18 | 10 | 71 | 100: 127 |
| | Ireland | 19 | 9 | 1 | 30 | 60 | 100: 198 |

| Product | Importing Country | Total World Imports | PRINCIPAL SUPPLIERS SHARE OF IMPORTS | | | | Export:Import Ratio |
|---|---|---|---|---|---|---|---|
| | | | U.K. | E.E.C. | U.S. | Other | |
| | | $ million | % | % | % | % | |
| Miscellaneous Food Preparations | Bel./Lux. | 37 | — | 91 | — | 9 | 100: 138 |
| | Netherlands | 19 | 3 | 77 | 9 | 11 | 100: 29 |
| | Germany | 23 | 6 | 63 | 5 | 26 | 100: 93 |
| | France | 14 | 3 | 64 | 2 | 31 | 100: 49 |
| | Italy | 8 | 3 | 77 | 8 | 12 | 100: 17 |
| | U.K. | 55 | — | 35 | 33 | 32 | 100: 134 |
| | Norway | 4 | 25 | 12 | 6 | 57 | 100: 61 |
| | Denmark | 7 | 23 | 25 | 11 | 41 | 100: 53 |
| | Ireland | 8 | 96 | 1 | 1 | 2 | 100: 297 |
| Hides and Skins | Bel./Lux. | 41 | 12 | 48 | 4 | 36 | 100: 258 |
| | Netherlands | 36 | 12 | 39 | 6 | 43 | 100: 92 |
| | Germany | 253 | 3 | 9 | 11 | 77 | 100: 598 |
| | France | 120 | 1 | 7 | 4 | 88 | 100: 205 |
| | Italy | 185 | 3 | 19 | 7 | 71 | 100:1553 |
| | U.K. | 187 | — | 8 | 9 | 83 | 100: 804 |
| | | | | 6 | | 71 | 100: 15 |

| | | | | | | |
|---|---|---|---|---|---|---|
| | Netherlands | 95 | — | 8 | 11 | 81 | 100: 700 |
| | Germany | 241 | 1 | 9 | 14 | 76 | 100:1200 |
| Pulp and | France | 179 | — | 7 | 11 | 82 | 100: 650 |
| Paper | Italy | 211 | — | 7 | 16 | 77 | — |
| | U.K. | 397 | — | 2 | 9 | 89 | 100: 630 |
| | Norway | 24 | — | — | — | 99 | — |
| | Denmark | 13 | — | — | — | 99 | 100: 193 |
| | Ireland | 6 | 6 | — | 6 | 88 | 100: 920 |
| | Bel./Lux. | 217 | 6 | 65 | 19 | 10 | 100: 84 |
| | Netherlands | 368 | 11 | 56 | 18 | 15 | 100: 92 |
| | Germany | 637 | 4 | 46 | 25 | 25 | 100: 59 |
| Chemical | France | 467 | 8 | 57 | 16 | 19 | 100: 85 |
| Elements and | Italy | 330 | 5 | 63 | 13 | 19 | 100: 114 |
| Compounds | U.K. | 485 | — | 36 | 18 | 46 | 100: 121 |
| | Norway | 125 | 7 | 22 | 18 | 53 | 100: 208 |
| | Denmark | 95 | 10 | 47 | 13 | 30 | 100: 111 |
| | Ireland | 23 | 63 | 25 | 4 | 8 | 100: 800 |

| Product | Importing Country | Total World Imports | PRINCIPAL SUPPLIERS OF IMPORTS | | | | Export:Import Ratio |
|---|---|---|---|---|---|---|---|
| | | | U.K. | E.E.C. | U.S. | Other | |
| | | $ million | % | % | % | % | |
| Dyeing, Tanning and Colouring Materials | Bel./Lux. | 53 | 7 | 79 | 5 | 9 | 100: 160 |
| | Netherlands | 60 | 13 | 68 | 5 | 14 | 100: 74 |
| | Germany | 84 | 9 | 45 | 10 | 36 | 100: 18 |
| | France | 97 | 8 | 67 | 8 | 17 | 100: 118 |
| | Italy | 90 | 8 | 64 | 7 | 21 | 100: 348 |
| | U.K. | 66 | — | 38 | 13 | 49 | 100: 36 |
| | Norway | 14 | 21 | 40 | 5 | 34 | 100: 118 |
| | Denmark | 22 | 11 | 42 | 5 | 42 | 100: 114 |
| | Ireland | 7 | 67 | 24 | 3 | 6 | 100: 860 |
| Medicines and Pharmaceutical Goods | Bel./Lux. | 117 | 17 | 59 | 11 | 13 | 100: 180 |
| | Netherlands | 92 | 4 | 70 | 5 | 21 | 100: 77 |
| | Germany | 130 | 9 | 42 | 9 | 40 | 100: 31 |
| | France | 129 | 11 | 35 | 17 | 37 | 100: 56 |
| | Italy | 115 | 11 | 49 | 10 | 30 | 100: 99 |
| | U.K. | 61 | — | 38 | 14 | 48 | 100: 21 |
| | Norway | 23 | 12 | 24 | 6 | 58 | 100: 445 |

| | | | | | | |
|---|---|---|---|---|---|---|
| Perfumery, Toilet and Cleansing Preparations | Netherlands | 64 | 6 | 81 | 7 | 6 | 100: 82 |
| | Germany | 85 | 5 | 64 | 10 | 21 | 100: 50 |
| | France | 98 | 8 | 51 | 9 | 32 | 100: 45 |
| | Italy | 60 | 8 | 67 | 9 | 16 | 100: 162 |
| | U.K. | 52 | — | 44 | 22 | 34 | 100: 36 |
| | Norway | 19 | 21 | 14 | 2 | 63 | 100: 499 |
| | Denmark | 17 | 26 | 31 | 5 | 38 | 100: 102 |
| | Ireland | 8 | 89 | 6 | 3 | 2 | 100: 238 |
| Manufactured Fertilisers | Bel./Lux. | 48 | — | 82 | — | 18 | 100: 30 |
| | Netherlands | 20 | — | 67 | 2 | 31 | 100: 23 |
| | Germany | 37 | — | 84 | 5 | 11 | 100: 25 |
| | France | 104 | — | 83 | 6 | 11 | 100: 150 |
| | Italy | 19 | — | 46 | 21 | 33 | 100: 33 |
| | U.K. | 58 | — | 62 | 5 | 33 | 100: 458 |
| | Norway | 1 | — | — | — | — | 100: — |
| | Denmark | 35 | — | 34 | — | 66 | 100:1708 |
| | Ireland | 16 | 24 | 54 | 5 | 17 | 100:1311 |

| Product | Importing Country | Total World Imports | PRINCIPAL SUPPLIERS OF IMPORTS | | | | Export:Import Ratio |
|---|---|---|---|---|---|---|---|
| | | | U.K. | E.E.C. | U.S. | Other | |
| Plastic Materials | Bel./Lux. | 148 | 5 | 80 | 11 | 4 | 100: 80 |
| | Netherlands | 192 | 8 | 70 | 15 | 7 | 100: 55 |
| | Germany | 373 | 3 | 70 | 15 | 12 | 100: 45 |
| | France | 281 | 4 | 79 | 11 | 6 | 100: 118 |
| | Italy | 155 | 5 | 79 | 11 | 5 | 100: 87 |
| | U.K. | 222 | — | 49 | 28 | 23 | 100: 72 |
| | Norway | 52 | 20 | 38 | 11 | 31 | 100: 172 |
| | Denmark | 105 | 16 | 52 | 8 | 24 | 100: 483 |
| | Ireland | 33 | 72 | 18 | 4 | 6 | 100:2081 |
| Leather and Leather Manufactures | Bel./Lux. | 31 | 10 | 66 | 3 | 21 | 100: 59 |
| | Netherlands | 39 | 9 | 72 | 2 | 17 | 100: 108 |
| | Germany | 202 | 6 | 57 | 3 | 34 | 100: 157 |
| | France | 82 | 5 | 33 | 2 | 60 | 100: 64 |
| | Italy | 72 | 6 | 30 | 3 | 61 | 100: 79 |
| | U.K. | 89 | — | 10 | 3 | 87 | 100: 81 |
| | Norway | 12 | 20 | 24 | 2 | 54 | 100: 150 |
| | Denmark | 25 | 28 | 17 | 2 | 53 | 100: 294 |
| | Ireland | 10 | 72 | 17 | 4 | 7 | 100: 83 |
| Rubber Manufactures | Bel./Lux. | 83 | 6 | 83 | 5 | 6 | 100: 133 |
| | Netherlands | 66 | 10 | 75 | 7 | 8 | 100: 108 |
| | Germany | 180 | 6 | 65 | 7 | 22 | 100: 80 |
| | France | 87 | 11 | 65 | 9 | 17 | 100: 38 |
| | Italy | 58 | 10 | 73 | 5 | 12 | 100: 51 |
| | U.K. | 59 | — | 29 | 15 | 56 | 100: 34 |
| | Norway | 28 | 23 | 22 | 5 | 50 | 100: 311 |

| | | | | | | |
|---|---|---|---|---|---|---|
| **Paper and Paperboard and Manufactures thereof** | | | | | | |
| Netherlands | 234 | 3 | 53 | 7 | 37 | 100: 118 |
| Germany | 584 | 2 | 33 | 10 | 55 | 100: 195 |
| France | 296 | 3 | 52 | 9 | 36 | 100: 166 |
| Italy | 108 | 5 | 36 | 26 | 33 | 100: 102 |
| U.K. | 488 | — | 5 | 11 | 84 | 100: 380 |
| Norway | 29 | 9 | 16 | 5 | 70 | 100: 17 |
| Denmark | 128 | 4 | 12 | 4 | 80 | 100: 556 |
| Ireland | 39 | 45 | 5 | 8 | 42 | 100: 390 |
| **Textile Yarns, Fabrics and Made-up Articles** | | | | | | |
| Bel./Lux. | 440 | 3 | 82 | 6 | 9 | 100: 51 |
| Netherlands | 644 | 3 | 83 | 3 | 11 | 100: 94 |
| Germany | 1303 | 4 | 69 | 2 | 25 | 100: 103 |
| France | 614 | 4 | 79 | 3 | 14 | 100: 74 |
| Italy | 313 | 7 | 66 | 4 | 23 | 100: 35 |
| U.K. | 572 | — | 25 | 6 | 69 | 100: 68 |
| Norway | 134 | 18 | 30 | 1 | 51 | 100: 498 |
| Denmark | 230 | 20 | 36 | 2 | 42 | 100: 273 |
| Ireland | 92 | 61 | 15 | 5 | 19 | 100: 213 |
| **Iron and Steel** | | | | | | |
| Bel./Lux. | 347 | 3 | 72 | 6 | 19 | 100: 21 |
| Netherlands | 546 | 3 | 88 | 1 | 8 | 100: 13 |
| Germany | 1397 | 2 | 66 | 2 | 30 | 100: 66 |
| France | 991 | 2 | 83 | 3 | 12 | 100: 113 |
| Italy | 635 | 3 | 62 | 7 | 28 | 100: 148 |
| U.K. | 417 | — | 33 | 10 | 57 | 100: 60 |
| Norway | 170 | 16 | 48 | 2 | 34 | 100: 110 |
| Denmark | 248 | 10 | 55 | 1 | 34 | 100: 808 |
| Ireland | 47 | 61 | 29 | 2 | 8 | 100: 2300 |

| Product | Importing Country | Total World Imports | PRINCIPAL SUPPLIERS SHARE OF IMPORTS | | | | Export:Import Ratio |
|---|---|---|---|---|---|---|---|
| | | | U.K. | E.E.C. | U.S. | Other | |
| | | $ million | % | % | % | % | |
| Non-ferrous Metals | Bel./Lux. | 720 | 3 | 23 | 4 | 70 | 100: 82 |
| | Netherlands | 337 | 9 | 60 | 4 | 29 | 100: 183 |
| | Germany | 1758 | 9 | 26 | 8 | 57 | 100: 258 |
| | France | 909 | 6 | 40 | 7 | 47 | 100: 272 |
| | Italy | 647 | 7 | 21 | 11 | 61 | 100: 543 |
| | U.K. | 1461 | — | 8 | 9 | 83 | 100: 195 |
| | Norway | 87 | 20 | 22 | 4 | 54 | 100: 20 |
| | Denmark | 100 | 12 | 33 | — | 55 | 100: 555 |
| | Ireland | 27 | 74 | 7 | — | 19 | 100: 420 |
| Manufactures of Metal n.e.s. | Bel./Lux. | 221 | 5 | 82 | 5 | 8 | 100: 90 |
| | Netherlands | 292 | 7 | 77 | 6 | 10 | 100: 148 |
| | Germany | 330 | 8 | 53 | 9 | 30 | 100: 31 |
| | France | 383 | 5 | 76 | 7 | 12 | 100: 112 |
| | Italy | 148 | 8 | 65 | 10 | 17 | 100: 37 |
| | U.K. | 182 | — | 34 | 20 | 46 | 100: 35 |
| | Norway | 77 | 18 | 28 | 4 | 50 | 100: 179 |
| | Denmark | 99 | 15 | 44 | 3 | 48 | 100: 180 |

|  | Country | | | | | | |
|---|---|---|---|---|---|---|---|
| Machinery other than Electric | Netherlands | 1015 | 12 | 62 | 13 | 13 | 100: 150 |
| | Germany | 1760 | 11 | 42 | 20 | 27 | 100: 27 |
| | France | 2227 | 10 | 61 | 16 | 13 | 100: 117 |
| | Italy | 1181 | 12 | 58 | 17 | 13 | 100: 58 |
| | U.K. | 1634 | — | 43 | 32 | 25 | 100: 48 |
| | Norway | 331 | 16 | 33 | 12 | 39 | 100: 300 |
| | Denmark | 433 | 17 | 42 | 13 | 28 | 100: 105 |
| | Ireland | 197 | 59 | 20 | 7 | 14 | 100:1320 |
| Electrical Machinery | Bel./Lux. | 423 | 5 | 79 | 8 | 8 | 100: 119 |
| | Netherlands | 792 | 7 | 71 | 10 | 12 | 100: 90 |
| | Germany | 995 | 7 | 49 | 20 | 24 | 100: 41 |
| | France | 843 | 6 | 64 | 21 | 9 | 100: 101 |
| | Italy | 563 | 7 | 61 | 20 | 12 | 100: 67 |
| | U.K. | 639 | — | 33 | 37 | 30 | 100: 57 |
| | Norway | 178 | 13 | 43 | 7 | 37 | 100: 317 |
| | Denmark | 244 | 14 | 46 | 7 | 33 | 100: 123 |
| | Ireland | 69 | 61 | 25 | 7 | 7 | 100: 222 |

| Product | Importing Country | Total World Imports | PRINCIPAL SUPPLIERS SHARE OF IMPORTS | | | | Export:Import Ratio |
|---|---|---|---|---|---|---|---|
| | | | U.K. | E.E.C. | U.S. | Other | |
| | | $ million | % | % | % | % | |
| Transport Equipment | Bel./Lux. | 1116 | 7 | 80 | 5 | 8 | 100: 106 |
| | Netherlands | 817 | 8 | 74 | 11 | 7 | 100: 167 |
| | Germany | 1184 | 5 | 75 | 10 | 10 | 100: 39 |
| | France | 1144 | 7 | 75 | 11 | 7 | 100: 61 |
| | Italy | 621 | 4 | 66 | 20 | — | 100: 49 |
| | U.K. | 892 | — | 36 | 53 | 11 | 100: 34 |
| | Norway | 499 | 12 | 37 | 10 | 41 | 100: 137 |
| | Denmark | 392 | 19 | 46 | 9 | 26 | 100: 250 |
| | Ireland | 139 | 50 | 20 | 27 | 3 | 100:4600 |
| of which Road Motor Vehicles | Bel./Lux. | 990 | 7 | 85 | 2 | 6 | 100: 105 |
| | Netherlands | 607 | 8 | 85 | 2 | 5 | 100: 386 |
| | Germany | 849 | 3 | 91 | 2 | 4 | 100: 21 |
| | France | 835 | 7 | 84 | 4 | 5 | 100: 61 |
| | Italy | 413 | 5 | 90 | 1 | 4 | 100: 41 |
| | U.K. | 285 | — | 73 | 9 | 18 | 100: 15 |
| | Norway | 191 | 16 | 52 | 3 | 29 | 100:1364 |
| | Denmark | 259 | 25 | 47 | 1 | 27 | 100:1517 |

| Clothing | | | | | | |
|---|---|---|---|---|---|---|
| Netherlands | 397 | 2 | 83 | 1 | 14 | 100: 245 |
| Germany | 809 | 2 | 60 | 2 | 36 | 100: 211 |
| France | 296 | 4 | 81 | 3 | 12 | 100: 82 |
| Italy | 72 | 11 | 72 | 1 | 16 | 100: 8 |
| U.K. | 299 | — | 11 | 3 | 86 | 100: 115 |
| Norway | 188 | 12 | 11 | 2 | 75 | 100: 830 |
| Denmark | 88 | 19 | 19 | 2 | 60 | 100: 102 |
| Ireland | 23 | 87 | 5 | — | 8 | 100: 60 |
| Footwear | | | | | | |
| Bel./Lux. | 59 | 1 | 90 | — | 9 | 100: 327 |
| Netherlands | 53 | 1 | 86 | — | 13 | 100: 206 |
| Germany | 212 | 1 | 82 | 1 | 16 | 100: 270 |
| France | 86 | 1 | 82 | — | 17 | 100: 81 |
| Italy | 4 | 9 | 56 | 2 | 33 | 100: 1 |
| U.K. | 85 | — | 31 | — | 69 | 100: 106 |
| Norway | 23 | 17 | 33 | — | 50 | 100: 768 |
| Denmark | 27 | 17 | 38 | — | 45 | 100: 385 |
| Ireland | 3 | 63 | 23 | — | 14 | 100: 33 |

| Product | Importing Country | Total World Imports | PRINCIPAL SUPPLIERS SHARE OF IMPORTS | | | | Export:Import Ratio |
|---|---|---|---|---|---|---|---|
| | | | U.K. | E.E.C. | U.S. | Other | |
| | | $ million | % | % | % | % | |
| Scientific Instruments, Photographic Goods and Clocks | Bel./Lux. | 124 | 7 | 62 | 13 | 18 | 100: 84 |
| | Netherlands | 182 | 18 | 50 | 16 | 16 | 100: 131 |
| | Germany | 376 | 9 | 38 | 21 | 34 | 100: 36 |
| | France | 338 | 11 | 53 | 16 | 20 | 100: 122 |
| | Italy | 215 | 5 | 54 | 18 | 23 | 100: 127 |
| | U.K. | 277 | — | 30 | 34 | 36 | 100: 64 |
| | Norway | 48 | 16 | 35 | 12 | 37 | 100: 900 |
| | Denmark | 78 | 18 | 44 | 11 | 27 | 100: 268 |
| | Ireland | 24 | 46 | 17 | 25 | 12 | 100: 126 |

# APPENDIX II

*The Extraction of Statistics of Production, Consumption,
Imports and Exports of the Common Market Countries
by the use of Input-Output Tabulations*

Input-Output statistics involve long and complicated calculations.
In the following tables, use has been made of computer listings
prepared by the Statistical Office of the European Communities
in 1970 for 1965 figures.

Their usefulness lies in the information they give of the size of
each industry in Germany, France, Belgium, The Netherlands and
Italy, and the relation of Imports and Exports to Production and
Consumption.

The table for each of these countries sets out:

(1)  The value (in $ million) of the Production.
(2)  The value of Imports.
(3)  The value of Domestic Consumption.
(4)  The value of Exports.
(5)  The percentages which Imports of similar goods bear to
     Consumption.
(6)  The percentages which Exports of similar goods bear to
     Production.
(7)  The Export:Import Ratio, i.e. the index of the value of Imports
     to Exports (Exports = 100).

The list of industries varies from country to country because of
their different statistical methods.

The last column (column 7) in each table gives a valuable indication, by means of an index of the Export:Import Ratio, of the extent
of the industry's need to import, or of its strength to export its
products.

GERMANY

| Product | $ million | | | | Imports as % of Consumption | Exports as % of Production | Export: Import Ratio |
| --- | --- | --- | --- | --- | --- | --- | --- |
| | Production | Imports | Exports | Consumption | | | |
| Agricultural and industrial machinery | 10,098 | 1,890 | 3,371 | 8,617 | 21·9 | 33·4 | 100: 56 |
| Base metals—iron and steel | 11,496 | 869 | 1,309 | 11,056 | 7·9 | 11·2 | 100: 66 |
| non-ferrous metals | 2,575 | 1,325 | 471 | 3,429 | 38·6 | 18·3 | 100:355 |
| Chemicals | 9,740 | 1,227 | 2,333 | 8,634 | 14·2 | 20·0 | 100: 53 |
| Clothing | 3,192 | 285 | 128 | 3,349 | 8·5 | 4·0 | 100:223 |
| Cocoa, chocolate and confectionery | 910 | 68 | 18 | 960 | 7·1 | 2·0 | 100:380 |
| Electrical machinery including electronic and office | 8,078 | 749 | 1,641 | 7,186 | 10·4 | 20·3 | 100: 47 |
| Footwear and leather | 1,348 | 161 | 83 | 1,426 | 11·3 | 6·2 | 100:194 |
| Hides and skins | 420 | 114 | 65 | 469 | 24·3 | 15·5 | 100:176 |
| Metal manufactures | 7,465 | 281 | 795 | 6,951 | 4·0 | 10·6 | 100: 35 |
| Motor vehicles | 7,732 | 500 | 2,537 | 5,195 | 9·6 | 35·0 | 100: 19 |
| Paper manufactures | 2,780 | 618 | 146 | 3,250 | 19·0 | 5·2 | 100:418 |
| Printing and publishing | 3,015 | 64 | 108 | 2,971 | 2·1 | 3·6 | 100: 59 |
| Plastics | 1,275 | 97 | 172 | 1,200 | 8·0 | 12·9 | 100: 56 |
| Precision instruments, optical and photographic equipment | 1,656 | 249 | 598 | 1,307 | 19·0 | 36·1 | 100: 41 |
| Rubber | 1,199 | 142 | 133 | 1,208 | 11·8 | 10·8 | 100:107 |
| Textiles | 5,812 | 1,356 | 638 | 6,530 | 20·1 | 11·0 | 100:212 |

# NETHERLANDS

| Product | $ million | | | | Imports as % of Consumption | Exports as % of Production | Export: Import Ratio |
|---|---|---|---|---|---|---|---|
| | Production | Imports | Exports | Consumption | | | |
| Agricultural and industrial machinery | 847 | 774 | 703 | 918 | 84·3 | 85·9 | 100:110 |
| Base Metals: iron and steel | 662 | 382 | 233 | 811 | 47·1 | 35·0 | 100:164 |
| non-ferrous metals | 192 | 209 | 108 | 293 | 71·3 | 56·2 | 100:193 |
| Chemicals and plastics | 1,502 | 639 | 724 | 1,417 | 45·1 | 48·6 | 100: 87 |
| Clothing and furs | 435 | 137 | 63 | 509 | 27·0 | 14·5 | 100:233 |
| Cocoa, chocolate and confectionery | 204 | 23 | 99 | 128 | 18·0 | 50·0 | 100: 22 |
| Electrical machinery | 1,285 | 648 | 820 | 1,113 | 58·2 | 63·8 | 100: 78 |
| Electronic calculating and office machinery | 50 | 58 | 47 | 61 | 95·0 | 84·0 | 100:123 |
| Footwear | 111 | 33 | 18 | 126 | 26·0 | 17·5 | 100:183 |
| Furniture and bedding | 634 | 169 | 65 | 738 | 26·6 | 10·2 | 100:260 |
| Glass and glassware | 48 | 65 | 9 | 104 | 62·5 | 18·7 | 100:722 |
| Hides and skins | 43 | 23 | 21 | 45 | 51·1 | 48·9 | 100:110 |
| Leather other than footwear | 29 | 14 | 7 | 36 | 38·9 | 24·1 | 100:200 |
| Metal manufactures | 863 | 233 | 139 | 957 | 24·5 | 16·6 | 100:167 |
| Motor vehicles | 226 | 549 | 83 | 692 | 79·3 | 34·7 | 100:661 |
| Paper manufactures | 248 | 50 | 40 | 258 | 19·3 | 16·7 | 100:125 |
| Printing and publishing | 520 | 28 | 48 | 500 | 5·6 | 9·2 | 100: 58 |
| Pulp and paper | 218 | 177 | 72 | 323 | 54·8 | 33·0 | 100:246 |
| Precision instruments, optical and photographic equipment | 349 | 147 | 47 | 449 | 32·7 | 13·5 | 100:313 |
| Rubber and asbestos | 104 | 51 | 43 | 112 | 45·7 | 40·0 | 100:109 |
| Textiles: fibre and yarn | 264 | 154 | 100 | 318 | 48·4 | 37·7 | 100:154 |
| Textiles: woven | 551 | 280 | 238 | 593 | 47·2 | 43·2 | 100:118 |
| Textiles: knitted and knitwear | 149 | 127 | 58 | 217 | 58·5 | 39·3 | 100:218 |

BELGIUM

| Product | Production | $ million Imports | $ million Exports | Consumption | Imports as % of Consumption | Exports as % of Production | Export: Import Ratio |
|---|---|---|---|---|---|---|---|
| Agricultural and industrial machinery | 769 | 539 | 476 | 832 | 64·8 | 61·9 | 100:113 |
| Base Metals: iron and steel | 1,732 | 240 | 794 | 1,178 | 20·3 | 45·6 | 100: 30 |
| non-ferrous metals | 626 | 459 | 536 | 549 | 83·6 | 85·6 | 100: 86 |
| Chemicals: basic chemicals for industrial products | 424 | 231 | 247 | 408 | 56·6 | 60·0 | 100: 93 |
| Chemicals for domestic products | 282 | 86 | 132 | 236 | 36·4 | 46·7 | 100: 65 |
| Petrochemicals | 69 | 67 | 43 | 93 | 72·0 | 72·8 | 100:156 |
| Clothing and furs | 387 | 59 | 88 | 358 | 16·5 | 22·7 | 100: 67 |
| Cocoa, chocolate and confectionery | 99 | 27 | 26 | 100 | 27·0 | 26·0 | 100:104 |
| Electrical machinery | 628 | 336 | 257 | 707 | 47·5 | 41·2 | 100:130 |
| Electronic calculating and office machinery | 14 | 36 | 8 | 42 | 87·5 | 57·1 | 100:178 |
| Footwear | 81 | 42 | 18 | 105 | 40·0 | 23·4 | 100:233 |
| Furniture and bedding | 255 | 27 | 40 | 242 | 11·1 | 2·2 | 100:371 |
| Glass and glassware | 164 | 38 | 129 | 73 | 52·1 | 78·7 | 100: 30 |
| Hides and skins | 44 | 30 | 21 | 53 | 56·6 | 47·7 | 100:143 |
| Leather other than footwear | 30 | 14 | 13 | 31 | 45·2 | 40·3 | 100:109 |
| Metal manufactures | 613 | 216 | 112 | 717 | 30·1 | 18·3 | 100:193 |
| Motor vehicles | 685 | 685 | 416 | 954 | 71·7 | 60·1 | 100: 60 |
| Paper manufactures | 179 | 42 | 40 | 181 | 23·2 | 22·3 | 100:105 |
| Printing and publishing | 275 | 46 | 42 | 279 | 16·5 | 15·3 | 100:109 |
| Pulp and paper | 161 | 119 | 45 | 235 | 50·7 | 27·9 | 100:267 |
| Plastics | 106 | 72 | 56 | 122 | 59·0 | 50·0 | 100:125 |
| Precision instruments, optical and photographic equipment | 29 | 96 | 24 | 101 | 95·5 | 82·7 | 100:400 |
| Rubber and asbestos | 64 | 78 | 22 | 120 | 65·0 | 40·0 | 100:335 |
| Synthetics including rubber | 114 | 121 | 85 | 150 | 80·0 | 74·4 | 100:142 |
| Textiles: fibre and yarn | 626 | 149 | 298 | 477 | 31·4 | 47·6 | 100: 50 |
| Textiles: woven | 535 | 194 | 358 | 371 | 52·3 | 67·1 | 100: 54 |
| Textiles: knitted and knitwear | 153 | 63 | 69 | 147 | 42·8 | 45·1 | 100: 91 |

FRANCE

| Product | $ million | | | | Imports as % of Consumption | Exports as % of Production | Export: Import Ratio |
|---|---|---|---|---|---|---|---|
| | Production | Imports | Exports | Consumption | | | |
| Agricultural and industrial machinery | 7,069 | 1,271 | 895 | 7,445 | 17·0 | 12·7 | 100:142 |
| Base Metals: iron and steel | 3,297 | 655 | 892 | 3,060 | 21·4 | 26·8 | 100: 74 |
| non-ferrous metals | 1,718 | 568 | 337 | 1,949 | 29·1 | 19·6 | 100:169 |
| Chemicals: basic chemicals for industrial products | 2,714 | 472 | 440 | 2,746 | 17·0 | 16·6 | 100:107 |
| Chemicals for domestic products | 2,079 | 88 | 236 | 1,931 | 4·5 | 11·3 | 100: 38 |
| Petrochemicals | 357 | 265 | 183 | 439 | 60·3 | 47·3 | 100:145 |
| Clothing and furs | 1,988 | 62 | 126 | 1,924 | 3·2 | 6·3 | 100: 50 |
| Cocoa, chocolate and confectionery | 423 | 54 | 32 | 445 | 12·1 | 7·6 | 100:107 |
| Electrical machinery | 4,565 | 518 | 560 | 4,523 | 11·2 | 12·2 | 100: 92 |
| Electronic calculating and office machinery | 335 | 213 | 150 | 398 | 53·5 | 44·8 | 100:142 |
| Footwear | 620 | 33 | 77 | 576 | 5·8 | 13·6 | 100: 43 |
| Furniture and bedding | 967 | 78 | 21 | 1,024 | 7·6 | 2·2 | 100:371 |
| Glass and glassware | 514 | 52 | 117 | 449 | 11·6 | 22·8 | 100: 44 |
| Hides and skins | 532 | 83 | 123 | 492 | 16·9 | 23·1 | 100: 65 |
| Leather other than footwear | 281 | 11 | 30 | 262 | 4·2 | 10·7 | 100: 37 |
| Metal manufactures | 3,997 | 249 | 250 | 3,996 | 6·2 | 6·2 | 100:100 |
| Motor vehicles | 3,928 | 512 | 769 | 3,671 | 14·0 | 19·8 | 100: 66 |
| Paper manufactures | 1,064 | 79 | 66 | 1,077 | 7·3 | 6·2 | 100:120 |
| Printing and publishing | 2,336 | 106 | 109 | 2,333 | 4·5 | 4·7 | 100: 97 |
| Pulp and paper | 1,159 | 250 | 69 | 1,340 | 18·6 | 6·0 | 100:362 |
| Plastics | 922 | 43 | 41 | 924 | 4·7 | 4·4 | 100:105 |
| Precision instruments, optical and photographic equipment | 724 | 283 | 150 | 857 | 33·0 | 20·7 | 100:188 |
| Rubber and asbestos | 926 | 65 | 158 | 833 | 7·8 | 15·8 | 100: 41 |
| Synthetics including rubber | 939 | 358 | 235 | 1,062 | 33·7 | 25·0 | 100:153 |
| Textiles, fibre and yarn | 2,104 | 103 | 328 | 1,879 | 5·5 | 15·0 | 100: 31 |
| Textiles, woven | 2,208 | 236 | 433 | 2,011 | 11·7 | 19·6 | 100: 54 |
| Textiles, knitted and knitwear | 856 | 78 | 121 | 813 | 9·6 | 14·1 | 100: 65 |

# ITALY

| Product | $ million | | | | Imports as % of Consumption | Exports as % of Production | Export: Import Ratio |
|---|---|---|---|---|---|---|---|
| | Production | Imports | Exports | Consumption | | | |
| Agricultural and industrial machinery | 2,108 | 537 | 924 | 1,721 | 31·2 | 43·8 | 100: 57 |
| Base Metals: iron and steel | 3,135 | 273 | 349 | 3,059 | 8·9 | 11·1 | 100: 79 |
| non-ferrous metals | 769 | 443 | 112 | 1,100 | 40·0 | 14·6 | 100:396 |
| Chemicals for domestic products | 1,230 | 120 | 91 | 1,259 | 9·6 | 7·4 | 100:132 |
| Petrochemicals | 2,522 | 382 | 390 | 2,514 | 15·2 | 15·4 | 100: 98 |
| Clothing and furs | 1,811 | 28 | 137 | 1,702 | 1·6 | 7·6 | 100: 20 |
| Cocoa, chocolate and confectionery | 394 | 6 | 17 | 383 | 1·6 | 4·3 | 100: 35 |
| Electrical machinery | 1,810 | 327 | 412 | 1,725 | 19·0 | 22·7 | 100: 79 |
| Footwear | 596 | 19 | 213 | 407 | 1·2 | 35·9 | 100: 2 |
| Furniture and bedding | 651 | 5 | 25 | 631 | 0·8 | 3·9 | 100: 20 |
| Glass and glassware | 349 | 58 | 51 | 356 | 16·3 | 14·6 | 100:114 |
| Hides and skins | 256 | 38 | 33 | 261 | 14·6 | 12·9 | 100:116 |
| Leather other than footwear | 153 | 3 | 42 | 114 | 2·7 | 27·4 | 100: 7 |
| Metal manufactures | 1,192 | 106 | 257 | 1,041 | 10·0 | 21·5 | 100: 41 |
| Motor vehicles | 2,021 | 218 | 482 | 1,757 | 12·4 | 23·8 | 100: 45 |
| Paper manufactures | 356 | 35 | 29 | 262 | 9·6 | 8·1 | 100:121 |
| Printing and publishing | 1,015 | 26 | 54 | 987 | 2·6 | 5·3 | 100: 48 |
| Pulp and paper | 565 | 180 | 24 | 721 | 25·0 | 4·2 | 100:750 |
| Plastics | 393 | 45 | 66 | 372 | 12·1 | 17·0 | 100: 71 |
| Precision instruments, optical and photographic equipment | 263 | 146 | 90 | 319 | 45·7 | 34·2 | 100:162 |
| Rubber and asbestos | 498 | 33 | 73 | 458 | 7·2 | 13·7 | 100: 44 |
| Synthetics including rubber | 790 | 194 | 316 | 668 | 29·0 | 40·0 | 100: 61 |
| Textiles: fibre and yarn | 1,208 | 92 | 105 | 1,195 | 7·7 | 8·7 | 100: 87 |
| Textiles: woven | 1,492 | 137 | 391 | 1,238 | 11·0 | 26·2 | 100: 35 |
| Textiles: knitted and knitwear | 600 | 20 | 282 | 338 | 5·9 | 47·0 | 100: 7 |

# APPENDIX III

*Who produces most in the Common Market?*

This appendix gives production figures for 21 basic commodities in the Six shown as totals for the Common Market and as the amounts for each member country, for 1969.

It also gives parallel statistics for the new member-countries and, for purposes of comparison, for the United States, Japan and the U.S.S.R.

Source: Basic Statistics of the Community (E.E.C., 1970).

| Product | Total Common Market production | Shares of each Common Market country | | | | | Production of new member-countries | | | Production of other countries | | |
|---|---|---|---|---|---|---|---|---|---|---|---|---|
| | | Ger. | Fra. | B./L. | Neth. | It. | U.K. | Nor. | Den. | U.S. | Japan | U.S.S.R. |
| | (000 Tons) | | | | | | | | | | | |
| *Steel* | | | | | | | | | | | | |
| Crude steel | 107,319 | 45,316 | 22,510 | 18,353 | 4,712 | 16,428 | 26,845 | 854 | 482 | 128,150 | 82,166 | 110,290 |
| Rolled steel products | 78,870 | 31,918 | 17,246 | 13,473 | 3,039 | 12,894 | 20,243 | 392 | 423 | 90,177 | 68,060 | 73,310 |
| *Non-ferrous metals* | | | | | | | | | | | | |
| Aluminium | 847 | 262 | 372 | — | 69 | 144 | 34 | 512 | — | 3,441 | 569 | 1,450 |
| Copper, refined | 742 | 402 | 37 | 287 | — | 16 | 198 | 22 | — | 2,034 | 692 | 1,020 |
| Lead, refined | 655 | 303 | 156 | 97 | 15 | 84 | 260 | 1 | 12 | 714 | 186 | 520 |
| Zinc | 969 | 281 | 254 | 258 | 46 | 130 | 151 | 59 | — | 1,042 | 713 | 550 |
| Tin | 12·5 | 2·4 | — | 4·6 | 5·5 | — | 28·7 | — | — | 6·4 | 2·2 | 46·5 |
| Passenger cars (000 units) | 7,298 | 3,312 | 2,168 | 87·1 | 784 | 1,477 | 1,717 | — | — | 8,224 | 2,611 | 294 |
| Commercial vehicles (000 units) | 772 | 292 | 299 | 174 | 46 | 119 | 466 | — | — | 1,981 | 2,063 | 540 |
| Cotton yarn | 1,039 | 367 | 267 | 96 | 55 | 254 | 166 | 4 | 5 | 1,683 | 527 | 1,437 |
| Fabrics | 783 | 259 | 201 | 71 | 75 | 177 | 106 | 4 | 3 | 1,023 | 374 | 955 |
| Wool yarn | 638 | 135 | 145 | 81 | 22 | 254 | 242 | 6 | 3 | 420 | 175 | 302 |
| Wool fabrics | 267 | 52 | 66 | 16 | 19 | 115 | 95 | 2 | — | 94 | 138 | n.a. |
| *Man-made fibres* | | | | | | | | | | | | |
| Cellulosic yarn | 276 | 76 | 53 | 16 | 37 | 93 | 97 | — | — | 361 | 142 | 212 |
| staple | 394 | 185 | 78 | 25 | — | 106 | 156 | 29 | — | 364 | 355 | 220 |
| Non-cellulosic yarn | 497 | 239 | 76 | 20 | 58 | 105 | 162 | — | 4 | 802 | 360 | 104 |
| staple | 474 | 213 | 81 | 15 | 33 | 132 | 139 | — | — | 780 | 447 | 46 |
| Wood pulp | 4,897 | 1,670 | 1,715 | 335 | 218 | 959 | 422 | 1,955 | 89 | 34,268 | 7,137 | 4,975 |
| Newsprint | 1,296 | 314 | 423 | 84 | 171 | 304 | 790 | 511 | — | 2,878 | 1,614 | 1,016 |
| Kraft paper and board | 1,091 | 303 | 352 | 84 | 81 | 307 | 275 | 193 | 22 | 13,454 | 2,846 | n.a. |
| Other paper and board | 12,419 | 4,693 | 3,220 | 569 | 1,110 | 2,827 | 3,872 | 659 | 219 | 29,816 | 6,850 | n.a. |

# APPENDIX IV

*Population of the Six and the Four by Country, Age and Sex, 1969 (in thousands).*

| | Under 15 | | 15 to 64 | | 65 and over | | Total | |
|---|---|---|---|---|---|---|---|---|
| | M | F | M | F | M | F | M | F |
| Germany | 7,207 | 6,864 | 18,518 | 20,123 | 2,991 | 4,760 | 28,716 | 31,347 |
| France | 6,395 | 6,154 | 15,797 | 15,710 | 2,472 | 4,018 | 24,664 | 25,881 |
| Belgium | 1,169 | 1,114 | 3,033 | 3,056 | 528 | 761 | 4,730 | 4,931 |
| Luxembourg | 38·2 | 36·7 | 110·2 | 111·3 | 17·7 | 24·3 | 166·2 | 172·3 |
| Netherlands | 1,816 | 1,733 | 4,070 | 4,027 | 579 | 732 | 6,465 | 6,493 |
| Italy | 6,743 | 6,486 | 16,589 | 17,437 | 2,203 | 2,875 | 25,535 | 26,800 |
| Community | 23,368 | 22,390 | 58,117 | 60,484 | 8,791 | 13,170 | 90,276 | 96,024 |
| U.K. | 6,828 | 6,483 | 17,583 | 17,715 | 2,679 | 4,355 | 27,090 | 28,553 |
| Norway | 481 | 458 | 1,209 | 1,190 | 211 | 270 | 1,901 | 1,918 |
| Denmark | 590 | 562 | 1,570 | 1,573 | 258 | 326 | 2,418 | 2,461 |
| Ireland | | | | | | | 1,449 | 1,434 |

| Enlarged Community | Total population 253·5 million |
|---|---|

Source: Basic Statistics of the Community (E.E.C. 1970).

# APPENDIX V

*Average monthly unemployment in the Common Market Countries, 1962 to 1969 (thousands)*

|  | *1962* | *1966* | *1967* | *1968* | *1969* |
|---|---|---|---|---|---|
| France | 125 | 147 | 365 | 254 | 223 |
| West Germany | 155 | 161 | 459 | 323 | 179 |
| Belgium | 81·2 | 68·8 | 92 | 118·7 | 97·7 |
| Luxembourg | 0·08 | 0·02 | 0·02 | 0·09 | 0·04 |
| Netherlands | 34·6 | 36·4 | 86 | 84·3 | 55·9 |
| Italy | 1,162 | 1,115 | 699 | 961 | 887 |

Source: E.E.C. Social Statistics 1970

| U.K. | 463·2 | 359·7 | 560 | 564·1 | 559·3 |
|---|---|---|---|---|---|

Source: Ministry of Employment and Productivity

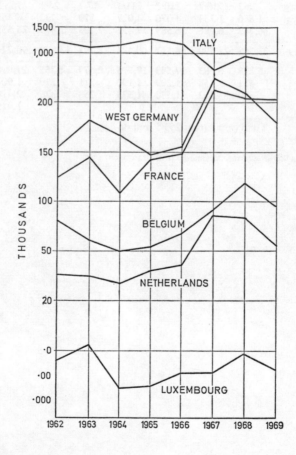

# APPENDIX VI

*Employment in the Common Market Countries in the
Principal Manufacturing Industries, 1969* (*thousands*)

| | Germany | France | Italy | Nether-lands | Belgium |
|---|---|---|---|---|---|
| Food manufacturing | 593 | n.a. | 233 | 147 | 78 |
| Textiles | 562 | 410 | 455 | 81 | 125 |
| Footwear, apparel, made-up textile goods | 569 | 384 | 365 | 97 | 90 |
| Wood and cork manufactures | 243 | 106 | 158 | 33 | 19 |
| Wooden furniture manufacture | 297 | 83 | 109 | 22 | 30 |
| Paper and paper products | 171 | 129 | 80 | 34 | 27 |
| Printing, publishing and allied industries | 392 | 205 | 93 | 76 | 38 |
| Leather and leather products | 80 | 48 | 44 | 8 | 7 |
| Rubber, plastics, man-made fibres, starch and its products | 327 | 216 | 193 | 44 | 24 |
| Chemicals and chemical products | 534 | 311 | 196 | 76 | 66 |
| Non-metallic mineral products | 382 | 225 | 236 | 49 | 70 |
| Basic metal manufactures | 750 | 406 | 235 | 45 | 117 |
| Metal products | 881 | 508 | 385 | 111 | 85 |
| Machinery, other than electric | 1,339 | 372 | 319 | 91 | 69 |
| Electrical machinery and apparatus | 989 | 431 | 278 | 116 | 80 |
| Transport equipment | 748 | 649 | 430 | 127 | 99 |
| Total manufacturing | 9,426 | 5,180 | 3,957 | 1,212 | 1,098 |
| Construction | 2,023 | 1,686 | 851 | 409 | 242 |
| Total salaried employees and wage-earners | 11,841 | 7,081 | 4,876 | 1,649 | 1,401 |
| Average employers' expenditure on wages and related costs, per hour (Belgian francs) | 80·31 | 68·56 | 63·20 | 74·37 | 76·32 |

Source: Basic Statistics of the Community (E.E.C. 1970).

# Index